Test Bank

Financial Accounting

NINTH EDITION

OR

Accounting: Concepts and Applications

NINTH EDITION

W. Steve Albrecht
Brigham Young University

James D. Stice
Brigham Young University

Earl K. Stice
Brigham Young University

Monte Swain
Brigham Young University

Prepared by

Jeffrey D. Ritter
St. Norbert College

THOMSON
™
SOUTH-WESTERN

Australia · Canada · Mexico · Singapore · Spain · United Kingdom · United States

THOMSON
SOUTH-WESTERN

Test Bank for **Financial Accounting, 9e** or **Accounting: Concepts and Applications, 9e**

W. Steve Albrecht, James D. Stice, Earl K. Stice, and Monte R. Swain

VP/Editorial Director:
Jack W. Calhoun

VP/Editor-in-Chief:
George Werthman

Executive Editor:
Sharon Oblinger

Developmental Editor:
Carol Bennett

Technology Project Editor:
Amy Wilson

Marketing Manager:
Keith Chasse

Senior Production Editor:
Kara ZumBahlen

Media Editor:
Kelly Reid

Manufacturing Coordinator:
Doug Wilke

Printer:
Globus Printing, Minster, OH

CONTENTS

Chapter 1—Accounting Information: Users and Uses

MULTIPLE CHOICE

The Purpose of Accounting

1. Which of the following is NOT typically true of accounting information?
   a. The information is quantitative in nature.
   b. The information relates to future time periods.
   c. The information relates to specific accounting entities.
   d. The information is primarily financial in nature.

   ANS: B

2. Businesses use accounting systems to
   a. Analyze transactions
   b. Handle routine bookkeeping tasks
   c. Evaluate the performance and health of the business
   d. All of the above

   ANS: D

3. Which of the following is NOT a function of accounting?
   a. Accumulating economic information about organizations
   b. Measuring economic information about organizations
   c. Executing sales transactions for organizations
   d. Communicating economic information about organizations

   ANS: C

4. Which of the following is NOT a key component of the definition of accounting?
   a. Financial
   b. Qualitative
   c. Useful
   d. Decision-oriented

   ANS: B

The Relationship of Accounting to Business

5. Accounting can be best described as a
   a. Manufacturing activity
   b. Service activity
   c. Retailing activity
   d. All of the above

   ANS: B

1

6. Which of the following is NOT a typical way business organizations acquire monetary resources?
   a. Business purchases
   b. Business earnings
   c. Investments by owners
   d. Loans from creditors

   ANS: A

7. Accountants typically perform what action related to the results of business activities?
   a. Measurement
   b. Reporting
   c. Both a and b
   d. None of the above

   ANS: C

8. The accounting cycle includes all of the following, EXCEPT
   a. Recording
   b. Summarizing
   c. Analyzing
   d. Interpreting

   ANS: D

Users of Accounting Information

9. The emphasis in financial accounting is on which of the following user groups?
   a. Management
   b. Certified public accountants
   c. Investors and creditors
   d. Educators

   ANS: C

10. The primary internal group that uses accounting information is
    a. The Securities and Exchange Commission
    b. The Internal Revenue Service
    c. Creditors
    d. Management

    ANS: D

11. Which of the following is NOT an important aspect of management accounting?
    a. Planning
    b. Product design
    c. Implementing plans
    d. Controlling costs

    ANS: B

12. Accounting reports are the output of the accounting process. Which of the following is NOT one of the four main categories of accounting reports?
    a. General-purpose financial statements
    b. Income tax returns
    c. Management reports
    d. Stock market reports

    ANS: D

13. The area of accounting that is concerned with providing information for external users is referred to as
    a. Financial accounting
    b. Governmental accounting
    c. Management accounting
    d. Nonprofit accounting

    ANS: A

14. Which of the following is NOT one of the three primary financial statements?
    a. Statement of cash flows
    b. Income statement
    c. Retained earnings statement
    d. Balance sheet

    ANS: C

15. Which of the following is NOT an external user of financial information?
    a. Competitors
    b. Employees
    c. Management
    d. Suppliers

    ANS: C

The Financial Accounting Standards Board

16. Which of the following is NOT true of the FASB?
    a. It consists of seven full-time members.
    b. It is a government agency.
    c. It seeks consistency for its proposed standards.
    d. It has no legal power to enforce the standards it sets.

    ANS: B

17. Generally accepted accounting principles are
    a. Natural laws
    b. Based on scientific proofs
    c. Developed by accounting rulemakers
    d. Both b and c

    ANS: C

18. The Financial Accounting Standards Board was established in
    a. 1983
    b. 1973
    c. 1963
    d. 1953

    ANS: B

19. The predecessor to the Financial Accounting Standards Board was the
    a. Accounting Research Committee
    b. Accounting Principles Board
    c. Committee on Accounting Procedures
    d. Securities and Exchange Commission

    ANS: B

20. The initials GAAP stand for
    a. General Accounting Principles
    b. Generally Accepted Procedures
    c. Generally Accepted Accounting Principles
    d. Generally Accepted Accounting Practices

    ANS: C

Other Organizations

21. The initials CPA stand for
    a. Certified Professional Appraiser
    b. Certified Professional Accountant
    c. Certified Public Accountant
    d. Certified Public Auditor

    ANS: C

22. The current standard-setting board for accounting in the private sector is the
    a. Financial Accounting Standards Board (FASB)
    b. Securities and Exchange Commission (SEC)
    c. Accounting Principles Board (APB)
    d. American Accounting Association (AAA)

    ANS: A

23. Within a CPA firm, you will most likely work as a(n)
    a. Controller
    b. Chief financial executive
    c. Auditor
    d. IRS agent

    ANS: C

24. Which of the following is NOT a service typically provided by large public accounting firms?
    a. Auditing
    b. Forecasting
    c. Consulting
    d. Tax accounting

    ANS: B

25. Which of the following organizations has specific legal authority to establish accounting standards for publicly held companies?
    a. Financial Accounting Standards Board (FASB)
    b. Securities and Exchange Commission (SEC)
    c. Internal Revenue Service (IRS)
    d. American Institute of Certified Public Accountants (AICPA)

    ANS: B

26. The Sarbanes-Oxley Act created the
    a. Financial Accounting Standards Board
    b. Public Company Accounting Oversight Board
    c. Arthur Andersen CPA firm
    d. Enron-WorldCom Fraud Committee

    ANS: B

International Business

27. Accountants are MOST concerned with
    a. Foreign companies operating in the United States
    b. U.S. companies with domestic customers
    c. U.S. companies with foreign customers
    d. All of the above

    ANS: D

28. The organization that develops worldwide accounting standards is the
    a. International Committee on Accounting Standards (ICAS)
    b. International Accounting Standards Board (IASB)
    c. International Board of Accounting Standards (IBAS)
    d. International Accounting Standards Committee (IASC)

    ANS: B

29. Standards established by the International Accounting Standards Board are NOT accepted in
    a. The United States
    b. China
    c. Germany
    d. Switzerland

    ANS: A

Ethics in Accounting

30. Ethics are especially important in accounting because
    a. Independent accountants represent the public interest
    b. Accountants can steal money more easily than other employees
    c. Accountants have historically committed more company thefts than other employees
    d. The accounting profession does not have a code of professional conduct

    ANS: A

31. What organization has established the Code of Professional Conduct for the accounting profession?
    a. FASB
    b. SEC
    c. AICPA
    d. GAAP

    ANS: C

PROBLEMS

1. Identify and describe the functions of an accounting system.

    ANS: The functions of an accounting system are analysis, bookkeeping, and evaluation. Analysis involves analyzing business transactions to determine what information should be captured by the accounting system. Bookkeeping is tracking activities on a day-to-day basis. Evaluation uses summary information to evaluate the financial health and performance of a business.

2. List the steps involved in the decision-making process.

    ANS:

    Step 1:   Identify the issue.
    Step 2:   Gather information.
    Step 3:   Identify alternatives.
    Step 4:   Select the alternative that will most likely result in the desired objective.

3. Identify the three primary financial statements and discuss the content of each.

    ANS: The balance sheet reports the assets, liabilities, and owners' equity of a business.

    The income statement reports the net income or net loss of a company, which represents the difference between revenues and expenses.

    The statement of cash flows reports the cash inflows and outflows from operating, investing, and financing activities.

4. List six users of accounting information and indicate whether they are an internal or external user.

    ANS:

Management	internal
Creditors (Lenders)	external
Investors	external
Suppliers	external
Customers	external
Employees	external
Competitors	external
Government agencies	external
The press	external

5. It is often said that companies must keep two sets of books. Isn't this dishonest? Explain.

    ANS: No, it is not dishonest. Companies are subject to both the rules governing financial accounting and those governing tax accounting. One set of books must be maintained according to GAAP, from which the company's financial statements are prepared. The other set of books is maintained in compliance with income tax regulations, from which the company's tax return is prepared.

Chapter 1—Accounting Information: Users and Uses—Quiz A

Name_____   Section_____

TRUE/FALSE

Circle T or F to indicate whether each of the following statements is true or false.

T F   1.   Accounting is a service activity.

T F   2.   A major function of accounting is to accumulate reliable economic and analytical data that reflect the progress and status of an enterprise's activities.

T F   3.   Creditors and investors are usually considered the most important internal users of accounting information.

T F   4.   The Financial Accounting Standards Board is part of the Securities and Exchange Commission.

T F   5.   CPAs have adopted a Code of Professional Conduct to guide their actions.

T F   6.   U.S. accounting practices are adopted by all other countries in the world.

T F   7.   The environment of accounting is one of an international economy.

T F   8.   The AICPA Code of Conduct requires CPAs to be independent of their clients.

T F   9.   Since accountants only work with numbers, they need not be concerned about ethical considerations in business dealings.

T F   10.   Management accounting typically refers to reports a company's management sends to shareholders to describe management's actions during the year.

Name_____   Section_____

MATCHING

In the spaces provided, write the letter of the definition for each of the following terms:

   a. A system for providing quantitative information about economic entities that is useful for making sound economic decisions.
   b. The area of accounting concerned with reporting information to interested external parties.
   c. Reports summarizing the financial operations of business entities.
   d. Authoritative guidelines that define accounting practice at a particular time.
   e. The procedures for analyzing, recording, classifying, summarizing, and reporting accounting data.
   f. The area of accounting concerned with providing internal financial reports for decision-making purposes.
   g. The national organization of CPAs in the United States.
   h. The preservation of a systematic, quantitative record of an activity.
   i. The private organization responsible for establishing standards for financial accounting and reporting in the United States.
   j. The government body responsible for regulating financial reporting practices used by public corporations in connection with the buying and selling of stocks and bonds.

1. _____   Financial statements

2. _____   Financial Accounting Standards Board (FASB)

3. _____   Management accounting

4. _____   Securities and Exchange Commission (SEC)

5. _____   Accounting

6. _____   Bookkeeping

7. _____   American Institute of Certified Public Accountants (AICPA)

8. _____   Accounting cycle

9. _____   Financial accounting

10. _____   Generally accepted accounting principles (GAAP)

Quiz Solutions

Quiz A

1. T
2. T
3. F
4. F
5. T
6. F
7. T
8. T
9. F
10. F

Quiz B

1. c
2. i
3. f
4. j
5. a
6. h
7. g
8. e
9. b
10. d

MULTIPLE CHOICE

The Balance Sheet

1. The basic accounting equation is
   a. Assets = Liabilities + Owners' equity
   b. Assets + Liabilities = Owners' equity
   c. Assets + Owners' equity = Liabilities
   d. Liabilities – Owners' equity = Assets

   ANS: A

2. The idea that an increase or decrease on one side of the accounting equation must be offset exactly by an increase or decrease on the other side of the accounting equation is
   a. The additive concept
   b. The going concern assumption
   c. The monetary measurement concept
   d. Double-entry accounting

   ANS: D

3. A transaction that causes an increase in an asset may also cause a(n)
   a. Decrease in owners' equity
   b. Increase in another asset
   c. Decrease in a liability
   d. Increase in either a liability or owners' equity

   ANS: D

4. The three major types of business entities are
   a. Profit, nonprofit, and corporate organizations
   b. Corporations, associations, and nonprofit organizations
   c. Corporations, partnerships, and proprietorships
   d. Institutions, partnerships, and corporations

   ANS: C

5. A business owned by one person is called a
   a. Nonprofit organization
   b. Partnership
   c. Corporation
   d. Proprietorship

   ANS: D

6. A business owned by two or more individuals or entities is called a(n)
   a. Nonprofit organization
   b. Partnership
   c. Institution
   d. Proprietorship

   ANS: B

7. Owners of a corporation are referred to as
   a. Debtors
   b. Partners
   c. Stockholders
   d. Creditors

   ANS: C

8. Which of the following is a separate legal entity from its owners?
   a. Proprietorship
   b. Partnership
   c. Corporation
   d. All of the above

   ANS: C

9. Which of the following is true of the balance sheet?
   a. It includes revenue and expense accounts.
   b. It identifies a company's assets and liabilities as of a specific date.
   c. It shows the results of operations for an accounting period.
   d. It discloses the amount of dividends paid.

   ANS: B

10. Distributions by a corporation to its stockholders are called
    a. Dividends
    b. Retained earnings
    c. Income
    d. Withdrawals

    ANS: A

11. The financial statement that reports resources owned, the obligations to transfer resources to other organizations, and the claims by the entity's owners is known as the
    a. Income statement
    b. Statement of retained earnings
    c. Balance sheet
    d. Statement of cash flows

    ANS: C

12. Another name for the balance sheet is the
    a. Statement of cash flows
    b. Statement of earnings
    c. Statement of financial position
    d. Retained earnings statement

    ANS: C

13. Which of the following financial statements reports information as of a specific date?
    a. Income statement
    b. Statement of retained earnings
    c. Statement of cash flows
    d. Balance sheet

    ANS: D

14. Which of the following financial statements provides a picture of the enterprise at a particular point in time?
    a. Balance sheet
    b. Income statement
    c. Statement of cash flows
    d. All of the above

    ANS: A

15. Which of the following types of accounts are NOT found on the balance sheet?
    a. Revenues
    b. Assets
    c. Liabilities
    d. Owners' equity

    ANS: A

16. The heading of formal financial statements should include
    a. The name of the company
    b. The title of the statement
    c. The date of, or period covered by, the statement
    d. All of the above

    ANS: D

17. Current assets usually are listed on a balance sheet in
    a. Decreasing order of liquidity
    b. Increasing order of liquidity
    c. A random fashion
    d. Decreasing order of profitability

    ANS: A

18. Which of the following would be classified as a current asset?
    a. Accounts payable
    b. Land
    c. Capital stock
    d. Accounts receivable

    ANS: D

19. Economic resources that are owned or controlled by an enterprise are called
    a. Assets
    b. Liabilities
    c. Revenues
    d. Gains

    ANS: A

20. Which of the following is NOT normally considered to be an asset?
    a. Cash
    b. Accounts receivable
    c. Land
    d. Accounts payable

    ANS: D

21. Which of the following generally is NOT considered to be a liability?
    a. Notes payable
    b. Mortgage payable
    c. Accounts receivable
    d. Accounts payable

    ANS: C

22. An enterprise's obligations to pay cash or other economic resources to others are called
    a. Liabilities
    b. Expenses
    c. Losses
    d. Assets

    ANS: A

23. Which of the following types of accounts show how resources came into a firm?
    a. Liabilities
    b. Owners' equity
    c. Assets
    d. Both a and b

    ANS: D

24. Which of the following usually is NOT considered to be an owners' equity account?
    a. Capital Stock
    b. Retained Earnings
    c. Inventory
    d. All the above are owners' equity accounts

    ANS: C

25. Companies prepare classified and comparative financial statements because
    a. They are required by international accounting principles
    b. They provide financial statement readers with useful information about trends in financial position and operating performance
    c. They are required by the IRS
    d. They show changes in a company's management policies

    ANS: B

26. A corporation's periodic cash payments to its shareholders are called
    a. Withdrawals
    b. Retained earnings
    c. Income
    d. Dividends

    ANS: D

27. The total amount invested to acquire an ownership interest in a corporation is called
    a. Retained earnings
    b. Capital stock
    c. Net assets
    d. Owners' equity

    ANS: B

28. Economic resources that are owned or controlled by an enterprise are called
    a. Gains
    b. Liabilities
    c. Revenues
    d. Assets

    ANS: D

29. Which of the following is generally considered to be an asset?
    a. Notes payable
    b. Mortgage payable
    c. Accounts receivable
    d. Accounts payable

    ANS: C

30. Net assets are equal to
    a. Total assets minus owners' equity
    b. Total assets minus net income
    c. Total assets minus dividends paid
    d. Total assets minus total liabilities

    ANS: D

31. Which of the following is normally considered to be a liability?
    a. Cash
    b. Accounts receivable
    c. Land
    d. Accounts payable

    ANS: D

32. The debts, or obligations, of a company are called
    a. Assets
    b. Liabilities
    c. Owners' equity
    d. Net income

    ANS: B

33. Which of the following is generally considered to be a liability?
    a. Accounts receivable
    b. Capital stock
    c. Notes payable
    d. Retained earnings

    ANS: C

34. Which of the following accounts is NOT an asset account?
    a. Equipment
    b. Accounts Receivable
    c. Accounts Payable
    d. Supplies

    ANS: C

35. What is the primary limitation of the balance sheet?
    a. It does not reflect the net assets of a company.
    b. It does not reflect the current value of the company.
    c. It does not reflect the number of shares issued.
    d. It does not reflect the undistributed earnings of a company.

    ANS: B

36. If a corporation has assets of $200,000, liabilities of $30,000, and retained earnings of $100,000, what is the amount of capital stock?
   a. $30,000
   b. $0
   c. $70,000
   d. $130,000

   ANS: C

37. The following data were taken from the records of Moss Corporation for the year ending December 31, 2006.

	01/01/06	12/31/06
Assets	$7,500	?
Liabilities	5,720	$6,910
Owners' equity	?	4,310

   Given the above information, owners' equity on January 1, 2006, was
   a. $13,220
   b. $1,780
   c. $590
   d. $5,130

   ANS: B

38. The following data were taken from the records of Moss Corporation for the year ending December 31, 2006:

	01/01/06	12/31/06
Assets	$7,500	?
Liabilities	5,720	$6,910
Owners' equity	?	4,310

   Given the above information, assets on December 31, 2006, were
   a. $11,220
   b. $3,350
   c. $12,040
   d. $7,500

   ANS: A

The Income Statement

39. Expense and revenue accounts appear on the
   a. Balance sheet
   b. Income statement
   c. Retained earnings statement
   d. Funds statement

   ANS: B

40. Resource increases from the sale of goods or services are called
    a. Net income
    b. Assets
    c. Gains
    d. Revenues

    ANS: D

41. Revenues cause
    a. An increase in net assets
    b. A decrease in net assets
    c. No change in net assets
    d. An increase in liabilities

    ANS: A

42. Costs that are incurred during the normal operations of a business to generate revenues are called
    a. Losses
    b. Liabilities
    c. Expenses
    d. Assets

    ANS: C

43. Which of the following is an overall measure of the performance of a business entity's activities?
    a. Revenues
    b. Net income (or net loss)
    c. Assets
    d. Owners' equity

    ANS: B

44. The beginning balance of retained earnings will be greater than the ending balance if
    a. The company has a net income greater than dividends paid
    b. The company issues additional shares of stock during the period
    c. The company has a net income less than dividends paid
    d. The revenues earned for the period are greater than the expenses incurred and dividends
        paid

    ANS: C

45. Earnings per share is equal to
    a. Net income divided by total number of shares of stock outstanding
    b. Total revenues divided by total number of shares of stock outstanding
    c. Total revenues divided by the number of shares of stock sold during the year
    d. Net income divided by the number of shares of stock sold during the year

    ANS: A

46. Another name for the income statement is
    a. Statement of cash flows
    b. Statement of financial position
    c. Statement of earnings
    d. Retained earnings statement

    ANS: C

47. Which of the following would be included on an income statement?
    a. Cash
    b. Accounts receivable
    c. Land
    d. Rent expense

    ANS: D

48. Which of the following is the correct way to date an income statement?
    a. For the Year Ended December 31, 2006
    b. At December 31, 2006
    c. As of December 31, 2006
    d. Either b or c

    ANS: A

49. The difference between sales and cost of goods sold is called
    a. Gross profit
    b. Intermediate profit
    c. Net income
    d. Gross income

    ANS: A

50. If a company sells its equipment for more than it is valued on the balance sheet, the difference is called a(n)
    a. Income
    b. Revenue
    c. Profit
    d. Gain

    ANS: D

51. Which of the following is NOT included in comprehensive income?
    a. Changes in the value of certain derivative financial instruments
    b. Net income
    c. Changes in owners' investment
    d. Changes in foreign currency exchange rates

    ANS: C

52. If a company has $200,000 of sales revenue, pays $10,000 in dividends, and has net income of $60,000, how much were the expenses for the year?
    a. $130,000
    b. $160,000
    c. $150,000
    d. $140,000

    ANS: D

53. During the year, Reese Company earned revenues of $114,000 and incurred $98,000 for various operating expenses. There are 1,280 shares of stock outstanding. Earnings per share is
    a. $12.80
    b. $12.50
    c. $8.80
    d. $8.50

    ANS: B

54. The financial statement that presents a summary of the revenues and expenses of a business for a specific period of time, such as a month or year, is called a(n)
    a. Statement of cash flows
    b. Statement of retained earnings
    c. Income statement
    d. Balance sheet

    ANS: C

55. The following information was taken from the records of Merle Corporation for the period ending December 31, 2006:

Advertising expense	$1,200
Equipment	800
Accounts receivable	1,500
Notes payable	6,000
Retained earnings	8,420
Utilities expense	1,385
Revenues	4,620
Dividends	975
Interest receivable	125
Rent expense	655

    Assuming that 3,450 shares of stock are outstanding, earnings per share is approximately
    a. $1.40
    b. $0.40
    c. $0.27
    d. $0.23

    ANS: B

56. Eddy Corporation reported the following data for the period: Earnings per share, $3.00; Retained Earnings, $27,000; Revenues, $75,000; Capital Stock, $15,000; Expenses, $64,500. With this information, how many shares of stock are outstanding?
   a. 9,000
   b. 5,000
   c. 4,000
   d. 3,500

   ANS: D

57. The following information was taken from the records of Tellers Corporation for the month ended December 31, 2006:

Advertising expense	$20,625
Income tax expense	13,095
Accounts payable	13,450
Dividends paid	14,125
Retained earnings (12/01/06)	57,860
Consulting fees revenue	93,550
Rent expense	11,728
Supplies expense	16,917

   Given the above information, net income is
   a. $45,110
   b. $35,310
   c. $31,185
   d. $11,385

   ANS: C

58. The following information was taken from the records of Tellers Corporation for the month ended December 31, 2006:

Advertising expense	$20,625
Income tax expense	13,095
Accounts payable	13,450
Dividends paid	14,125
Retained earnings (12/01/06)	57,860
Consulting fees revenue	93,550
Rent expense	11,728
Supplies expense	16,917

   If Tellers has 2,100 shares of stock outstanding, earnings per share is approximately
   a. $46.51
   b. $14.85
   c. $16.81
   d. $4.67

   ANS: B

The Statement of Retained Earnings

59. Which of the following is NOT included in the statement of retained earnings?
    a. Dividends
    b. Net income
    c. Net loss
    d. Owner investment

    ANS: D

60. The following information was taken from the records of McDyce Corporation for the year ended December 31, 2006:

Dividends paid	$ 2,560
Service revenue	18,100
Accounts payable	27,950
Capital stock	75,750
Total expenses	13,400
Retained earnings (01/01/06)	8,680

    The retained earnings balance at December 31, 2006, was
    a. $86,570
    b. $10,820
    c. $58,620
    d. $13,380

    ANS: B

The Statements of Cash Flows

61. A major source of cash from operating activities is
    a. Receipts from sale of goods
    b. Receipts from borrowing
    c. Receipts from sale of building
    d. Receipts from investment by owner

    ANS: A

62. The financial statement that shows the origin and disposition of an enterprise's cash flows is called the
    a. Balance sheet
    b. Statement of cash flows
    c. Income statement
    d. Retained earnings statement

    ANS: B

63. Which of the following is a primary use of cash?
    a. Borrowing
    b. Investment by owners
    c. Operating expenses
    d. Sale of equipment

    ANS: C

64. Which of the following financial statements shows an entity's cash receipts and payments?
    a. The statement of financial position
    b. The statement of cash flows
    c. The statement of earnings
    d. The statement of changes in owners' equity

    ANS: B

65. Which of the following classifications does NOT appear on the statement of cash flows?
    a. Investing
    b. Operating
    c. Borrowing
    d. Financing

    ANS: C

How the Financial Statements Tie Together

66. The idea that certain figures on an operating statement help to explain changes in figures on comparative balance sheets is referred to as
    a. Liquidity
    b. Double entry
    c. Articulation
    d. Classification

    ANS: C

67. During 2006, Cabrera Corporation had revenues of $99,000 and expenses of $78,000. Dividends of $14,000 were paid during the year and additional stock was issued for $10,700. If total assets and total liabilities on January 1, 2006, were $65,000 and $28,000, respectively, how much is owners' equity on December 31, 2006?
    a. $68,700
    b. $54,700
    c. $40,700
    d. $32,700

    ANS: B

68. The following information was taken from the records of Hart Corporation for the month ended December 31, 2006:

Advertising expense	$20,625
Income tax expense	13,095
Accounts payable	13,450
Dividends paid	14,125
Retained earnings (12/01/06)	57,860
Consulting fees revenue	97,875
Rent expense	11,728
Supplies expense	16,917

Given the above information, retained earnings as of December 31, 2006, is
a. $79,045
b. $79,245
c. $55,795
d. $33,895

ANS: B

69. The transactions carried out by Blue Waters Corporation during the year caused an increase in total assets of $25,650 and a decrease in total liabilities of $12,250. If no additional stock was issued during the year and dividends of $7,850 were paid, what was the net income for the year?
a. $53,600
b. $45,750
c. $29,100
d. $13,400

ANS: B

70. On April 1, Bonita Corporation's retained earnings account had a balance of $785,000. During April, Bonita had revenues of $135,000 and expenses of $93,000. On April 30, retained earnings had a balance of $811,500. What amount of dividends were paid during April?
a. $42,500
b. $30,750
c. $15,500
d. $13,250

ANS: C

71. The following data were taken from the records of Mendez Corporation for the year ended December 31, 2006:

	01/01/06	12/31/06
Assets	$3,750	?
Liabilities	2,860	$3,455
Owners' equity...........	?	3,455
Dividends paid		1,230

Given the above information, net income for the year ended December 31, 2006, is
a. $1,675
b. $2,120
c. $2,905
d. $3,795

ANS: D

72. If a company has assets of $230,000, liabilities of $50,000, and capital stock of $105,000, what is the amount of retained earnings?
a. $75,000
b. $105,000
c. $55,000
d. $155,000

ANS: A

Notes to the Financial Statements

73. Vital information that CANNOT be captured solely by dollar amounts is reported in a firm's
a. Balance sheet
b. Notes to financial statements
c. Income statement
d. Statement of retained earnings

ANS: B

74. Which of the following is NOT one of the four general types of financial statement notes?
a. Summary of significant accounting policies
b. Additional information about the summary totals found in the financial statements
c. Disclosure of important information that is not recognized in the financial statements
d. Supplementary information required by the Internal Revenue Service

ANS: D

The External Audit

75. An independent audit report is usually issued by
a. Management
b. A government accountant
c. A private detective
d. A certified public accountant

ANS: D

76. In completing an audit of a company's financial statements, auditors
    a. Guarantee that the financial statements are accurate
    b. Examine every transaction underlying the financial statements
    c. Assume responsibility for the accuracy of the financial statements
    d. Provide some assurance that the financial statements are not misleading

    ANS: D

77. The accuracy of the information contained in the financial statements is the responsibility of the
    a. Stockholders
    b. Certified public accountant
    c. Management
    d. Securities and Exchange Commission

    ANS: C

The Separate Entity Concept

78. For accounting purposes, which of the following is considered to be a separate entity from its owner(s)?
    a. Proprietorship
    b. Partnership
    c. Corporation
    d. All of the above

    ANS: D

79. The idea that only transactions of the business being accounted for are entered in the accounting records is the
    a. Separate entity concept
    b. Arm's-length transaction assumption
    c. Money measurement concept
    d. Going concern assumption

    ANS: A

Assumption of Arm's-Length Transactions

80. The idea that both parties to a transaction must be rational and free to act independently is the
    a. Monetary measurement concept
    b. Arm's-length transaction assumption
    c. Going concern assumption
    d. Cost principle

    ANS: B

81. Suppose you decide to purchase a stereo and an independent store dealer offers to sell you a system that retails for $4,000 for a price of $3,695. After some negotiation, you purchase the system for $3,400. The $3,400 is considered the accounting measurement for the transaction because of the
    a. Going concern assumption
    b. Fair value assumption
    c. Double-entry assumption
    d. Arm's-length transaction assumption

    ANS: D

The Cost Principle

82. The idea that transactions are recorded at their exchange prices at the transaction date is referred to as the
    a. Arm's-length transaction assumption
    b. Monetary measurement principle
    c. Cost principle
    d. Going concern assumption

    ANS: C

83. Lange Company purchased land for $60,000 in 2004. In 2006, the land is valued at $75,000. The land would appear on the company's books in 2006 at
    a. $15,000
    b. $60,000
    c. $45,000
    d. $75,000

    ANS: B

The Monetary Measurement Concept

84. The accounting idea that only items quantifiable in terms of U.S. currency are recorded is the
    a. Monetary measurement concept
    b. Arm's-length transaction assumption
    c. Going concern concept
    d. Double-entry assumption

    ANS: A

Going Concern Assumption

85. Which of the following is an essential characteristic of the traditional accounting model?
    a. Going concern assumption
    b. Cost principle
    c. Entity concept
    d. All are essential characteristics

    ANS: D

86. The idea that businesses must be accounted for as though they will exist at least for the foreseeable future is the
    a. Going concern concept
    b. Entity concept
    c. Monetary measurement concept
    d. Arm's-length transaction assumption

    ANS: A

PROBLEMS

1. The following financial statement was prepared by Schenck Corporation's accountant.

Schenck Corporation
Balance Sheet
December 31, 2006

Assets		Liabilities and Stockholders' Equity	
Cash	$ 6,000	Accounts Payable	$ 4,000
Accounts Receivable	6,500	Notes Payable	?
Inventory	15,000	Total liabilities	$ 9,500
Building	?	Capital Stock (10,000	
Total assets	$165,000	shares @ $10 per share)	$120,000
		Retained Earnings	?
		Total stockholders' equity	?
		Total liabilities and	
		stockholders' equity	?

Based on the above balance sheet for Schenck Corporation, what are the correct balances for the items listed below:

1. Building
2. Notes Payable
3. Total liabilities and stockholders' equity
4. Total stockholders' equity
5. Retained Earnings

ANS:

1.	$137,500	($165,000 – $6,000 – $6,500 – $15,000)
2.	$5,500	($9,500 – $4,000)
3.	$165,000	(same as Total assets)
4.	$155,500	($165,000 – $9,500)
5.	$35,500	($155,500 – $120,000)

2. Identify the three major types of business entities and discuss the characteristics of each.

ANS: Proprietorship. A proprietorship is a business owned by one person. The owner also manages the business. Additionally, the business is not a separate legal entity from the owner (i.e., the owner is responsible for all the debts and obligations of the business).

Partnership. A partnership is a business owned by two or more individuals. The owners generally manage the business and are legally responsible for the debts and obligations of the business (i.e., it is not a separate legal entity).

Corporation. A corporation is a business owned by stockholders. It is chartered (incorporated) as a separate legal entity under the laws of a particular state or country. The stockholders elect a board of directors, which hires executives to manage the business.

3. The comparative balance sheet for Brooks Company is presented below.

Brooks Company
Comparative Balance Sheet
December 31, 2006 and 2005

Assets	12/31/06	12/31/05
Cash	$30,000	$25,000
Supplies	?	7,000
Land	40,000	40,000
Equipment	25,000	20,000
Liabilities and Stockholders' Equity		
Accounts payable	$18,000	$15,000
Notes payable	20,000	22,000
Capital stock	40,000	40,000
Retained earnings	27,000	?

Additional information for Brooks' 2006 operations revealed that the company had revenues of $50,000 for the year and no dividends were paid. Based on this information, compute the balances below.

1. Retained Earnings balance at 12/31/05
2. Supplies balance at 12/31/06
3. Total current assets as of 12/31/06
4. Total expenses incurred for 2006

ANS:

1. $15,000 = [Total assets at 12/31/05 of $92,000 – ($15,000 + $22,000 + $40,000)]
2. $10,000 = [Total liabilities and stockholders' equity at 12/31/06 of $105,000 – ($30,000 + $40,000 + $25,000)]
3. $40,000 = ($30,000 + $10,000)
4. $38,000 = (R/E at 12/31/05 + revenue – R/E at 12/31/06) = ($15,000 + $50,000 – $27,000)

4. The following information was taken from the Hall Corporation's books:

Accounts receivable	$ 98,000	Salaries expense	$165,000
Income tax expense	62,000	Accounts payable	50,000
Retained earnings	252,000	Supplies expense	46,000
Service revenue	450,000	Utilities expense	3,000
Advertising expense	18,000	Rent expense	12,000

Prepare an income statement for the year ended December 31, 2006 (assume that 10,000 shares of stock are outstanding).

ANS:

Hall Corporation
Income Statement
For the Year Ended December 31, 2006

Service revenue..		$450,000
Expenses:		
Advertising expense...	$ 18,000	
Salaries expense...	165,000	
Supplies expense..	46,000	
Utilities expense...	3,000	
Rent expense	12,000	244,000
Income before taxes		$206,000
Income tax expense...		62,000
Net income...		$144,000
EPS ($144,000/10,000 shares)		$ 14.40

5. For each of the following items, indicate whether it would be classified as an operating activity (OA), an investing activity (IA), or a financing activity (FA) on the statement of cash flows.

_____ a. Cash payments for taxes

_____ b. Cash proceeds from the sale of land

_____ c. Cash receipts from providing services

_____ d. Cash proceeds from a long-term loan

_____ e. Issuance of stock for cash

_____ f. Cash payments for interest

_____ g. Cash payments for the purchase of equipment

_____ h. Cash payments for dividends paid to stockholders

ANS:

a. OA
b. IA
c. OA
d. FA
e. FA
f. OA
g. IA
h. FA

6. While the three financial statements contain a lot of information, they don't tell the readers everything they may need to know about a company. Additional information can be found in the notes to the financial statements. Identify the four types of notes (be specific).

ANS:

1. Summary of significant accounting policies.
2. Additional information about the summary totals found in the financial statements.
3. Disclosure of important information that is not recognized in the financial statements.
4. Supplementary information required by the FASB or the SEC.

7. Financial accounting is based on certain fundamental concepts and assumptions. The importance of these items is that they allow the accountant to determine which events to account for and in what manner. Define the following:

a. Separate entity concept
b. Arm's-length transactions
c. Cost principle
d. Monetary measurement concept
e. Going concern assumption

ANS:

a. The idea that the activities of an entity are to be separated from those of the individual owners.
b. Business dealings between independent and rational parties who are looking out for their own interests.
c. The idea that transactions are recorded at their historical costs or exchange prices at the transaction date.
d. The idea that money is the accounting unit of measurement, and that only economic activities measurable in monetary terms are included in the accounting model.
e. The idea that an accounting entity will have a continuing existence for the foreseeable future.

Chapter 2—Financial Statements: An Overview—Quiz A

Name_____   Section_____

TRUE/FALSE

Circle T or F to indicate whether each of the following statements is true or false.

T F   1.   Financial statements are designed to provide useful information about specific entities. As a result, they must serve many different users.

T F   2.   The balance sheet does not include all the resources of a firm.

T F   3.   Another name for owners' equity in a corporation is stockholders' equity.

T F   4.   The balance in owners' equity represents the current value of the business entity.

T F   5.   Retained earnings is equal to the total earnings of a corporation since it began operations.

T F   6.   Another name for net income is earnings.

T F   7.   Retained earnings is reported on the income statement.

T F   8.   All outflows of cash from an entity are considered to be expenses.

T F   9.   Earnings-per-share amounts are reported on a company's income statement.

T F   10.   The statement of cash flows and the income statement cover the same period of time.

Name_____   Section_____

MATCHING

In the spaces provided, write the letter of the statement on which each of the following items is normally found.

      a. Balance sheet
      b. Income statement
      c. Statement of retained earnings

1. _____   Cash

2. _____   Income taxes (expense)

3. _____   Gross profit

4. _____   Dividends declared

5. _____   Accounts receivable

6. _____   Sales revenue

7. _____   Accounts payable

8. _____   Capital stock

9. _____   Land

10. _____   Advertising expense

Name_____   **Section**_____

MATCHING

In the spaces provided, write the letter of the proper classification for each of the following items:

   a. Asset
   b. Liability
   c. Owners' equity
   d. Revenue
   e. Expense

1. _____ Accounts receivable

2. _____ Inventory

3. _____ Sale of merchandise

4. _____ Rent paid for the current period

5. _____ Mortgage payable

6. _____ Retained earnings

7. _____ Accounts payable

8. _____ Land

9. _____ Utilities paid for the current period

10. _____ Capital stock

Quiz Solutions

Quiz A	Quiz B	Quiz C
1. T	1. a	1. a
2. T	2. b	2. a
3. T	3. b	3. d
4. F	4. c	4. e
5. F	5. a	5. b
6. T	6. b	6. c
7. F	7. a	7. b
8. F	8. a	8. a
9. T	9. a	9. e
10. T	10. b	10. c

MULTIPLE CHOICE

How Can We Collect All This Information?

1. Which of the following is NOT a step in the accounting cycle?
    a. Journalizing transactions
    b. Posting to accounts
    c. Forecasting sales
    d. Preparing financial statements

    ANS: C

2. Which of the following steps is normally first in the accounting cycle?
    a. Transactions are journalized.
    b. Journal accounts are posted.
    c. A trial balance is prepared.
    d. Business documents are analyzed.

    ANS: D

3. Which of the following is NOT an advantage of a computerized accounting system over a manual accounting system?
    a. A computerized system is faster.
    b. A computerized system is more accurate once the data are correctly entered.
    c. Data can be managed more easily in a computerized system.
    d. A computerized system can analyze the information for decision making.

    ANS: D

The Accounting Equation

4. The basic accounting equation is
    a. Assets – Liabilities = Owners' equity
    b. Assets + Owners' equity = Liabilities
    c. Assets + Liabilities = Owners' equity
    d. Both a and b

    ANS: A

5. Borrowing money from a bank
    a. Increases assets and decreases liabilities
    b. Increases liabilities and decreases assets
    c. Decreases assets and decreases liabilities
    d. Increases assets and increases liabilities

    ANS: D

6. The basic accounting equation
   a. Is out of balance after each journal entry
   b. Should always balance
   c. Is balanced only at the end of the period with closing entries
   d. Is balanced only at the end of the period with adjusting entries

   ANS: B

7. Which of the following would usually NOT happen in a single transaction?
   a. Increase assets, decrease liabilities
   b. Increase assets, increase liabilities
   c. Increase liabilities, decrease owners' equity
   d. Decrease assets, decrease owners' equity

   ANS: A

8. The purchase of supplies on account
   a. Increases assets and decreases liabilities
   b. Decreases assets and increases liabilities
   c. Increases assets and increases liabilities
   d. Decreases assets and decreases liabilities

   ANS: C

9. If a company purchased equipment for cash, the accounting equation would show a(n)
   a. Increase in assets and a decrease in assets
   b. Decrease in liabilities and an increase in assets
   c. Increase in liabilities and an increase in assets
   d. Decrease in liabilities and a decrease in assets

   ANS: A

10. A credit sale of merchandise for a price that exceeds the cost of the merchandise
    a. Increases net assets and increases liabilities
    b. Decreases net assets and increases revenues
    c. Increases liabilities and increases revenues
    d. Increases net assets and increases revenues

    ANS: D

11. If a company paid off a loan, the accounting equation would show a(n)
    a. Increase in assets and a decrease in liabilities
    b. Decrease in assets and a decrease in liabilities
    c. Increase in liabilities and a decrease in assets
    d. Increase in assets and an increase in liabilities

    ANS: B

12. If a company purchased equipment by borrowing money, the accounting equation would show a(n)
    a. Increase in assets and a decrease in assets
    b. Decrease in liabilities and an increase in assets
    c. Increase in assets and an increase in liabilities
    d. Decrease in liabilities and a decrease in assets

    ANS: C

13. The purchase of supplies with cash would show a(n)
    a. Increase in assets and a decrease in assets
    b. Decrease in liabilities and an increase in assets
    c. Increase in assets and an increase in liabilities
    d. Decrease in liabilities and a decrease in assets

    ANS: A

14. If a company purchased a building with a cash down payment and the balance with a loan, the accounting equation will show a(n)
    a. Decrease in assets and an increase in liabilities
    b. Increase in assets and an increase in liabilities
    c. Increase in assets and a decrease in liabilities
    d. Decrease in assets and a decrease in liabilities

    ANS: B

15. If a company issues stock for cash, the accounting equation will show a(n)
    a. Increase in liabilities and a decrease in owners' equity
    b. Decrease in liabilities and a decrease in owners' equity
    c. Decrease in assets and an increase in owners' equity
    d. Increase in assets and an increase in owners' equity

    ANS: D

Using Accounts to Categorize Transactions

16. An entry to the left side of an account is always called a(n)
    a. Debit
    b. Credit
    c. Increase
    d. Decrease

    ANS: A

17. Which of the following types of accounts shows how resources came into a firm?
    a. Liabilities
    b. Owners' equity
    c. Assets
    d. Both a and b

    ANS: D

18. Liability accounts are increased
    a. By debits
    b. By credits
    c. On the left side
    d. Below the balance line

    ANS: B

19. The inventory account is increased by
    a. Credits
    b. Debits
    c. Either a or b
    d. Neither a nor b

    ANS: B

20. Owners' equity accounts are decreased with
    a. Debit entries
    b. Credit entries
    c. Liabilities
    d. Assets

    ANS: A

21. The capital stock account is
    a. Increased with a debit
    b. Increased with a credit
    c. An asset account
    d. A liability account

    ANS: B

22. Usually, when accounts receivable are collected, an asset is debited and
    a. Another asset is debited
    b. Another asset is credited
    c. A liability is debited
    d. A liability is credited

    ANS: B

23. When accounts receivable are collected,
    a. Total assets are increased
    b. Total assets are decreased
    c. Total assets remain constant
    d. Owners' equity increases

    ANS: C

24. When equipment is purchased with a cash down payment and a signed note for the balance, the net effect will be
    a. An increase in assets
    b. A decrease in liabilities
    c. A decrease in assets
    d. Both b and c

    ANS: A

25. When a note payable is given to settle an existing account payable,
    a. There is no net change in assets, liabilities, or owners' equity
    b. Net assets are increased
    c. Net liabilities are increased
    d. Net owners' equity is increased

    ANS: A

26. Which of the following types of entries would NOT usually be made?
    a. A credit to an asset account, a debit to a liability account
    b. A debit to an asset account, a credit to a liability account
    c. A debit to an asset account, a credit to an owners' equity account
    d. A debit to an asset account, a debit to a liability account

    ANS: D

27. An entry to the right side of an account is called a(n)
    a. Increase
    b. Credit
    c. Debit
    d. Decrease

    ANS: B

28. Owners' equity accounts are increased by
    a. Debits
    b. Expenses
    c. Credits
    d. The payment of dividends

    ANS: C

29. The inventory account is decreased with
    a. Debits
    b. Credits
    c. Both a and b
    d. None of the above

    ANS: B

30. Which of the following is true of the cash account?
    a. It normally has a credit balance.
    b. It is increased with credit entries.
    c. It is an owners' equity account.
    d. It is increased with debit entries.

    ANS: D

31. The debit and credit analysis of a transaction normally takes place
    a. When the entry is posted to a subsidiary ledger
    b. When the entry is recorded in a journal
    c. When the trial balance is prepared
    d. When the financial statements are prepared

    ANS: B

32. Capital Stock has what kind of a balance?
    a. Credit
    b. Left-side
    c. Debit
    d. Capital stock accounts can have either type of balance

    ANS: A

33. Which of the following is true?
    a. Assets + Liabilities = Owners' equity
    b. Credits = Assets
    c. Debits = Credits
    d. Assets = Liabilities – Owners' equity

    ANS: C

34. Which of the following types of accounts have a normal credit balance?
    a. Assets and expenses
    b. Liabilities and dividends
    c. Revenues and liabilities
    d. Owners' equity and dividends

    ANS: C

Expanding the Accounting Equation

35. Revenue accounts are
    a. Increased with debit entries
    b. Assets
    c. Increased with credit entries
    d. Maintained from period to period

    ANS: C

36. Which of the following types of accounts are affected when a company pays dividends to its shareholders?
    a. Assets
    b. Liabilities
    c. Owners' equity
    d. Both a and c

    ANS: D

37. A company's retained earnings balance would decrease by
    a. The declaration and payment of dividends
    b. Sales
    c. Investments by owners
    d. Net income

    ANS: A

38. Revenues
    a. Decrease assets
    b. Decrease owners' equity
    c. Increase liabilities
    d. Do none of the above

    ANS: D

39. Expense and revenue accounts can be considered to be subcategories of
    a. An asset account
    b. A liability account
    c. An owners' equity account
    d. None of the above

    ANS: C

40. Which of the following accounts would normally NOT have a credit balance?
    a. Accounts Payable
    b. Cost of Goods Sold
    c. Sales Revenue
    d. Retained Earnings

    ANS: B

41. The entry to record the payment of a note with interest usually includes a
    a. Debit to Cash
    b. Credit to Note Payable
    c. Debit to Interest Expense
    d. Credit to Note Receivable

    ANS: C

42. When dividends are paid,
    a. Assets are decreased and liabilities are decreased
    b. Assets are increased and owners' equity is increased
    c. Assets are decreased and owners' equity is increased
    d. Assets are decreased and owners' equity is decreased

    ANS: D

43. The supplies expense account
    a. Normally has a credit balance
    b. Is increased with a credit entry
    c. Is increased with a debit entry
    d. Is decreased with a debit entry

    ANS: C

44. The fees earned account in a dry cleaning business would be considered
    a. Revenue
    b. Expense
    c. Asset
    d. Liability

    ANS: A

45. Which of the following is true of revenue accounts?
    a. They are increased by debit entries.
    b. They are assets.
    c. They are increased by credit entries.
    d. They are subtracted from capital stock.

    ANS: C

46. Which of the following types of accounts would normally have a debit balance?
    a. Liabilities
    b. Retained earnings
    c. Expenses
    d. Capital stock

    ANS: C

47. Which of the following accounts is decreased with a debit?
    a. Rent Expense
    b. Retained Earnings
    c. Equipment
    d. Accounts Receivable

    ANS: B

48. The dividends account
    a. Is increased with a credit entry
    b. Is decreased with a debit entry
    c. Normally has a credit balance
    d. Normally has a debit balance

    ANS: D

49. Expense accounts
    a. Are increased with credit entries
    b. Are increased with debit entries
    c. Normally have credit balances
    d. Are closed to the capital stock account

    ANS: B

50. During March, Groh Corporation completed the following transactions:

    • Purchased inventory for $18,000 on credit.
    • Issued additional capital stock for $10,000.
    • Purchased equipment for $7,950 cash.

    As a result of these transactions, Groh's total assets would
    a. Increase by $28,000
    b. Increase by $20,050
    c. Increase by $17,950
    d. Increase by $10,050

    ANS: A

51. Assuming no other changes except a decrease in assets of $20,000, increase in liabilities of $10,000, and expenses of $60,000, by how much did owners' equity increase or decrease, and what were revenues for the period?
    a. Owners' equity increased $30,000; revenues were $90,000
    b. Owners' equity decreased $30,000; revenues were $30,000
    c. Owners' equity increased $10,000; revenues were $70,000
    d. Owners' equity decreased $10,000; revenues were $70,000

    ANS: B

52. Assuming that capital stock increased $5,000, net income was $100,000, and dividends were $120,000, if total assets increased by $25,000, what was the change in liabilities?
    a. Liabilities increased by $40,000.
    b. There was no change in liabilities.
    c. Liabilities decreased by $10,000.
    d. The answer cannot be determined from the data given.

    ANS: A

53. On May 1, James Corporation had total assets of $877,000. During May, the company completed the following transactions:

   • Barry Saunder, an owner in the firm, donated equipment to James Corporation. The equipment had a value of $6,700 at the time it was acquired by the firm.
   • Purchased a building for $78,000 and signed a note for the purchase.
   • Purchased $1,500 of supplies for cash.

   After these transactions were recorded, total assets would have a balance of
   a. $963,200
   b. $961,700
   c. $963,000
   d. $945,700

   ANS: B

54. As of June 1, Mega Corporation had total assets of $53,000. During June, the company had the following transactions:

   • Collected receivables of $8,700 from previous periods.
   • Generated revenues of $25,000, of which 40 percent were cash.
   • Incurred total expenses of $18,000, 60 percent of which were paid.

   After these transactions have been recorded, Mega would have total assets of
   a. $67,200
   b. $66,700
   c. $60,800
   d. $69,500

   ANS: A

55. Miles Motor Supplies had the following transactions during December:

   • Paid a note of $17,000 owed since March plus $425 for interest.
   • Sold $36,525 of merchandise to customers on account. Cost of goods sold was $21,250.
   • Paid accounts payable of $2,050.

   As a result of these transactions, at year-end, liabilities and owners' equity would show a total
   a. Decrease by $4,575
   b. Decrease by $4,200
   c. Decrease by $4,800
   d. Increase by $13,425

   ANS: B

56. During the period, Ritter Company completed the following transactions:

- Purchased $1,500 of supplies for cash.
- Signed a note with Firstland Bank for a $15,000 loan (ignore interest).
- Paid $6,600 of accounts payable.

As a result of these transactions, Ritter's total assets would
a. Increase by $24,000
b. Increase by $22,800
c. Increase by $8,400
d. Increase by $7,200

ANS: C

57. On June 30, the balances in the general ledger accounts of Pancho Company resulted in the following totals:

Assets	$517,600
Liabilities	323,400
Owners' equity	200,500

Total assets do not equal total liabilities plus owners' equity because the following errors were made:

- Supplies of $500 were on hand but were not included in assets because all purchases were debited to Supplies Expense.
- Credit sales of $15,700 were posted to the sales revenue account as $17,500. The accounts receivable account was posted correctly.
- Equipment purchased on credit for $51,600 was incorrectly posted to Notes Payable as $56,100. No error was made in the equipment account.

The correct balances in the asset, liability, and owners' equity accounts, respectively, should be

	Assets	Liabilities	Owners' Equity
a.	$518,100;	$318,900;	$199,200
b.	$517,850;	$327,900;	$189,950
c.	$517,350;	$327,900;	$189,450
d.	$517,850;	$318,900;	$198,950

ANS: A

How Do We Record the Effects of Transactions?

58. Transactions are typically entered into the general journal in which order?
a. Alphabetically by account
b. By account number, lowest to highest
c. By dollar amount, lowest to highest
d. By transaction date

ANS: D

59. Which of the following is NOT usually part of an entry in the general journal?
    a. Account numbers for the debit and credit entry
    b. Account titles for the debit and credit entry
    c. The transaction date
    d. An explanation of the transaction

    ANS: A

60. A book of original entry is called a
    a. Journal
    b. Ledger
    c. Trial balance
    d. Check register

    ANS: A

61. A chronological listing of all economic transactions is maintained in a company's
    a. Work sheets
    b. Ledgers
    c. Journals
    d. Balance sheets

    ANS: C

62. Kiu Company received and immediately paid a $7,500 utility bill from Chula Vista Gas and Electric Company. The entry by Chula Vista Gas and Electric Company to record receipt of the payment would include
    a. A credit to Accounts Payable
    b. A debit to Cash
    c. A credit to Utilities Expense
    d. Both a and b

    ANS: B

63. Deano Inc. purchased $27,000 of merchandise from Jeri Co. by making a 25 percent cash down payment and signing a 90-day note for the balance. The cost of the merchandise to Jeri Co. was $22,000. The entry by Deano Inc. to record the transaction would
    a. Increase total assets
    b. Decrease total liabilities
    c. Decrease total assets
    d. Decrease total owners' equity

    ANS: A

64. Deano Inc. purchased $27,000 of merchandise from Jeri Co. by making a 25 percent cash down payment and signing a 90-day note for the balance. The cost of the merchandise to Jeri Co. was $22,000. The entry by Jeri Co. to record the transaction would include a
    a. Credit to Cash
    b. Credit to Inventory
    c. Debit to Sales Revenue
    d. Credit to Notes Receivable

    ANS: B

65. Alma Co. paid $18,000 of accounts payable owed to Sylvia Inc. by giving cash of $4,500 and issuing a note payable for the balance. The entry by Sylvia Inc. to record the transaction would
    a. Increase assets
    b. Decrease liabilities
    c. Increase owners' equity
    d. Not change total assets, liabilities, or owners' equity

    ANS: D

66. A journal entry that includes more than two accounts is called a(n)
    a. Simple journal entry
    b. Compound journal entry
    c. Complex journal entry
    d. Essential journal entry

    ANS: B

67. Cost of Goods Sold is what type of account?
    a. Expense
    b. Asset
    c. Liability
    d. Revenue

    ANS: A

68. Christopher Company purchased $20,000 of equipment for cash. The correct entry to record the purchase of equipment is

a. Cash..	20,000	
Equipment		20,000
b. Equipment	20,000	
Accounts Payable		20,000
c. Equipment	20,000	
Cash		20,000
d. Accounts Payable	20,000	
Equipment		20,000

    ANS: C

69. On September 4, Brittany Corporation bought merchandise from a supplier for $800 on account. On September 30, Brittany paid the $800 owed to the supplier. The correct entry to record the purchase on September 4 is

a. Cost of Goods Sold	800	
Inventory		800
b. Accounts Payable	800	
Inventory		800
c. Inventory	800	
Cost of Goods Sold		800
d. Inventory	800	
Accounts Payable		800

    ANS: D

70. On September 4, Brittany Corporation bought merchandise from a supplier for $800 on account. On September 30, Brittany paid the $800 owed to the supplier. The correct entry to record the payment to the supplier on September 30 is

a. Accounts Payable 800
      Inventory   800
b. Cash 800
      Accounts Payable   800
c. Accounts Payable 800
      Cash   800
d. Cost of Goods Sold 800
      Accounts Payable   800

ANS: C

71. Solo Company borrowed $4,000 from National City Bank on June 1. On August 31, Solo Company paid off the loan plus $100 interest. The correct entry to record the borrowing transaction on June 1 is

a. Notes Payable 4,000
      Cash   4,000
b. Notes Payable 4,100
      Cash   4,100
c. Cash 4,000
      Notes Payable   4,000
d. Cash 4,100
      Notes Payable   4,100

ANS: C

72. Solo Company borrowed $4,000 from National City Bank on June 1. On August 31, Solo Company paid off the loan plus $100 interest. The correct entry to record the August 31 payment of the loan plus interest is

a. Cash 4,000
      Interest Expense 100
      Notes Payable   4,100
b. Notes Payable 4,000
      Interest Expense   100
      Cash   3,900
c. Cash 4,000
      Notes Payable 100
      Interest Expense   4,100
d. Notes Payable 4,000
      Interest Expense 100
      Cash   4,100

ANS: D

73. The accounting record where all accounts are maintained is the
    a. General ledger
    b. General journal
    c. Balance sheet
    d. Posting reference

    ANS: A

74. Which of the following groups of accounts have a normal debit balance?
    a. Revenues and liabilities
    b. Owners' equity and assets
    c. Liabilities and expenses
    d. Assets and expenses

    ANS: D

Posting Journal Entries to Accounts and Preparing a Trial Balance

75. Gore Company paid a $2,500 cash dividend to its stockholders. The transaction would be posted as

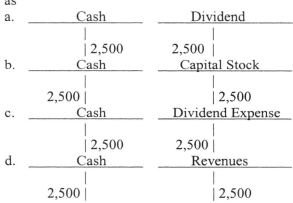

    ANS: A

76. Grbac Corporation issued stock to John Grbac for $4,000 cash. This transaction would be posted to the ledger accounts of Grbac Corporation as

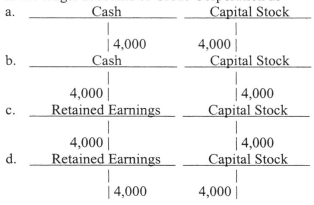

    ANS: B

77. Valenzuala Company purchased a truck for $38,000 cash. This transaction would be posted to the ledger accounts of Valenzuala Company as

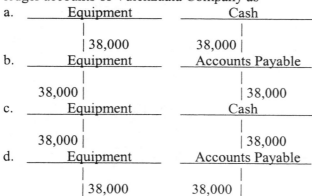

a.
Equipment	Cash
| 38,000	38,000 |

b.
Equipment	Accounts Payable
38,000 |	| 38,000

c.
Equipment	Cash
38,000 |	| 38,000

d.
Equipment	Accounts Payable
| 38,000	38,000 |

ANS: C

78. Perez Company received and immediately paid a $500 utility bill. Payment of the utility bill would be posted to the ledger accounts as

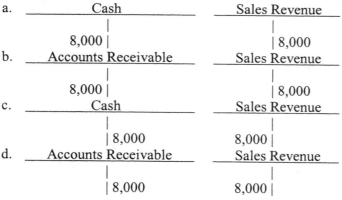

a.
Accounts Payable	Utility Expense
500 |	| 500

b.
Utility Expense	Cash
500 |	| 500

c.
Utility Expense	Cash
| 500	500 |

d.
Accounts Payable	Utility Expense
| 500	500 |

ANS: B

79. Ayala Inc. sold merchandise to a customer for $8,000 cash. The sale would be posted to the ledger accounts as

a.
Cash	Sales Revenue
8,000 |	| 8,000

b.
Accounts Receivable	Sales Revenue
8,000 |	| 8,000

c.
Cash	Sales Revenue
| 8,000	8,000 |

d.
Accounts Receivable	Sales Revenue
| 8,000	8,000 |

ANS: A

80. Mila Company paid $900 for merchandise previously purchased on credit. The payment would be posted to the ledger accounts as

a.   Accounts Payable   Cash

                       | 900   900 |

b.   Accounts Payable   Cash

             900 | 900 |

c.   Accounts Payable   Cash

             900 | | 900

d.   Accounts Payable   Cash

               | 900 | 900

ANS: C

81. During July 2006, Hasan Corporation incurred but did NOT pay a $500 utility expense. This transaction would be posted as

a.   Accounts Payable   Utility Expense

             500 | | 500

b.   Utility Expense   Cash

               | 500   500 |

c.   Utility Expense   Cash

             500 | 500 |

d.   Accounts Payable   Utility Expense

               | 500   500 |

ANS: D

82. During July 2006, Gutierrez Corporation sold $9,000 of merchandise on account. The revenue portion of this transaction would be posted as

a.   Cash   Sales Revenue

        9,000 | | 9,000

b. Accounts Receivable   Sales Revenue

        9,000 | | 9,000

c.   Cash   Sales Revenue

          | 9,000   9,000 |

d. Accounts Receivable   Sales Revenue

          | 9,000   9,000 |

ANS: B

83. During January 2006, Wells Corporation paid off $700 of wages payable that were incurred in the prior year. This transaction would be posted as

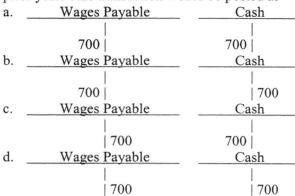

    a.   Wages Payable   Cash

                    | |
              700 | 700 |
    b.   Wages Payable   Cash

                    | |
              700 | | 700
    c.   Wages Payable   Cash

                    | |
                  | 700   700 |
    d.   Wages Payable   Cash

                    | |
                  | 700 | 700

    ANS: B

84. Each account is assigned a number. This systematic listing of all accounts is called a
    a. Trial balance
    b. General journal
    c. General ledger
    d. Chart of accounts

    ANS: D

85. A trial balance shows that
    a. No transactions have been omitted
    b. All transactions have been properly recorded
    c. Journal entries have not been posted to the wrong accounts
    d. Total debits equal total credits

    ANS: D

86. After all transactions have been journalized and posted to the accounts, a trial balance will be prepared. The purpose of this is to
    a. Determine whether there is enough cash to pay dividends
    b. Check that total debits equal total credits
    c. Close the books
    d. Obtain unadjusted balances that can be transferred directly to the financial statements

    ANS: B

87. Which of the following can be demonstrated by a trial balance?
    a. The firm is making a profit.
    b. All transactions have been recorded.
    c. Journal entries have been correctly posted.
    d. Total debits equal total credits.

    ANS: D

Where Do Computers Fit in All This?

88. Computers CANNOT do which of the following?
    a. Analyze transactions
    b. Post journal entries
    c. Summarize accounting data
    d. Prepare a variety of reports

    ANS: A

89. Which of the following is a disadvantage of computers?
    a. Increased accuracy in the posting process.
    b. Data are accepted without question.
    c. Reports can be prepared with increased efficiency.
    d. Elimination of the need to specify the terms debit and credit.

    ANS: B

PROBLEMS

1. The basic accounting equation can be used to show the changes in assets, liabilities, and owners' equity. Reynolds Corporation recently had the following transactions:

    a. Owners invested $80,000.
    b. Purchased equipment for $50,000 on credit.
    c. Borrowed $60,000 from the bank.
    d. Purchased $25,000 of inventory for cash.
    e. Paid for the equipment purchased above.

    Record the monetary consequences of these transactions under the appropriate columns shown below. Also indicate the column totals.

Transaction	Assets	=	Liabilities	+	Owners' Equity

    ANS:

Transaction	Assets	=	Liabilities	+	Owners' Equity
a.	+80,000				+80,000
b.	+50,000		+50,000		
c.	+60,000		+60,000		
d.	+25,000				
	−25,000				
e.	−50,000		−50,000		
	+140,000		+60,000		+80,000

2. The basic accounting equation can be broken into accounts that represent a firm's assets, liabilities, and owners' equity. Zuleger Company had the following transactions during a recent week:

   a. Received $25,000 cash from the issuance of capital stock.
   b. Purchased equipment for $20,000. Paid $5,000 down and signed a note for the balance.
   c. Purchased $500 of supplies, 40 percent cash and 60 percent on credit.
   d. Paid $3,000 on the note payable.

Record these transactions in the appropriate columns shown below. Also, include account balances.

Transaction	Cash	Supplies	Equipment	Accounts Payable	Notes Payable	Capital Stock

ANS:

Transaction	Cash	Supplies	Equipment	Accounts Payable	Notes Payable	Capital Stock
a.	+25,000					+25,000
b.	−5,000		+20,000		+15,000	
c.	−200	+500		+300		
d.	−3,000				−3,000	
	+16,800	+500	+20,000	+300	+12,000	+25,000

3. Give the effect the following transactions would have on EACH side of the accounting equation. Be specific in the description of the accounts. The first transaction's effect is noted as an example for you to follow.

Transaction	Effect
Payment of account owed with cash	Decrease in assets (Cash), decrease in liabilities (Accounts Payable)

1. Borrowing money from a bank

2. Purchase of a truck for cash and a note

3. Receipt of interest revenue

4. Sale of stock

5. Payment of dividends to shareholders

6. Payment of electric bill

7. Sale of merchandise for cash

ANS:

1. Increase in assets (Cash), increase in liabilities (Note Payable)
2. Increase in assets (Truck), decrease in assets (Cash), increase in liabilities (Note Payable)
3. Increase in assets (Cash), increase in owners' equity (Interest Revenue)
4. Increase in assets (Cash), increase in owners' equity (Stock)
5. Decrease in assets (Cash), decrease in owners' equity (Dividends)
6. Decrease in assets (Cash), decrease in owners' equity (Utilities Expense)
7. Increase in assets (Cash), decrease in assets (Inventory), increase in owners' equity (Sales Revenue), decrease in owners' equity (Cost of Goods Sold)

4. Using the format provided, for each account identify (a) whether the account would be reported on a balance sheet (B/S), on an income statement (I/S), or on neither statement (N); (b) whether it is an asset (A), a liability (L), owners' equity (OE), a revenue (R), or an expense (E); and (c) whether the account has a debit or a credit balance. An example is provided.

Account Title	(a) B/S, I/S or N	(b) A, L, OE R, or E	(c) Debit/ Credit
Cash	B/S	A	Debit

1. Sales Revenue
2. Dividends
3. Cost of Goods Sold
4. Utilities Expense
5. Notes Payable
6. Accounts Receivable
7. Capital Stock
8. Supplies

ANS:

Account Title	(a) B/S, I/S or N	(b) A, L, OE R, or E	(c) Debit/ Credit
1. Sales Revenue	I/S	R	Credit
2. Dividends	N	OE	Debit
3. Cost of Goods Sold	I/S	E	Debit
4. Utilities Expense	I/S	E	Debit
5. Notes Payable	B/S	L	Credit
6. Accounts Receivable	B/S	A	Debit
7. Capital Stock	B/S	OE	Credit
8. Supplies	B/S	A	Debit

5. Record the following transactions in journal entry form (omit explanations).

1. Sold merchandise for $2,000 on account; cost of merchandise sold was $1,000.
2. Borrowed $20,000 from a bank.
3. Issued stock for $4,500.
4. Purchased equipment costing $75,000; gave cash of $20,000 and a note for the remainder.
5. Paid off the loan in transaction 2 plus $250 interest.

ANS:

1.	Accounts Receivable...	2,000	
	Sales Revenue		2,000
	Cost of Goods Sold	1,000	
	Inventory..		1,000
2.	Cash	20,000	
	Notes Payable		20,000
3.	Cash	4,500	
	Capital Stock..		4,500
4.	Equipment...	75,000	
	Cash		20,000
	Notes Payable		55,000
5.	Notes Payable	20,000	
	Interest Expense...	250	
	Cash		20,250

6. Miron, Inc., experienced the following transactions during May 2006. Prepare the appropriate journal entries to record these transactions (omit explanations).

May 3	Purchased $80,000 of inventory, paying 40% in cash and the balance on account.
8	Paid monthly rent of $2,800.
11	Purchased equipment for $100,000, paying 75% in cash and signing a note for the balance.
15	Sold inventory costing $20,000 for $30,000 cash.
21	Purchased a 2-year insurance policy for $8,000.
25	Paid $6,000 on account.
28	Collected $9,000 in accounts receivable.
29	Sold an additional 1,000 shares of capital stock for $12,000.
30	Paid utilities for $1,500.

ANS:

May 3	Inventory..	80,000	
	Cash		32,000
	Accounts Payable		48,000
8	Rent Expense	2,800	
	Cash		2,800
11	Equipment..	100,000	
	Cash		75,000
	Notes Payable		25,000
15	Cash	30,000	
	Sales Revenue..		30,000
	Cost of Goods Sold.......................................	20,000	
	Inventory..		20,000
21	Prepaid Insurance	8,000	
	Cash		8,000
25	Accounts Payable	6,000	
	Cash		6,000
28	Cash	9,000	
	Accounts Receivable		9,000
29	Cash	12,000	
	Capital Stock..		12,000
30	Utilities Expense..	1,500	
	Cash		1,500

7. Cloveridge, Inc. had the following transactions during a recent period:
    a. Received $80,000 cash from the issuance of capital stock.
    b. Purchased inventory for $37,000 cash.
    c. Purchased $7,500 of equipment on account.
    d. Sold merchandise on account for $44,000; cost of goods sold was $28,500.
    e. Purchased land and a building for $30,000 and $100,000, respectively, for $25,000 cash, signing a note for the balance.
    f. Collected $23,750 from customers who had previously purchased inventory on account.

Use the T-accounts below to record these transactions. Use the alphabetical character representing each transaction to cross-reference your entries.

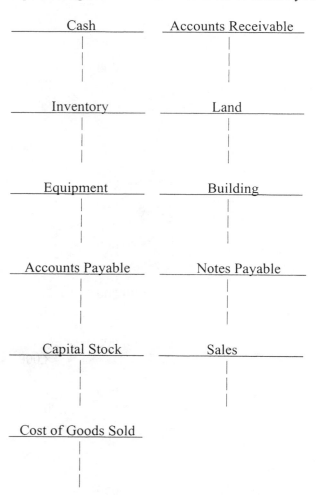

ANS:

Cash		Accounts Receivable	
80,000	37,000 b	d 44,000	23,750 f
f 23,750	25,000 e		

Inventory		Land	
b 37,000	28,500 d	e 30,000	

Equipment		Building	
c 7,500		e 100,000	

Accounts Payable		Notes Payable	
	7,500 c		105,000 e

Capital Stock		Sales	
	80,000 a		44,000 d

Cost of Goods Sold	
d 28,500	

8. Based on the following account balances at December 31, 2006, prepare a trial balance for Uniflex Company.

Accounts Payable	575	Notes Payable	7,000
Accounts Receivable	1,800	Rent Expense	1,500
Building	19,000	Retained Earnings	2,275
Capital Stock	10,000	Sales Revenue	35,684
Cash	1,160	Supplies	556
Cost of Goods Sold	17,969	Utilities Expense	849
Equipment	6,700	Wages Expense	2,000
Inventory	4,000		

ANS:

Uniflex Company
Trial Balance
December 31, 2006

Cash	1,160	
Accounts Receivable	1,800	
Inventory	4,000	
Supplies	556	
Building	19,000	
Equipment	6,700	
Accounts Payable		575
Notes Payable		7,000
Capital Stock		10,000
Retained Earnings		2,275
Sales Revenue		35,684
Wages Expense	2,000	
Rent Expense	1,500	
Utilities Expense	849	
Cost of Goods Sold	17,969	
	55,534	55,534

Chapter 3—The Mechanics of Accounting—Quiz A

Name_____   Section_____

TRUE/FALSE

Circle T or F to indicate whether each of the following statements is true or false.

T F   1.   Capital stock is a liability.

T F   2.   Assets are usually decreased with credit entries.

T F   3.   The payment of a debt usually involves crediting an asset account.

T F   4.   The word credit means to increase.

T F   5.   In the general journal for a manual system, the credit entry is always listed first.

T F   6.   A trial balance includes only balance sheet accounts.

T F   7.   Dividends reduce retained earnings and, therefore, owners' equity.

T F   8.   Net income always equals the ending balance in Retained Earnings.

T F   9.   Expense accounts are usually increased with credit entries.

T F   10.   The total debit and total credit amounts of all journal entries must be equal.

Chapter 3—The Mechanics of Accounting—Quiz B

Name_____   Section_____

MATCHING

In the spaces provided, write the letter of the term for each of the following definitions.

    a. Journal entry
    b. Dividends account
    c. Credit
    d. Posting
    e. Journal
    f. Electronic data processing (EDP)
    g. Compound journal entry
    h. Ledger
    i. Debit
    j. Trial balance

1. _____ An accounting record in which transactions are first entered; provides a chronological record of all business activities.

2. _____ The use of computers in recording, classifying, manipulating, and summarizing data.

3. _____ An entry on the left side of an account.

4. _____ A journal entry that involves more than one debit or more than one credit or both.

5. _____ A listing of all account balances; provides a means of testing whether total debits equal total credits for all accounts.

6. _____ An account used to reflect periodic distributions of earnings to the owners (stockholders) of a corporation.

7. _____ An entry on the right side of an account.

8. _____ The process of transferring amounts from the journal to the ledger.

9. _____ A recording of a transaction where debits equal credits; usually includes a date and an explanation of the transaction.

10. _____ A book of accounts in which data from transactions recorded in journals are posted and thereby classified and summarized.

Quiz Solutions

Quiz A		Quiz B	
1.	F	1.	e
2.	T	2.	f
3.	T	3.	i
4.	F	4.	g
5.	F	5.	j
6.	F	6.	b
7.	T	7.	c
8.	F	8.	d
9.	F	9.	a
10.	T	10.	h

MULTIPLE CHOICE

Accrual Accounting

1. Under accrual-basis accounting, revenues are always recognized when
   a. Earned
   b. Cash is received
   c. The manufacture of the product to be sold is completed
   d. The selling price is firmly established

   ANS: A

2. The idea that all expenses incurred in generating revenues should be recognized in the same period as those revenues is called the
   a. Time period concept
   b. Realization concept
   c. Matching concept
   d. Revenue recognition concept

   ANS: C

3. When are expenses usually recognized?
   a. When cash is paid
   b. When assets are purchased
   c. When incurred
   d. When assets are ordered

   ANS: C

4. The matching concept requires that
   a. Cash outflows be matched with cash inflows
   b. Expenses incurred be matched with revenues earned
   c. Assets be matched with liabilities
   d. Assets be matched with owners' equity

   ANS: B

5. A 12-month accounting period ending on December 31 is known as a
   a. Calendar year
   b. Reporting period
   c. Fiscal year
   d. All of the above

   ANS: D

6. The idea that a company's life can be divided into distinct time periods so that accounting information can be reported on a timely basis is
   a. Accrual-basis accounting
   b. The time period concept
   c. The fiscal year concept
   d. The revenue recognition concept

   ANS: B

7. A system of accounting in which revenues and expenses are recorded as they are earned and incurred is called
   a. Revenue recognition accounting
   b. Accrual-basis accounting
   c. Realization accounting
   d. Cash-basis accounting

   ANS: B

8. A system of accounting in which revenues and expenses are recorded only when cash is received or paid is called
   a. Revenue recognition accounting
   b. Accrual-basis accounting
   c. Realization accounting
   d. Cash-basis accounting

   ANS: D

9. Under accrual-basis accounting, revenue is recognized
   a. When cash is received without regard to when the services are rendered
   b. When the services are rendered without regard to when cash is received
   c. When cash is received before the time services are rendered
   d. If cash is received after the services are rendered

   ANS: B

10. Under accrual-basis accounting, expenses are recognized
    a. When they are incurred, whether or not cash is paid
    b. When they are incurred and paid at the same time
    c. If they are paid before they are incurred
    d. If they are paid after they are incurred

    ANS: A

11. During 2006, Rumbo Corporation had cash and credit sales of $21,760 and $15,225, respectively. The company also collected accounts receivable of $9,765 and incurred operating expenses of $27,700, 80 percent of which were paid during the year. In addition, Rumbo paid $4,500 for an 18-month advertising campaign that began on September 30. Rumbo's accrual-basis net income (loss) for 2006 was
    a. $9,285
    b. $8,535
    c. $14,075
    d. ($775)

    ANS: B

12. The 2006 accrual-basis income statement for Mason Corporation reports sales revenue of $18,000. The related balance sheet accounts for the beginning and end of the year were:

	Jan. 1, 2006	Dec. 31, 2006
Unearned Sales Revenue.....................................	$ 0	$6,500
Accounts Receivable...	1,500	500

Based on this information, the amount of cash collected during 2006 from Mason's customers was
a. $27,000
b. $26,500
c. $25,500
d. $22,000

ANS: C

13. Nona Corporation, a calendar-year company, had the following transactions during 2006:

- Rented an office building to Erma Company. On September 1, Erma paid $27,000 for the year ending August 31, 2007.
- Received notice that a $1,200 dividend would be paid on January 2, 2007, by Leslie Corporation.
- Received a check for $13,000 from a client on December 31 for services that will be performed during 2007.

Assuming cash-basis accounting for Nona Corporation, how much income should be reported on its 2006 income statement?
a. $21,000
b. $27,000
c. $40,000
d. $41,200

ANS: C

Adjusting Entries

14. Adjusting entries are
a. Recorded on a daily basis as transactions occur
b. Not posted to the general ledger
c. Made at the end of an accounting period
d. Not required under accrual-basis accounting

ANS: C

15. What is the first step accountants should perform to determine which adjusting entries are necessary?
a. Determine what original entries have been made
b. Determine what the correct account balances should be
c. Determine what adjusting entries are needed to bring the accounts to the proper balances
d. The order of the above steps is not important

ANS: A

16. Which of the following are usually NOT directly affected by adjusting entries?
    a. Asset accounts
    b. Liability accounts
    c. Revenue accounts
    d. Capital stock accounts

    ANS: D

17. Which of the following statements about adjusting entries is NOT true?
    a. They are recorded on a daily basis as transactions occur.
    b. They are posted to the general ledger.
    c. They do not affect the cash account.
    d. None of the above is true.

    ANS: A

18. In analyzing accounts to determine which adjusting entries are necessary, accountants should determine
    a. What original entries have been made
    b. What the correct account balances should be
    c. What adjusting entries are needed to bring the accounts to the proper balances
    d. All of the above

    ANS: D

19. Each adjusting entry will always affect
    a. Only balance sheet accounts
    b. At least one income statement account and one retained earnings statement account
    c. At least one balance sheet account and one income statement account
    d. Only income statement accounts

    ANS: C

Unrecorded Receivables

20. Which of the following types of accounts will always be debited to adjust for an unrecorded revenue?
    a. Liabilities
    b. Revenues
    c. Receivables
    d. Expenses

    ANS: C

21. Revenue items that are earned but have NOT been collected or recognized are called
    a. Unearned revenues
    b. Deferred revenues
    c. Unrecorded revenues
    d. Prepaid revenues

    ANS: C

22. Which of the following will occur if an adjusting entry to record an earned but unrecorded revenue is NOT made?
   a. Both revenues and assets will be understated.
   b. Both revenues and assets will be overstated.
   c. Revenues will be understated, but assets will be overstated.
   d. Assets will be understated, but revenues will be overstated.

   ANS: A

23. What is the effect on account balances when an adjusting entry to record an earned but unrecorded revenue is made?
   a. Both revenues and assets will be increased.
   b. Both revenues and assets will be decreased.
   c. Revenues will be increased, but assets will be decreased.
   d. Assets will be increased, but revenues will be decreased.

   ANS: A

24. If rent revenue of $5,000 is earned in 2005 but will NOT be received until 2006, what is the appropriate adjusting entry at December 31, 2006?

a. Rent Receivable	5,000	
Cash		5,000
b. Cash	5,000	
Rent Revenue		5,000
c. Rent Revenue	5,000	
Rent Receivable		5,000
d. Rent Receivable	5,000	
Rent Revenue		5,000

   ANS: D

25. On October 1, Woods Sporting Supplies, a calendar-year company, sold inventory that cost $30,000 for $50,000. The customer signed a four-month, 15 percent note in payment. On December 31, Woods should
   a. Debit Interest Receivable for $1,875
   b. Debit Interest Revenue for $1,875
   c. Credit Interest Revenue for $7,500
   d. Debit Interest Receivable for $7,500

   ANS: A

Unrecorded Liabilities

26. Which of the following types of accounts will always be debited to adjust for an unrecorded expense?
   a. Liabilities
   b. Revenues
   c. Receivables
   d. Expenses

   ANS: D

27. Which of the following will occur if an adjusting entry to record an accrued but unrecorded expense is NOT made?
    a. Both expenses and liabilities will be understated.
    b. Both expenses and liabilities will be overstated.
    c. Expenses will be understated, but liabilities will be overstated.
    d. Liabilities will be understated, but expenses will be overstated.

    ANS: A

28. Unrecognized interest expense on a note is an example of a(n)
    a. Unrecorded revenue
    b. Unearned revenue
    c. Unrecorded expense
    d. Prepaid expense

    ANS: C

29. If on December 31, 2005, interest expense of $600 is owed on a bank note that will NOT be paid until July 2006, what is the appropriate adjusting entry at the end of 2005?
    a. Interest Expense   600
         Cash......................................   600
    b. Interest Expense   600
         Interest Payable   600
    c. Cash..   600
         Interest Expense   600
    d. Interest Payable   600
         Interest Expense   600

    ANS: B

30. The failure to adjust unearned revenue that has been partly earned and was originally recorded as a unearned revenue would result in an
    a. Overstatement of revenues and an overstatement of liabilities
    b. Overstatement of revenues and an understatement of liabilities
    c. Understatement of revenues and an understatement of liabilities
    d. Understatement of revenues and an overstatement of liabilities

    ANS: D

31. An adjusting entry to record an unrecorded expense usually includes a credit to a(n)
    a. Liability account
    b. Asset account
    c. Revenue account
    d. Expense account

    ANS: A

32. For which of the following types of adjusting entries is there no original entry?
    a. Prepaid expenses
    b. Unearned revenues
    c. Unrecorded expenses
    d. None of the above

    ANS: C

33. Mathis Company reported the following balances in the wages payable account at the beginning and end of 2006:

	Jan. 1, 2006	Dec. 31, 2006
Wages Payable..	$600	$3,200

    If wages expense reported on the 2006 income statement was $29,300, how much cash was paid for wages during 2006?
    a. $26,700
    b. $28,000
    c. $30,600
    d. $31,200

    ANS: A

34. Boudin Corporation, a calendar-year company, obtained a $15,000, one-year, 10 percent bank loan on October 31 of the current year. Interest is payable at the end of the loan term. The adjusting entry needed on December 31 is
    a. A debit to Interest Expense of $1,500 and a credit to Cash of $1,500
    b. A debit to Interest Payable of $1,500 and a credit to Interest Expense of $1,500
    c. A debit to Interest Expense of $250 and a credit to Interest Payable of $250
    d. A debit to Interest Expense of $250 and a credit to Cash of $250

    ANS: C

35. Bay Graphics pays its employees each Friday for a five-day total workweek. The payroll is $9,000 per week. If the end of the accounting period occurs on a Wednesday, the adjusting entry to record wages payable would include a
    a. Debit to Salary Expense of $3,600
    b. Debit to Salary Expense of $5,400
    c. Credit to Cash of $9,000
    d. Credit to Salaries Payable of $3,600

    ANS: B

Prepaid Expenses

36. Which of the following types of accounts will always be credited when a prepaid expense account is adjusted?
    a. Assets
    b. Liabilities
    c. Revenues
    d. Expenses

    ANS: A

37. Prepaid expense accounts are usually classified as
    a. Assets
    b. Liabilities
    c. Expenses
    d. Revenues

    ANS: A

38. The failure to adjust a prepaid expense that has partially expired and was originally recorded by debiting a prepaid expense for the entire amount will usually result in an
    a. Understatement of assets and an understatement of expenses
    b. Overstatement of assets and an overstatement of expenses
    c. Understatement of assets and an overstatement of expenses
    d. Overstatement of assets and an understatement of expenses

    ANS: D

39. An expired asset is called a(n)
    a. Revenue
    b. Expense
    c. Retained earning
    d. Cost

    ANS: B

40. An adjusting entry to record the expired portion of a prepaid expense that was originally debited to a prepaid expense account always includes a
    a. Debit to an asset
    b. Credit to Cash
    c. Debit to an expense
    d. Credit to an expense

    ANS: C

41. The original entry to record a prepaid expense will usually include
    a. A debit to an asset account and a credit to another asset account
    b. A debit to an asset account and a credit to an expense account
    c. A debit to an expense account and a credit to an asset account
    d. None of the above

    ANS: A

42. On May 1, Mora Company paid $4,800 for two years rent and recorded the entire amount as a debit to Prepaid Rent. The adjusting entry on December 31 of that year would include a
    a. Credit to Rent Expense of $1,600
    b. Credit to Prepaid Rent of $2,400
    c. Debit to Rent Expense of $2,400
    d. Debit to Rent Expense of $1,600

    ANS: D

43. On June 30, 2005, Sinise Co. purchased a three-year fire insurance policy at a cost of $18,000 and debited Prepaid Insurance for the entire amount. The policy covers the period July 1, 2005, to June 30, 2008. The adjusting entry needed on December 31, 2005, includes a credit to
    a. Insurance Expense for $6,000
    b. Insurance Expense for $3,000
    c. Prepaid Insurance for $3,000
    d. Prepaid Insurance for $6,000

    ANS: C

44. On August 1, 2006, Base Line Realty purchased a two-year insurance policy for $15,000. On that date, the company debited Prepaid Insurance for $15,000. The adjusting entry on December 31, 2006, would include a debit to
    a. Prepaid Insurance for $2,500
    b. Prepaid Insurance for $3,125
    c. Insurance Expense for $3,125
    d. Insurance Expense for $2,500

    ANS: C

45. Kim Company purchased a two-year insurance policy on October 1, 2005, for $6,000. The policy covers its buildings for the next two years. If Kim debited Prepaid Insurance to record the purchase of the policy, the adjusting entry on December 31, 2005, (year-end), would include a credit to
    a. Insurance Expense of $750
    b. Insurance Expense of $3,000
    c. Prepaid Insurance of $750
    d. Prepaid Insurance of $3,000

    ANS: C

46. At the beginning of the period, F. Mulder Corporation had $2,400 of supplies on hand. During the period, it purchased $900 of supplies and debited Supplies for the same amount. At the end of the period, F. Mulder determined that only $800 of supplies were still on hand. What adjusting entry should F. Mulder Corporation make at the end of the period?

a.	Supplies	2,500	
	Supplies Expense		2,500
b.	Supplies	800	
	Supplies Expense		800
c.	Supplies Expense	800	
	Supplies		800
d.	Supplies Expense	2,500	
	Supplies		2,500

    ANS: D

47. Scully Corporation purchased a three-year insurance policy on November 1 for $3,600. Assuming that Scully Corporation recorded the original transaction by debiting Prepaid Insurance, the adjusting entry on December 31 will include a
a. Debit to Insurance Expense for $200
b. Credit to Prepaid Insurance for $100
c. Debit to Prepaid Insurance for $100
d. Credit to Cash for $200

ANS: A

48. Payton Company reported the following balances in Prepaid Insurance at the beginning and end of 2006.

	Jan. 1, 2006	Dec. 31, 2006
Prepaid Insurance	$600	$900

If Insurance Expense reported on the 2006 income statement was $1,700, how much cash was paid for insurance in 2006?
a. $1,100
b. $1,400
c. $1,700
d. $2,000

ANS: D

49. Given the following data, what is the amount in the supplies account to be shown as an asset on the balance sheet at the end of the period?

Supplies (beginning of period)	$500
Supplies purchased (during period)	425
Supplies used (during period)	375

a. $350
b. $550
c. $375
d. $425

ANS: B

50. From the following data, determine the amount of supplies on hand at the beginning of the period.

Supplies on hand (end of period)	$1,025
Supplies expense (for period)	425
Supplies purchased (during period)	800

a. $650
b. $600
c. $1,450
d. $375

ANS: A

51. On December 31, the trial balance of Rice Company included the following account with a debit balance:

Advertising Expense $6,000

If it is determined that the cost of advertising applicable to future periods is $2,400, the correct adjusting entry would be
a. Debit Advertising Expense $2,400; credit Prepaid Advertising $2,400
b. Debit Prepaid Advertising $3,600; credit Advertising Expense $3,600
c. Debit Advertising Expense $3,600; credit Prepaid Advertising $3,600
d. Debit Prepaid Advertising $2,400; credit Advertising Expense $2,400

ANS: D

52. Montana Inc.'s fiscal year ended on December 31, 2005. The balance in the prepaid insurance account as of December 31, 2005, was $34,800 (before adjustment) and consisted of the following policies:

Policy Number	Date of Purchase	Date of Expiration	Balance in Account
279248	10/01/04	09/30/05	$14,400
694421	03/01/05	02/28/07	9,600
800616	07/01/04	06/30/06	10,800
			$34,800

The adjusting entry required on September 30, 2005, would be
a. Insurance Expense 22,000
       Prepaid Insurance 22,000
b. Insurance Expense 20,200
       Prepaid Insurance 20,200
c. Prepaid Insurance 17,600
       Insurance Expense 17,600
d. Prepaid Insurance 25,600
       Insurance Expense 25,600

ANS: D
Policy 279248—3 months expired last year, so all 14,400 expires this year; policy 694421—10 months expire this year (9,600/24) × 10 = 4,000; policy 800616—6 months expired last year, 12 months expire this year (10,800/18) × 12 = 7,200. 14,400 + 4,000 + 7,200 = 25,600.

53. Young Company paid $24,900 in insurance premiums during 2005. Young showed $3,600 in prepaid insurance on its December 31, 2004 balance sheet and $4,500 on December 31, 2005. The insurance expense on the income statement for 2005 was
a. $16,800
b. $24,000
c. $25,800
d. $33,000

ANS: B

Unearned Revenues

54. Which of the following types of accounts will always be debited when an unearned revenue account is adjusted?
    a. Assets
    b. Liabilities
    c. Revenues
    d. Expenses

    ANS: B

55. Amounts received before they are earned are called
    a. Unrecorded revenues
    b. Unrecorded expenses
    c. Prepaid expenses
    d. Unearned revenues

    ANS: D

56. An unearned revenue account is usually considered to be a(n)
    a. Liability
    b. Asset
    c. Revenue
    d. Expense

    ANS: A

57. If a company receives rent for January 2006 from a tenant in December 2005, that rent would be a(n)
    a. Revenue in 2005
    b. Asset in 2005
    c. Expense in 2005
    d. Liability in 2005

    ANS: D

58. The failure to adjust an unearned revenue that has been partially earned and was originally recorded as a credit to Unearned Revenue will usually result in an
    a. Overstatement of revenues and an overstatement of liabilities
    b. Overstatement of revenues and an understatement of liabilities
    c. Understatement of revenues and an understatement of liabilities
    d. Understatement of revenues and an overstatement of liabilities

    ANS: D

59. An adjusting entry to record the portion of unearned revenue that was earned in the current period usually includes a debit to a(n)
    a. Liability account
    b. Asset account
    c. Expense account
    d. Revenue account

    ANS: A

60. Garcia Company has received advance payment for services yet to be performed. This prepayment is an example of a(n)
    a. Unrecorded expense
    b. Unrecorded revenue
    c. Prepaid expense
    d. Unearned revenue

    ANS: D

61. Rent collected in advance is classified as a(n)
    a. Liability
    b. Expense
    c. Asset
    d. Revenue

    ANS: A

62. A company received an advance payment for services NOT yet performed. This prepayment can be described as a(n)
    a. Prepaid asset
    b. Liability
    c. Unrecorded expense
    d. Unrecorded revenue

    ANS: B

63. On June 1, 2006, Marino Corporation received $1,800 as advance payment for 12 months' advertising. The receipt was recorded as a credit to Unearned Fees. What adjusting entry is required at December 31, 2006?

a.	Unearned Fees.........................	1,050	
	Advertising Revenue...........		1,050
b.	Advertising Revenue..............	1,050	
	Unearned Fees.....................		1,050
c.	Cash.......................................	750	
	Advertising Revenue...........		750
d.	Unearned Fees.........................	750	
	Advertising Revenue...........		750

    ANS: A

64. Favre Company reported the following balances in Unearned Rent at the beginning and end of 2006:

	Jan. 1, 2006	Dec. 31, 2006
Unearned Rent	$1,800	$1,600

    If Rent Revenue reported on the 2006 income statement was $5,800, how much cash was received for rent during 2006?
    a. $5,600
    b. $6,000
    c. $6,200
    d. $7,800

    ANS: A

65. On December 16, 2005, DeLeon Company received $1,800 from Columbus Company for rent on an office building owned by DeLeon. The $1,800 covers the period December 16, 2005, through February 15, 2006. If DeLeon Company credited Unearned Rent to record the $1,800 rent collected on December 16, the adjusting entry needed on December 31, 2005, would include a
    a. Credit to Rent Revenue of $450
    b. Credit to Unearned Rent of $450
    c. Debit to Rent Revenue of $900
    d. Debit to Unearned Rent Revenue of $900

    ANS: A

Preparing Financial Statements

66. The notes to the financial statements tell all of the following, EXCEPT
    a. Details about specific items
    b. Assumptions used by the company
    c. Accounting methods used by the company
    d. Financial analysis

    ANS: D

67. The audit procedures conducted by the external auditor include all of the following, EXCEPT
    a. Review of adjustments
    b. Review of accounting systems
    c. Sample of financial ratios
    d. Sample of selected accounts

    ANS: C

68. Prior to making any adjusting entries, Testa Corporation had net income of $77,550. The following adjusting entries were made: salaries payable, $787; interest earned on short-term investments but not yet recorded or collected, $3,634; adjustment to prepaid insurance for $2,769 for an insurance policy that expired during the period; and fees of $293 collected in advance that have now been earned. Testa uses the asset approach to record prepaid expenses and the liability approach to record unearned revenues. After recording these adjustments, net income would be
    a. $85,042
    b. $79,004
    c. $77,921
    d. $77,918

    ANS: C

69. The December 31, 2006 adjusted account balances taken from the adjusted trial balance of Cajon Corporation are as follows:

	Debits	Credits
Cash	$150	
Store Supplies	300	
Service Fees Revenue		$600
Retained Earnings		50
Accounts Payable		70
Dividends	200	
Unearned Service Fees Revenue		180
Wages Expense	200	
Store Supplies Expense	50	

Cajon Corporation had net income in 2006 of
a. $150
b. $530
c. $330
d. $350

ANS: D

The Closing Process

70. The closing entry involving a net loss will include a
    a. Credit to Sales Revenue
    b. Debit to Retained Earnings
    c. Credit to Dividends
    d. Debit to Salaries Expense

ANS: B

71. Nominal accounts are NOT found on which of the following financial statements?
    a. Balance sheet
    b. Income statement
    c. Statement of cash flows
    d. Retained earnings statement

ANS: A

72. Which of the following accounts is NOT a real account?
    a. Dividends
    b. Cash
    c. Accounts Payable
    d. Retained Earnings

ANS: A

73. Closing entries are
    a. Required to bring all real accounts to a zero balance at the end of the accounting period
    b. Not required to be posted
    c. Required to bring all nominal accounts to a zero balance prior to starting a new accounting cycle
    d. Generally taken from the financial statements rather than from the work sheet or the accounts themselves

    ANS: C

74. The entry to close the revenue accounts normally includes a
    a. Debit to each revenue account
    b. Credit to each revenue account
    c. Debit to each expense account
    d. Credit to each expense account

    ANS: A

75. Closing entries usually
    a. Bring all real accounts to a zero balance
    b. Bring all nominal accounts to a zero balance
    c. Adjust all nominal accounts to their proper balances
    d. Adjust all real accounts to their proper balances

    ANS: B

76. Which of the following is NOT a true statement?
    a. Expenses are closed with a credit.
    b. Revenues are closed with a debit.
    c. Dividends are closed with a credit.
    d. Retained Earnings are closed with a debit.

    ANS: D

77. The entry to close the expense accounts normally includes a
    a. Debit to each revenue account
    b. Credit to each revenue account
    c. Debit to each expense account
    d. Credit to each expense account

    ANS: D

78. The dividends account is
    a. An asset
    b. An expense
    c. A revenue
    d. None of the above

    ANS: D

79. The dividends account is
    a. Not used in the closing process
    b. Not a permanent capital account
    c. Always closed by being debited
    d. Shown in the equity section of the balance sheet

    ANS: B

80. The dividends account is
    a. Used for partnerships
    b. Closed to Retained Earnings by being credited
    c. A real account
    d. Closed to Retained Earnings by being debited

    ANS: B

81. Which of the following accounts would be closed at year-end?
    a. Capital Stock
    b. Prepaid Rent
    c. Dividends
    d. Accounts Payable

    ANS: C

82. Long Company has the following income statement for 2006:

Revenues:		
Sales revenue	$300,000	
Interest revenue	10,000	$310,000
Expenses:		
Interest expense	$ 5,000	
Rent expense	60,000	
Utilities expense	20,000	
Salaries expense	230,000	315,000
Net loss		$ (5,000)

    Given this information, the entry to close revenues and expenses would include a
    a. Credit to Retained Earnings of $55,000
    b. Debit to Retained Earnings of $5,000
    c. Credit to Retained Earnings of $310,000
    d. Credit to Retained Earnings of $310,000

    ANS: B

83. Long Company has the following income statement for 2006:

Revenues:
Sales revenue	$300,000	
Interest revenue	10,000	$310,000

Expenses:
Interest expense	$ 5,000	
Rent expense	60,000	
Utilities expense	20,000	
Salaries expense	230,000	315,000
Net loss		$ (5,000)

Given this information, the entry to close expenses would include a
a.   Debit to Utilities Expense of $20,000
b.   Credit to Utilities Expense of $20,000
c.   Credit to Sales Revenue of $300,000
d.   None of the above

ANS: B

84. The December 31, 2006 adjusted account balances taken from the adjusted trial balance of Cajon Corporation are as follows:

	Debits	Credits
Cash	$150	
Store Supplies	300	
Service Fees Revenue		$600
Retained Earnings		50
Accounts Payable		70
Dividends	200	
Unearned Service Fees Revenue		180
Wages Expense	200	
Store Supplies Expense	50	

Given this information, after all closing entries have been made, the balance in Cajon's retained earnings account would be
a. $380
b. $400
c. $330
d. $200

ANS: D

85. The December 31, 2006 adjusted account balances taken from the adjusted trial balance of Cajon Corporation are as follows:

	Debits	Credits
Cash	$150	
Store Supplies	300	
Service Fees Revenue		$600
Retained Earnings...		50
Accounts Payable..		70
Dividends..	200	
Unearned Service Fees Revenue......................................		180
Wages Expense...	200	
Store Supplies Expense...	50	

Given this information, after all closing entries have been made, the balance in Cajon's cash account would be
a. $250
b. $200
c. $150
d. $0

ANS: C

86. The December 31, 2006 closing entries for Smith Corp. are as follows:

	Debits	Credits
Sales Revenue	$12,500	
Interest Revenue	1,250	
Cost of Goods Sold		$7,000
Wages Expense		2,250
Supplies Expense		1,575
Retained Earnings		2,925
Retained Earnings...	1,000	
Dividends...		1,000

Smith Corp. had net income in 2006 of
a. $13,750
b. $1,925
c. $12,750
d. $2,925

ANS: D

87. On December 31, 2005, the balance in the retained earnings account is $18,500. On December 31, 2006, the balance of Retained Earnings is $17,100. During 2006, dividends of $4,200 were declared and paid. Based on this information, net income for 2006 is
a. $2,800
b. $7,000
c. $2,100
d. $4,200

ANS: A

88. On December 31, 2005, the balance in Pacino Company's retained earnings account is $21,500. On December 31, 2006, the balance is $22,000. During 2006, dividends of $5,200 were declared and paid. Based on this information, net income for 2006 was
   a. $1,700
   b. $6,900
   c. $3,500
   d. $5,700

   ANS: D

Preparing a Post-Closing Trial Balance

89. A post-closing trial balance does NOT include the
   a. Real accounts
   b. Balance sheet accounts
   c. Permanent accounts
   d. Income statement accounts

   ANS: D

90. Which of the following statements is true of a post-closing trial balance?
   a. Its debits must equal its credits.
   b. It lists all real and nominal account balances.
   c. It may be prepared before the closing process to provide some assurance that the previous steps in the cycle have been performed properly.
   d. All of the above are true.

   ANS: A

91. Which of the following accounts would NOT appear in the post-closing trial balance?
   a. Unearned Service Fees Revenue
   b. Dividends
   c. Supplies
   d. Salaries Payable

   ANS: B

EXPANDED MATERIAL

Alternative Adjustments for Prepaid Expenses

92. The failure to adjust a prepaid expense that has partly expired and that was originally recorded using the expense approach will usually result in an
   a. Overstatement of assets and an understatement of expenses
   b. Overstatement of assets and an overstatement of expenses
   c. Understatement of assets and an overstatement of expenses
   d. Understatement of assets and an understatement of expenses

   ANS: C

93. The premium on a two-year insurance policy expiring on June 30, 2007, was paid in total on July 1, 2005. The original payment was debited to the insurance expense account. The appropriate journal entry has been recorded on December 31, 2005. The balance in the prepaid asset account on December 31, 2005, should be
   a. The same as the original payment
   b. Higher than if the original payment had been initially debited to an asset account
   c. Lower than if the original payment had been initially debited to an asset account
   d. The same as it would have been if the original payment had been initially debited to an asset account

   ANS: D

94. The failure to adjust an unearned revenue that has been partially earned and was originally recorded using the revenue approach will usually result in an
   a. Overstatement of revenues and an overstatement of liabilities
   b. Overstatement of revenues and an understatement of liabilities
   c. Understatement of revenues and an understatement of liabilities
   d. Understatement of revenues and an overstatement of liabilities

   ANS: B

95. When the revenue approach is used to record the receipt of revenues prior to their being earned, the adjusting entry at year-end will include a
   a. Debit to the revenue account for the portion earned during the period
   b. Debit to the revenue account for the portion unearned during the period
   c. Credit to the liability account for the portion earned during the period
   d. Debit to the liability account for the portion unearned during the period

   ANS: B

96. Tye Company uses the expense approach in recording prepaid expenses. On April 1, the company paid $3,600 for one year's rent and recorded the entire amount as a debit to Rent Expense. The adjusting entry on December 31 of that year would include a
   a. Debit to Cash of $3,600
   b. Credit to Prepaid Rent of $900
   c. Debit to Rent Expense of $3,600
   d. Debit to Prepaid Rent of $900

   ANS: D

97. On June 30, 2005, Cristo Company purchased a two-year fire insurance policy at a cost of
     $12,000. The policy covers the period July 1, 2005, to June 30, 2007. If Cristo Company used the
     expense approach to record the insurance purchased on June 30, the adjusting entry needed on
     December 31, 2005, would include a debit to
     a.   Insurance Expense for $3,000
     b.   Insurance Expense for $9,000
     c.   Prepaid Insurance for $3,000
     d.   Prepaid Insurance for $9,000

     ANS: D

98. On August 1, 2006, Mountain View Realty purchased a one-year insurance policy for $7,800. On
     that date, the company debited Insurance Expense for $7,800. The adjusting entry on December
     31, 2006, would include a credit to
     a.   Prepaid Insurance for $4,550
     b.   Prepaid Insurance for $3,250
     c.   Insurance Expense for $3,250
     d.   Insurance Expense for $4,550

     ANS: D

99. Pogo Company paid $1,704 on June 1, 2005, for a two-year insurance policy and recorded the
     entire amount as Insurance Expense. The December 31, 2005 adjusting entry is
     a.   Debit Prepaid Insurance and credit Insurance Expense, $497
     b.   Debit Insurance Expense and credit Prepaid Insurance, $497
     c.   Debit Insurance Expense and credit Prepaid Insurance, $1,207
     d.   Debit Prepaid Insurance and credit Insurance Expense, $1,207

     ANS: D

Alternative Adjustments for Unearned Revenues

100. On November 1, 2006, a client pays Cunningham Inc. $2,400 for consulting fees covering the
     next 12-month period. Cunningham records all cash receipts as revenues. What adjusting entry is
     required on December 31, 2006?
     a.   Cash   400
              Consulting Revenue   400
     b.   Consulting Revenue   2,000
              Unearned Revenue   2,000
     c.   Consulting Revenue   400
              Unearned Revenue   400
     d.   Unearned Revenue   2,000
              Cash   2,000

     ANS: B

101. Flutie Corporation rented a building to Johnson Company. On December 1, Flutie collected rent
      of $400 per month for December through March. If Flutie uses the revenue approach to record the
      receipt of $1,600 on December 1, the adjusting entry on December 31 will include a debit to
      a. Rent Revenue of $400
      b. Unearned Rent of $1,200
      c. Rent Revenue of $1,200
      d. Unearned Rent of $400

      ANS: C

102. On December 16, 2005, Wong, Inc. received $600 from Eichi Company for rent of an office
      building owned by Wong. The $600 covers the period December 16, 2005, through January 15,
      2006. If Wong Company used the revenue approach to record the $600 rent collected on
      December 16, the adjusting entry needed on December 31, 2005, would include
      a. A credit to Rent Revenue of $300
      b. A credit to Unearned Rent of $300
      c. A debit to Rent Revenue of $300
      d. Both b and c

      ANS: D

103. Al Sheik Company sublet a portion of its office space for 10 years at an annual rental of $36,000,
      beginning on May 1. The tenant is required to pay one year's rent in advance, which Al Sheik
      recorded as a credit to Rental Income. Al Sheik reports on a calendar-year basis. The adjustment
      on December 31 of the first year should be
      a. Rental Income   12,000
              Unearned Rental Income.....   12,000
      b. Rental Income   24,000
              Unearned Rental Income.....   24,000
      c. Unearned Rental Income........   12,000
              Rental Income   12,000
      d. Unearned Rental Income........   24,000
              Rental Income   24,000

      ANS: A

Appendix A: Using a Work Sheet

104. Which of the following is true of a work sheet?
      a. It is prepared for distribution to outsiders.
      b. It lists a trial balance, adds adjusting entries, and extends the combined amounts into
          appropriate financial statement columns.
      c. It is the next to last step in the accounting cycle.
      d. It is a required step in the accounting cycle.

      ANS: B

105. Which of the following statements about work sheets is NOT true?
    a. A work sheet is needed to complete the closing process.
    b. A work sheet facilitates the preparation of financial statements.
    c. Adjusting entries entered on a work sheet must still be journalized and posted.
    d. A work sheet may contain as many columns as are needed by a particular company.

    ANS: A

106. Financial statements may be prepared from
    a. A completed work sheet
    b. The unadjusted accounts
    c. The adjusted accounts
    d. Either a or c

    ANS: D

107. For which of the following accounts would an entry in the adjustments column of the work sheet be most unlikely?
    a. Income Taxes Payable
    b. Inventory
    c. Prepaid Insurance
    d. Capital Stock

    ANS: D

108. In completing a work sheet, if the balancing figure in the income statement columns is a credit, then the
    a. Company had a net loss for the period
    b. Company earned net income for the period
    c. Company had an increase in retained earnings
    d. Balancing figure in the balance sheet columns is also a credit

    ANS: A

109. Which of the following statements about work sheet preparation is true?
    a. The adjusted trial balance columns are added to the income statement columns.
    b. Total debits and credits per the income statement columns must equal total debits and credits per the balance sheet columns.
    c. The total debits and credits of the beginning trial balance columns do not have to be equal provided adjusting entries are made.
    d. None of the above are true.

    ANS: D

110. Adjusting entries are
    a. Made only on a work sheet
    b. Entered on a work sheet after the financial statements are prepared
    c. Required to update and correct both income statement and balance sheet accounts
    d. Generally not needed under accrual-basis accounting

    ANS: C

111. On a work sheet, if the subtotal in the income statement debit column exceeds the subtotal in the income statement credit column, the company has had
    a. A net income for the period
    b. A net loss for the period
    c. Can't tell whether an income or loss has been realized
    d. None of the above

    ANS: B

112. On a work sheet, a balance in Prepaid Rent would be shown as a
    a. Debit on the balance sheet
    b. Credit on the balance sheet
    c. Debit on the income statement
    d. Credit on the income statement

    ANS: A

113. On a work sheet, a balance in Rent Revenue would be shown as a
    a. Debit on the income statement
    b. Credit on the income statement
    c. Debit on the balance sheet
    d. Credit on the balance sheet

    ANS: B

114. On a work sheet, a balance in Rent Expense would be shown as a
    a. Debit on the income statement
    b. Credit on the income statement
    c. Debit on the balance sheet
    d. Credit on the balance sheet

    ANS: A

115. On a work sheet, a balance in Unearned Rent would be shown as a
    a. Debit on the income statement
    b. Credit on the income statement
    c. Debit on the balance sheet
    d. Credit on the balance sheet

    ANS: D

116. Brewski Corporation's work sheet shows the following totals in the income statement column: total credits of $42,500 and total debits of $24,300 (before taxes). If the tax rate is 25 percent, what is the adjustment for tax expense for the period?
    a. Corporations do not pay income taxes
    b. Income Tax Expense 10,625
        Income Taxes Payable......... 10,625
    c. Income Tax Expense 13,650
        Income Taxes Payable......... 13,650
    d. Income Tax Expense 4,550
        Income Taxes Payable......... 4,550

    ANS: D

117. When the income statement columns of the December 31, 2006 work sheet of Bruschi
     Corporation were initially subtotaled, the debit and credit entries had balances of $24,750 and
     $38,750, respectively, before income taxes were recorded. If the appropriate tax rate for Bruschi
     Corporation is 30 percent, the 2006 income tax expense would be
     a. $11,625
     b. $9,800
     c. $4,200
     d. $3,600

     ANS: C

118. When the income statement columns of the December 31, 2006 work sheet of Bruschi
     Corporation were initially subtotaled, the debit and credit entries had balances of $24,750 and
     $38,750, respectively, before income taxes were recorded. Assuming a 30 percent tax rate,
     Bruschi's 2006 net income (after taxes) would be
     a. $14,000
     b. $3,600
     c. $9,800
     d. $4,200

     ANS: C

Appendix B: Special Journals

119. Bradshaw Company uses the following special journals: sales, purchases, cash receipts, and cash
     disbursements. Most of Bradshaw's merchandise is sold on credit, but about 10 percent of sales
     are for cash. These cash sales should be recorded in the
     a. Cash receipts journal
     b. Sales journal
     c. General journal
     d. Both the sales and cash receipts journals

     ANS: A

120. The total amount in the sales journal would be posted as a
     a. Debit to Sales Revenue and credit to Accounts Receivable
     b. Debit to Accounts Receivable and credit to Sales Revenue
     c. Debit to Cash and credit to Sales Revenue
     d. Debit to Sales Revenue and credit to Inventory

     ANS: B

121. The accounts receivable control account
     a. Is not included in the general ledger
     b. Contains separate accounts for each customer
     c. Provides detailed information in support of the subsidiary ledger
     d. Summarizes the balances in all customer accounts

     ANS: D

122. Myles Corporation uses the following special journals: sales, purchases, cash receipts, and cash disbursements. The cash disbursements journal would be used to record
    a. All cash payments
    b. All cash payments except those for inventory purchases
    c. All cash payments except those for payroll
    d. All cash payments except those recorded in the general journal

    ANS: A

123. The sales journal is used to record
    a. Credit sales
    b. Cash sales
    c. Both credit sales and cash sales
    d. Only special sales

    ANS: A

124. If a company uses a subsidiary ledger for accounts receivable, a credit sale must be recorded in the subsidiary ledger and in the
    a. General ledger
    b. Sales journal
    c. Cash receipts journal
    d. Check register

    ANS: B

PROBLEMS

1. Match the following terms to the definitions listed below.
    a. Accrual-basis accounting
    b. Calendar year
    c. Cash-basis accounting
    d. Fiscal year
    e. Matching principle
    f. Revenue recognition principle
    g. Time period concept

    _____ 1. Recognizes revenue only when cash is received and expenses only when cash is paid.
    _____ 2. Any 12-month accounting period.
    _____ 3. The idea that revenue is recorded when the earnings process is completed and the cash has either been collected or collection is reasonably assured.
    _____ 4. Expenses are matched to the revenues they generated each period.
    _____ 5. The idea that the life of a company can be divided into distinct accounting periods.
    _____ 6. Provides the best measure of periodic net income.
    _____ 7. An accounting period that ends on December 31.

ANS:

1. c
2. d
3. f
4. e
5. g
6. a
7. b

2. In the course of your examination of the books and records of Griffin Company for the year ending December 31, 2006, you find the following data:

Salaries earned by employees	$ 40,000
Salaries paid to employees	50,000
Total sales revenue	700,000
Cash collected from sales	750,000
Utility expense incurred	4,500
Utility bills paid	4,200
Cost of goods sold	400,000
Cash paid on inventory purchases in 2006	370,000
Inventory at December 31, 2006	286,400
Tax assessment for 2006	5,000
Taxes paid in 2006	3,500
Rent expense for 2006	30,000
Rent paid in 2006	25,000

1. Compute Griffin Company's net income for 2006 using cash-basis accounting.
2. Compute Griffin Company's net income for 2006 using accrual-basis accounting.

ANS:

1.
Net income on cash basis:

Cash collected from sales		$750,000
Cash expenses:		
Cash paid on inventory purchases	$370,000	
Salaries paid	50,000	
Utility bills paid	4,200	
Taxes paid	3,500	
Rent paid	25,000	
Total cash expenses		452,700
Net cash income		$297,300

2.

Net income on accrual basis:

Total sales revenue		$700,000
Expenses:		
Cost of goods sold	$400,000	
Salaries expense...	40,000	
Utility expense...	4,500	
Tax assessment	5,000	
Rent expense..	30,000	
Total expenses		479,500
Net income...		$220,500

3. Griesbach, Inc., prepares monthly financial statements. The September 30, 2005 trial balance reveals the following:

	Debits	Credits
Supplies on Hand...	$1,200	
Unearned Rent Revenue		$ 1,800
Notes Payable		45,000

An inventory of supplies reveals that only $675 is on hand at the end of the month. Of the unearned rent revenue, $600 remains unearned. The note payable was taken out on September 1, 2005, at 10 percent. Lastly, the weekly payroll is $3,600. Employees are paid each Friday for a five-day work week, and September 30 is a Wednesday.

Prepare the appropriate adjusting journal entries.

ANS:

Supplies Expense...	525	
Supplies on Hand..		525
($1,200 – $675 = $525)		
Unearned Rent Revenue	1,200	
Rent Revenue..		1,200
($1,800 – $600 = $1,200)		
Interest Expense..	375	
Interest Payable...		375
($45,000 × 10% × 1/12 = $375)		
Wages Expense..	2,160	
Wages Payable..		2,160
($3,600 × 3/5 = $2,160)		

4. Jill Austinson, the bookkeeper of Packers Inc., thinks that the following journal entries may lead to adjusting entries at December 31, 2006.

2006

Mar. 1	Prepaid Insurance	768	
	Cash		768
Feb. 28	Cash	6,000	
	Rent Revenue		6,000
June 1	Legal Service Expense	1,800	
	Cash		1,800
Sept. 1	Property Tax Expense	4,800	
	Cash		4,800

Jill has gathered the following information:

1. The insurance premium is for the 12-month period ending March 1, 2007.
2. The rent revenue represents rent received from a tenant for the period February 28, 2006, to August 31, 2006.
3. The prepaid legal services are for the services of Dewey Cheatham, attorney-at-law, for the 12-month period ending May 31, 2007.
4. The property tax expense is for the county's fiscal year, which ends August 31, 2007.

Make any adjusting entries required at December 31, 2006. (Omit explanations.)

ANS:

1.	Insurance Expense	640	
	Prepaid Insurance		640

($768 ÷ 12 = $64/mo.; $64 × 10 = $640)

2. No adjusting entry required.

3.	Prepaid Legal Expense	750	
	Legal Service Expense		750

($1,800 ÷ 12 = $150/mo.; $150 × 5 = $750)

4.	Prepaid Property Tax	3,200	
	Property Tax Expense		3,200

($4,800 ÷ 12 = $400/mo.; $400 × 8 = $3,200)

5. Tenor Company's trial balance as of August 31, 2006, is shown below:

Tenor Company
Trial Balance
August 31, 2006

	Debits	Credits
Cash	$30,500	
Accounts Receivable	7,400	
Supplies	800	
Prepaid Rent	3,500	
Inventory	5,800	
Land	18,300	
Accounts Payable		$15,300
Unearned Consulting Revenue		5,000
Capital Stock		40,400
Dividends	500	
Retained Earnings	900	
Sales Revenue		35,200
Cost of Goods Sold	15,200	
Advertising Expense	1,000	
Salaries Expense	12,000	
	$95,900	$95,900

Adjustments:
  Supplies expense, $250
  Rent expense, $3,000
  Salaries payable, $1,800
  Consulting revenue, $5,000

Prepare the necessary adjusting entries. (Omit explanations for journal entries.)

ANS:

Adjusting entries:
Supplies Expense	250	
Supplies		250
Rent Expense	3,000	
Prepaid Rent		3,000
Salaries Expense	1,800	
Salaries Payable		1,800
Unearned Consulting Revenue	5,000	
Consulting Revenue		5,000

6. Palmer Pen Co. has the following adjusted trial balance:

Palmer Pen Co.
Adjusted Trial Balance
December 31, 2006

	Debits	Credits
Cash	$ 50,000	
Accounts Receivable	40,500	
Supplies	4,000	
Inventory	74,580	
Buildings	100,000	
Machinery and Equipment	30,000	
Land	20,000	
Accounts Payable		$ 37,400
Notes Payable		49,180
Capital Stock (100,000 shares outstanding as of 12/31/06)		150,000
Retained Earnings		76,000
Sales Revenue		480,750
Salaries Expense	125,000	
Insurance Expense	6,000	
Dividends	20,000	
Cost of Goods Sold	290,900	
Utilities Expense	12,000	
Income Tax Expense	20,350	
	$793,330	$793,330

Prepare an income statement and a balance sheet in good form.

ANS:

Palmer Pen Co.
Income Statement
For the Year Ended December 31, 2006

Sales revenue		$480,750
Less expenses:		
Cost of goods sold	$290,900	
Salaries expense	125,000	
Utilities expense	12,000	
Insurance expense	6,000	433,900
Income before taxes		$ 46,850
Income tax expense		20,350
Net income		$ 26,500
Earnings per share		$ 0.265

Palmer Pen Co.
Balance Sheet
December 31, 2006

Assets

Current assets:

Cash	$ 50,000
Accounts receivable	40,500
Supplies	4,000
Inventory	74,580
Total current assets	$169,080

Property, plant, and equipment:

Buildings	$100,000
Machinery and equipment	30,000
Land	20,000
Total property, plant, and equipment	$150,000
Total assets	$319,080

Liabilities and Owners' Equity

Current liabilities:

Accounts payable	$ 37,400
Notes payable	49,180
Total current liabilities	$ 86,580

Owners' equity:

Capital stock	$150,000
Retained earnings	82,500*
Total owners' equity	$232,500
Total liabilities and owners' equity	$319,080

Retained earnings balances:

Beginning retained earnings	*$ 76,000*
Add: Net income	*26,500*
	$102,500
Deduct: Dividends	*20,000*
Ending retained earnings	*$ 82,500*

7. Lincoln Company's adjusted trial balance as of August 31, 2006, is shown below:

Lincoln Company
Adjusted Trial Balance
August 31, 2006

	Debits	Credits
Cash	$30,500	
Accounts Receivable	7,400	
Supplies	800	
Prepaid Rent	3,500	
Inventory	5,000	
Accounts Payable		$15,300
Land	16,200	
Capital Stock (10,000 shares outstanding as of 08/31/06)		45,400
Dividends	800	
Retained Earnings	900	
Sales Revenue		37,800
Cost of Goods Sold	16,600	
Advertising Expense	1,800	
Salaries Expense	15,000	
	$98,500	$98,500

Prepare the income statement and a statement of retained earnings for the year ended August 31, 2006.

ANS:

Lincoln Company
Income Statement
For the Year Ended August 31, 2006

Sales revenue		$37,800
Less expenses:		
Cost of goods sold	$16,600	
Advertising expense	1,800	
Salaries expense	15,000	33,400
Net income		$ 4,400
Earnings per share		$ 0.44

Lincoln Company
Statement of Retained Earnings
For the Year Ended August 31, 2006

Beginning retained earnings	$ (900)
Add: Net income	4,400
	$3,500
Less: Dividends	800
Ending retained earnings	$2,700

8. Lincoln Company's trial balance as of August 31, 2006, is shown below:

Lincoln Company
Trial Balance
August 31, 2006

	Debits	Credits
Cash	$30,500	
Accounts Receivable	7,400	
Supplies	800	
Prepaid Rent	3,500	
Inventory	5,000	
Accounts Payable		$15,300
Land	16,200	
Capital Stock		45,400
Dividends	800	
Retained Earnings	900	
Sales Revenue		37,800
Cost of Goods Sold	16,600	
Advertising Expense	1,800	
Salaries Expense	15,000	
	$98,500	$98,500

Prepare the closing entries.

ANS:

Closing entries:

Sales Revenue	37,800	
Retained Earnings		4,400
Cost of Goods Sold		16,600
Advertising Expense		1,800
Salaries Expense		15,000
Retained Earnings	800	
Dividends		800

9. Palmer Pen Co. has the following adjusted trial balance:

Palmer Pen Co.
Adjusted Trial Balance
December 31, 2006

	Debits	Credits
Cash	$ 50,000	
Accounts Receivable	40,500	
Supplies	4,000	
Inventory	74,580	
Buildings	100,000	
Machinery and Equipment	30,000	
Land	20,000	
Accounts Payable		$ 37,400
Notes Payable		49,180
Capital Stock		150,000
Retained Earnings		76,000
Sales Revenue		480,750
Salaries Expense	125,000	
Insurance Expense	6,000	
Dividends	20,000	
Cost of Goods Sold	290,900	
Utilities Expense	12,000	
Income Tax Expense	20,350	
	$793,330	$793,330

1. Prepare the necessary closing entries.
2. Prepare the post-closing trial balance.

ANS:

Closing entries:

Sales Revenue	480,750	
Retained Earnings		26,500
Cost of Goods Sold		290,900
Salaries Expense		125,000
Utilities Expense		12,000
Insurance Expense		6,000
Income Tax Expense		20,350
Retained Earnings	20,000	
Dividends		20,000

Palmer Pen Co.
Post-Closing Trial Balance
December 31, 2006

	Debits	Credits
Cash	$ 50,000	
Accounts Receivable	40,500	
Supplies	4,000	
Inventory	74,580	
Buildings	100,000	
Machinery and Equipment	30,000	
Land	20,000	
Accounts Payable		$ 37,400
Notes Payable		49,180
Capital Stock		150,000
Retained Earnings		82,500
	$319,080	$319,080

10. For each account listed below, check whether it appears on the income statement or the balance sheet and whether it would normally have a debit or a credit balance. (*Note*: This covers the entire accounting cycle.) The first line has been completed as an example.

Account	Balance Sheet	Income Statement	Debit	Credit
Notes Payable	X			X
Prepaid Insurance				
Cash				
Land				
Interest Revenue				
Accounts Receivable				
Inventory				
Wages Payable				
Tax Expense				
Notes Receivable				
Common Stock				
Service Revenue				
Supplies				
Supplies Expense				
Rent Revenue				
Furniture				
Short-Term Investments				
Unearned Rent				
Plant and Equipment				
Retained Earnings				
Selling Expense				
Accounts Payable				
Long-Term Debt				
Miscellaneous Expense				

ANS:

Account	Balance Sheet	Income Statement	Debit	Credit
Notes Payable	X			X
Prepaid Insurance	X		X	
Cash	X		X	
Land	X		X	
Interest Revenue		X		X
Accounts Receivable	X		X	
Inventory	X		X	
Wages Payable	X			X
Tax Expense		X	X	
Notes Receivable	X		X	
Common Stock	X			X
Service Revenue		X		X
Supplies	X		X	
Supplies Expense		X	X	
Rent Revenue		X		X
Furniture	X		X	
Short-Term Investments	X		X	
Unearned Rent	X			X
Plant and Equipment	X		X	
Retained Earnings	X			X
Selling Expense		X	X	
Accounts Payable	X			X
Long-Term Debt	X			X
Miscellaneous Expense		X	X	

11. For each account listed below, mark the column that BEST describes the correct classification of the account and mark the column for the financial statement on which the account would appear. Assume that all accounts have normal balances. (*Note*: This problem covers the entire accounting cycle.) The first line has been completed as an example.

Account	Asset	Liability	Owners' Equity	Expense	Revenue	Balance Sheet	Income Statement
Notes Payable		X				X	
Prepaid Insurance							
Cash							
Land							
Interest Revenue							
Accounts Receivable							
Inventory							
Wages Payable							
Tax Expense							
Notes Receivable							
Common Stock							
Service Revenue							
Supplies							
Supplies Expense							
Rent Revenue							
Furniture							
Short-Term Investment							
Unearned Rent							
Plant and Equipment							
Retained Earnings							
Selling Expense							
Accounts Payable							
Long-Term Debt							
Miscellaneous Expense							

ANS:

Account	Asset	Liability	Owners' Equity	Expense	Revenue	Balance Sheet	Income Statement
Notes Payable		X				X	
Prepaid Insurance	X					X	
Cash	X					X	
Land	X					X	
Interest Revenue					X		X
Accounts Receivable	X					X	
Inventory	X					X	
Wages Payable		X				X	
Tax Expense				X			X
Notes Receivable	X					X	
Common Stock			X			X	
Service Revenue					X		X
Supplies	X					X	
Supplies Expense				X			X
Rent Revenue					X		X
Furniture	X					X	
Short-Term Investment	X					X	
Unearned Rent		X				X	
Plant and Equipment	X					X	
Retained Earnings			X			X	
Selling Expense				X			X
Accounts Payable		X				X	
Long-Term Debt		X				X	
Miscellaneous Expense				X			X

EXPANDED MATERIAL

12. Mycro Corporation, a computer service company, had the following transactions during 2006.

   a. George Hale, a salesman with Mycro, signed Datum Sales to a two-year service contract for $48,000. The contract was signed on June 1, 2006, with Datum paying the full amount on that date.

   b. Mycro hired Mighty Maid Cleaning for general cleaning services. The contract was signed on October 1 and Mycro paid for the full year ($2,400) on that date.

   c. Fire insurance on Mycro's office building was purchased on April 1. The insurance expires March 31, 2008, and costs $4,000.

   d. Mycro rented a floor of the office building to Gates Company for one year. Gates paid $12,000 on August 1, the rent for 12 months.

   e. Mycro paid Space Savers $1,800 to rent a storage facility for one year on December 1, 2006.

1. Journalize these transactions using the expense/revenue approach.
2. Make any adjusting entries necessary for the year ended December 31, 2006.

ANS:

1.	a.	Cash	48,000	
		Service Revenue		48,000
	b.	Cleaning Expense	2,400	
		Cash		2,400
	c.	Insurance Expense	4,000	
		Cash		4,000
	d.	Cash	12,000	
		Rent Revenue...		12,000
	e.	Rent Expense..	1,800	
		Cash..		1,800

2.	a.	Service Revenue...	34,000	
		Unearned Service Revenue.........................		34,000
		($48,000/24 = $2,000/mo.		
		Unearned for 17 months = $34,000)		
	b.	Prepaid Cleaning	1,800	
		Cleaning Expense		1,800
		($2,400/12 = $200/mo.		
		Prepaid is 9 × $200 = $1,800)		
	c.	Prepaid Insurance	2,500	
		Insurance Expense		2,500
		($4,000/24 = $166.67/mo.		
		Prepaid is 15 × $166.67 = $2,500)		
	d.	Rent Revenue	7,000	
		Unearned Rent Revenue.............................		7,000
		[$12,000/12 = $1,000/mo. 7 months		
		unearned (7 × $1,000)]		
	e.	Prepaid Rent...	1,650	
		Rent Expense...		1,650
		($1,800/12 = $150/mo. Prepaid		
		is 11 × $150 = $1,650)		

13. Mancheski and Sons Inc. reported net income of $45,600 in 2006. Carl, the company bookkeeper, neglected to make the necessary adjusting entries. The necessary adjustments are given below:

a. Supplies at the beginning of the year were $4,000. Supply purchases during the year totaled $2,500 and were recorded as an expense. Ending inventory was $1,000.

b. Insurance purchased during the year was $3,500, of which $1,000 remained unexpired at year-end. The company uses the expense approach when recording this type of expense.

c. Rent revenue for the year was $15,000. Only $5,000 of this was earned in 2006. The company uses the revenue approach in recording this revenue.

d. The company rents storage space from a local firm. Mancheski paid the rent for September 1, 2006, to August 31, 2007, a total of $1,500, in advance on September 1. This was recorded as an expense.

1. Prepare the necessary adjusting entries for December 31, 2006.
2. Determine Mancheski's corrected net income for 2006.

ANS:

1. a. Supplies Expense..   3,000
              Supplies   3,000

    b. Prepaid Insurance   1,000
              Insurance Expense   1,000

    c. Rent Revenue..   10,000
              Unearned Rent Revenue   10,000

    d. Prepaid Rent   1,000
              Rent Expense..   1,000
              ($1,500/12 = $125/mo.;
              8 months × $125/mo. = $1,000)

2.   Original net income $45,600

        Adjustments:
            Supplies expense..   (3,000)
            Insurance expense...   1,000
            Rent revenue ....   (10,000)
            Rent expense..   <u>1,000</u>
            Corrected net income ....   <u>$34,600</u>

14. Bolt, Inc. has retained you for its bookkeeper because the regular bookkeeper is seriously ill. All the necessary adjustments have been entered on the work sheet, and account balances have been extended to the adjusted trial balance columns. Complete the work sheet using the information given.

Bolt, Inc.
Work Sheet
December 31, 2006

Account Titles	Adjusted Trial Balance		Income Statement		Balance Sheet	
	Debit	Credit	Debit	Credit	Debit	Credit
Cash	3,200					
Inventory....................	1,100					
Prepaid Rent..............	500					
Accounts Receivable .	800					
Investments	300					
Equipment..................	1,000					
Accounts Payable.......		700				
Income Tax Payable ..		300				
Notes Payable		1,000				
Common Stock		2,700				
Retained Earnings......		700				
Dividends...................	800					
Sales		8,400				
Salary Expense...........	400					
Office Expense...........	300					
Income Tax Expense..	200					
Officers' Salaries	600					
Rent Expense	300					
Cost of Goods Sold....	4,300					
Interest Receivable.....	300					
Interest Revenue		300				
Totals	14,100	14,100				

ANS:

Bolt, Inc.
Work Sheet
December 31, 2006

Account Titles	Adjusted Trial Balance		Income Statement		Balance Sheet	
	Debit	Credit	Debit	Credit	Debit	Credit
Cash............................	3,200				3,200	
Inventory....................	1,100				1,100	
Prepaid Rent...............	500				500	
Accounts Receivable..	800				800	
Investments	300				300	
Equipment...................	1,000				1,000	
Accounts Payable.......		700				700
Income Tax Payable...		300				300
Notes Payable		1,000				1,000
Common Stock		2,700				2,700
Retained Earnings......		700				700
Dividends....................	800				800	
Sales...........................		8,400		8,400		
Salary Expense...........	400		400			
Office Expense...........	300		300			
Income Tax Expense..	200		200			
Officers' Salaries	600		600			
Rent Expense	300		300			
Cost of Goods Sold....	4,300		4,300			
Interest Receivable.....	300				300	
Interest Revenue		300		300		
Totals	14,100	14,100	6,100	8,700	8,000	5,400
Net Income (to balance)			2,600			2,600
			8,700	8,700	8,000	8,000

15. Indicate in which journal the following transactions would be recorded.

    a.   General journal
    b.   Purchases journal
    c.   Cash receipts journal
    d.   Cash disbursements journal
    e.   Sales journal

    _____   1.   Sale of merchandise on credit.

    _____   2.   Collection of an account receivable.

    _____   3.   Payment of an account payable.

    _____   4.   Purchase of merchandise on credit.

    _____   5.   Sale of merchandise for cash.

    _____   6.   Sales returns and allowances.

    _____   7.   Purchase of merchandise for cash.

    _____   8.   Purchase of equipment on credit.

    _____   9.   Borrowing from a bank.

    _____   10.   Purchase of supplies on credit.

ANS:

1. e
2. c
3. d
4. b
5. c
6. a
7. d
8. a
9. c
10. a

Chapter 4—Completing the Accounting Cycle—Quiz A

Name_____   **Section**_____

TRUE/FALSE

Circle T or F to indicate whether each of the following statements is true or false.

T F 1. Expenses that cannot be matched directly with revenues should be expensed in the accounting period in which they are incurred.

T F 2. Accrual-basis accounting provides a more realistic presentation than cash-basis accounting of a business's profitability.

T F 3. Adjusting entries are usually recorded in the general journal and then are posted to the accounts in the general ledger.

T F 4. Each adjusting entry will include at least one balance sheet and one income statement account.

T F 5. Closing entries are made at the beginning of the accounting period.

T F 6. The adjusting entry to record the expiration of a prepaid item originally recorded as an asset will always cause an expense account to increase and an asset account to decrease.

T F 7. Adjusting entries would be unnecessary if no errors were made in recording the original transactions.

T F 8. The adjusted trial balance will include fewer accounts than the post-closing trial balance.

T F 9. Adjusting entries must be made before closing entries.

T F 10. All nominal accounts are reduced to a zero balance.

Chapter 4—Completing the Accounting Cycle—Quiz B

Name_____   Section_____

MATCHING

For each of the following accounts, indicate in the space given whether it is real or a nominal account.

    a. Real account
    b. Nominal account

  1. _____ Capital Stock

  2. _____ Sales Revenue

  3. _____ Supplies

  4. _____ Dividends

  5. _____ Notes Payable

  6. _____ Prepaid Insurance

  7. _____ Cost of Goods Sold

  8. _____ Income Tax Payable

  9. _____ Interest Expense

10. _____ Retained Earnings

Quiz Solutions

Quiz A

1. T
2. T
3. T
4. T
5. F
6. T
7. F
8. F
9. T
10. T

Quiz B

1. a
2. b
3. a
4. b
5. a
6. a
7. b
8. a
9. b
10. a

Chapter 5—Introduction to Financial Statement Analysis

MULTIPLE CHOICE

Financial Statements Analysis

1. Which of the following statements best describes financial statement analysis?
   a. Financial statement analysis involves relationships and trends.
   b. Financial statement analysis evaluates future performance.
   c. Measurements for a specific company should be compared only with the past.
   d. All of the above are correct.

   ANS: A

2. What ratio is used to measure a firm's liquidity?
   a. Debt ratio
   b. Asset turnover
   c. Current ratio
   d. Return on equity

   ANS: C

3. What ratio is used to measure a firm's leverage?
   a. Debt ratio
   b. Current ratio
   c. Asset turnover
   d. Return on equity

   ANS: A

4. What ratio is used to measure a firm's efficiency at using its assets?
   a. Current ratio
   b. Asset turnover
   c. Return on sales
   d. Return on equity

   ANS: B

5. What ratio is used to measure the profit earned on each dollar invested in a firm?
   a. Current ratio
   b. Asset turnover
   c. Return on sales
   d. Return on equity

   ANS: D

6. What ratio represents an indication of investors' expectations concerning a firm's growth potential?
    a. Earnings per share
    b. Return on equity
    c. Price-earnings ratio
    d. Asset turnover

    ANS: C

7. A measure of the amount of profit earned per dollar of investment is called the
    a. Return on equity
    b. Profit margin
    c. Return on assets
    d. Gross profit

    ANS: A

8. Which of the following ratios measures liquidity?
    a. Current ratio
    b. Creditors' equity to total assets
    c. Return on investment
    d. Total asset turnover

    ANS: A

9. Which of the following transactions could increase a firm's current ratio?
    a. Purchase of inventory for cash
    b. Payment of accounts payable
    c. Collection of accounts receivable
    d. Purchase of temporary investments for cash

    ANS: B

10. In comparing the current ratios of two companies, why is it invalid to assume that the company with the higher current ratio is the better company?
    a. A high current ratio may indicate inadequate inventory on hand.
    b. A high current ratio may indicate inefficient use of various assets and liabilities.
    c. The two companies may define current assets and current liabilities in different terms.
    d. The two companies may be different sizes.

    ANS: B

11. Information from Blain Company's balance sheet is as follows:

Current assets:

Cash	$ 1,200,000
Marketable securities	3,750,000
Accounts receivable	28,800,000
Inventories	33,150,000
Prepaid expenses	600,000
Total current assets	$67,500,000

Current liabilities:

Notes payable	$ 750,000
Accounts payable	9,750,000
Accrued expenses	6,250,000
Income taxes payable	250,000
Payments due within one year on long-term debt	1,750,000
Total current liabilities	$18,750,000

What is Blain's current ratio?
a. 0.26 to 1
b. 0.30 to 1
c. 1.80 to 1
d. 3.60 to 1

ANS: D

12. Selected information for Henry Company is as follows:

	December 31	
	2004	2005
Common stock	$600,000	$600,000
Additional paid-in capital	250,000	250,000
Retained earnings	170,000	370,000
Net income for year	120,000	240,000

Henry's return on equity, rounded to the nearest percentage point, for 2005 is
a. 20 percent
b. 21 percent
c. 28 percent
d. 40 percent

ANS: A

13. On December 31, 2004 and 2005, Taft Corporation had 100,000 shares of common stock issued and outstanding. Additional information:

Stockholders' equity at 12/31/05	$4,500,000
Net income year ended 12/31/05	1,200,000
Market price per share of common stock at 12/31/05....................	144

The price-earnings ratio on common stock at December 31, 2005, was
a. 10 to 1
b. 12 to 1
c. 14 to 1
d. 16 to 1

ANS: B

14. Which of the following is a measure of the liquid position of a corporation?
a. Price-earnings ratio
b. Debt ratio
c. Current ratio
d. Asset turnover

ANS: C

15. The balance sheets at the end of each of the first two years of operations indicate the following:

	2006	2005
Total current assets	$600,000	$560,000
Total investments...	85,000	40,000
Total property, plant, and equipment..............................	900,000	700,000
Total current liabilities...	250,000	180,000
Total long-term liabilities	350,000	250,000
Common stock, $10 par..	600,000	600,000
Paid-in capital in excess of par—common stock..............	60,000	60,000
Retained earnings...	325,000	210,000

If net income is $115,000 for 2006, what is the return on equity for 2006 (round percent to one decimal point)?
a. 10.6 percent
b. 11.7 percent
c. 12.4 percent
d. 15.6 percent

ANS: B

16. In a common-size income statement, each item on the statement is expressed as a percentage of
a. Revenue
b. Expenses
c. Net income
d. Gross profit

ANS: A

17. In a common-size balance sheet, each item on the balance sheet is expressed as a percentage of
    a. Assets
    b. Net income
    c. Equity
    d. Revenue

    ANS: D

18. A useful tool in financial statement analysis is the common-size financial statement. What does this tool enable the financial analyst to do?
    a. Evaluate financial statements of companies within a given industry of approximately the same value
    b. Determine which companies in the same industry are at approximately the same stage of development
    c. Ascertain the relative potential of companies of similar size in different industries
    d. Compare the mix of revenue and expenses and determine efficient use of resources within a company over time or between companies within a given industry without respect to relative size

    ANS: D

19. When using common-size statements,
    a. Data may be selected for the same business as of different dates, or for two or more businesses as of the same date
    b. Relationships should be stated in terms of ratios
    c. Dollar changes are reported over a period of at least three years
    d. All of the above are correct

    ANS: A

20. Which of the following generally is the most useful in analyzing companies of different sizes?
    a. Comparative statements
    b. Common-size financial statements
    c. Price-level accounting
    d. Audit report

    ANS: B

21. Which of the following is NOT included in the DuPont framework of the return on equity ratio?
    a. Profit margin
    b. Current ratio
    c. Asset turnover
    d. Assets-to-equity ratio

    ANS: B

22. The return on equity ratio under the DuPont framework is computed as
    a. Net income/Revenue
    b. Revenue/Assets
    c. Assets/Equity
    d. Net income/Equity

    ANS: D

23. The following data came from the financial statements of the Bradshaw Co.:

Revenue	$900,000		Assets	$600,000
Expenses	600,000		Liabilities	100,000
Net income	300,000		Equity	500,000

The return on equity is
a.   40 percent
b.   50 percent
c.   30 percent
d.   60 percent

ANS: D

24. The following data came from the financial statements of the Bradshaw Co.:

Revenue	$900,000		Assets	$600,000
Expenses	600,000		Liabilities	100,000
Net income	300,000		Equity	500,000

The profit margin is
a.   25 percent
b.   33 percent
c.   40 percent
d.   50 percent

ANS: B

25. The following data came from the financial statements of the Bradshaw Co.:

Revenue	$900,000		Assets	$600,000
Expenses	600,000		Liabilities	100,000
Net income	300,000		Equity	500,000

The asset turnover is
a.   1.25
b.   1.40
c.   1.50
d.   1.60

ANS: C

26. The following data came from the financial statements of the Bradshaw Co.:

Revenue	$900,000		Assets	$600,000
Expenses	600,000		Liabilities	100,000
Net income	300,000		Equity	500,000

The assets-to-equity ratio is
a. 1.20
b. 1.40
c. 1.25
d. 1.15

ANS: A

27. The cash flow adequacy ratio is computed as
a. Cash from operations/Cash from investing activities
b. Cash from operations/Cash from financing activities
c. Cash from operations/Cash paid for capital expenditures
d. Cash from investing activities/Cash from operations

ANS: C

28. The following data came from the financial statements of the Green Co.:

Cash from operations	$900,000
Cash from investing activities	350,000
Cash from financing activities	220,000
Cash paid for capital expenditures	55,000
Net income	425,000

The cash flow adequacy ratio is
a. 2.57
b. 4.09
c. 16.36
d. 2.12

ANS: C

29. The following data came from the financial statements of the Green Co.:

Cash from operations	$900,000
Cash from investing activities	350,000
Cash from financing activities	220,000
Cash paid for capital expenditures	55,000
Net income	425,000

The cash flow-to-net income ratio is
a. 2.57
b. 4.09
c. 16.36
d. 2.12

ANS: D

30. The particular analytical measures chosen to analyze a company may be influenced by all but which of the following?
   a. Industry type
   b. Capital structure
   c. Diversity of business operations
   d. Product quality or service effectiveness

   ANS: D

PROBLEMS

1. The financial statements for Kobe Corporation revealed that sales revenue was $1,581,000 and that the following were the ending account balances:

Cash	$100,000	Accounts Payable............	$ 80,000
Accounts Receivable..........	130,000	Mortgage Payable	500,000
Land....................................	200,000	Capital Stock...................	300,000
Buildings............................	500,000	Retained Earnings	50,000

   Compute the following:

   a. Debt ratio
   b. Current ratio
   c. Asset turnover ratio

   ANS:

   a. 62.4% (rounded) = Total liabilities/Total assets = $580,000/$930,000
   b. 2.875 = Current assets/Current liabilities = $230,000/$80,000
   c. 1.7 = Sales/Total assets = $1,581,000/$930,000

2. MacroSoft, Inc.'s financial statements contained the following information:

Sales.....................................	$600,000	Owners' equity...............	$150,000
Expenses	$570,000	Market price per share....	$ 45
Number of shares outstanding	10,000		

   Calculate the following:

   a. Return on sales ratio
   b. Return on equity ratio
   c. Price-earnings ratio

   ANS:

   a. 5% = Net income/Sales = $30,000/$600,000
   b. 20% = Net income/Owners' equity = $30,000/$150,000
   c. 15 = Market price per share/Earnings per share = $45/$3

3. Match the following terms to the definitions listed below:

   a. Assets-to-equity ratio
   b. Asset turnover
   c. Current ratio
   d. Common-size financial statements
   e. Debt ratio
   f. Price-earnings ratio
   g. Return on sales
   h. Cash flow adequacy ratio
   i. Return on equity

   _____ 1. Measures the number of times current assets could cover current liabilities.

   _____ 2. Measures the amount of profit earned per dollar of investment.

   _____ 3. Achieved by dividing all financial statement amounts by total revenues.

   _____ 4. Measures the number of asset dollars a company is able to acquire for each dollar of equity.

   _____ 5. An indication of growth potential.

   _____ 6. Represents the proportion of borrowed funds used to acquire the company's assets.

   _____ 7. Determines the sufficiency of operating cash flows to pay for capital additions.

   _____ 8. Measures the number of revenue dollars generated for each dollar of assets.

   _____ 9. Measures the amount of profit generated for each dollar of revenue.

   ANS:

   1. c
   2. i
   3. d
   4. a
   5. f
   6. e
   7. h
   8. b
   9. g

4. The income statement and balance sheet for W. Gretsky Company for the year ended December 31, 2006, are presented below:

W. Gretsky Company
Income Statement
For the Year Ended December 31, 2006

Sales revenue		$360,000
Less: Cost of goods sold		200,000
Gross profit		$160,000
Less: Operating expenses		
Salaries expense	$60,000	
Advertising expense	14,000	74,000
Net income		$ 86,000

W. Gretsky Company
Balance Sheet
December 31, 2006

Assets
Current assets:
Cash	$ 66,000
Accounts receivable	30,000
Inventory	20,000
Buildings	300,000
Total assets	$416,000

Liabilities
Accounts payable	$ 20,000

Owners' equity
Capital stock	$270,000
Retained earnings	126,000
Total owners' equity	$396,000
Total liabilities and owners' equity	$416,000

1. Prepare a common-size income statement.
2. Prepare a common-size balance sheet.

ANS:

1.

W. Gretsky Company
Income Statement
For the Year Ended December 31, 2006

			% of Revenues
Sales	....	$360,000	100.0
Less:	Cost of goods sold................................	200,000	55.6
	Gross profit	$160,000	44.4
Less:	Operating expenses		
	Salaries expense................................	60,000	16.7
	Advertising expense................................	14,000	3.9
Net income	....	$ 86,000	23.9

2.

W. Gretsky Company
Balance Sheet
December 31, 2006

		% of Total Revenue
Assets		
Cash	$ 66,000	18.3
Accounts receivable................................	30,000	8.3
Inventory................................	20,000	5.6
Buildings................................	300,000	83.3
Total assets................................	$416,000	115.6
Liabilities		
Accounts payable................................	$ 20,000	5.6
Owners' Equity		
Capital stock	$270,000	75.0
Retained earnings................................	126,000	35.0
Total owners' equity	$396,000	110.0
Total liabilities and owners' equity	$416,000	115.6

5. The income statement and balance sheet for the W. Gretsky Company for the year ended December 31, 2006 are presented below:

W. Gretsky Company
Income Statement
For the Year Ended December 31, 2006

Sales revenue		$360,000
Less: Cost of goods sold		200,000
Gross profit		$160,000
Operating expenses:		
Advertising	$14,000	
Salaries	60,000	74,000
Net income		$ 86,000

W. Gretsky Company
Balance Sheet
December 31, 2006

Assets

Current assets:	
Cash	$ 66,000
Accounts receivable	30,000
Inventory	20,000
Total current assets	$116,000
Buildings	$300,000
Total assets	$416,000

Liabilities

Accounts payable	$ 20,000

Owners' equity

Capital stock	$270,000
Retained earnings	126,000
Total owners' equity	$396,000
Total liabilities and owners' equity	$416,000

Using the DuPont framework, compute:
a. The profit margin
b. The asset turnover
c. The assets-to-equity ratio
d. The return on equity

ANS:

a. Profit margin = $86,000/$360,000 = 23.9%
b. Asset turnover = $360,000/$416,000 = 0.865 time
c. Assets-to-equity ratio = $416,000/$396,000 = 1.05
d. Return on equity = $86,000/$396,000 = 21.7%

Name_____   Section_____

TRUE/FALSE

Circle T or F to indicate whether each of the following statements is true or false.

T F 1. Examining relationships among data in the company's financial statements can provide knowledge that cannot be gained from just looking at individual items in the statements.

T F 2. On a common-size income statement, all items are stated as a percent of total assets or equities at year-end.

T F 3. Statements in which all items are expressed in relative terms are called common-size statements.

T F 4. If a firm has a current ratio of 2.0, the subsequent receipt of a 60-day note receivable on account will cause the ratio to decrease.

T F 5. When you are interpreting financial ratios, it is useful to compare a company's ratios to some form of standard.

T F 6. GAAP require the calculation of financial ratios.

T F 7. The debt ratio is a measure of leverage.

T F 8. Asset turnover represents how effective management uses total assets.

T F 9. Return on equity is an overall measure of the performance of a company.

T F 10. Price-earnings ratio is an indication of growth potential.

Name_____   Section_____

MATCHING

In the spaces provided, write the letter of the ratio for each of the following calculations.

     a. Debt ratio
     b. Current ratio
     c. Return on sales
     d. Asset turnover
     e. Return on equity
     f. Price-earnings ratio
     g. Assets-to-equity ratio
     h. Cash flow-to-net income ratio
     i. Cash flow adequacy ratio

1. _____   Sales/Total assets

2. _____   Cash from operations/Net income

3. _____   Net income/Sales

4. _____   Net income/Shareholders' equity

5. _____   Cash from operations/Cash paid for capital expenditures

6. _____   Total liabilities/Total assets

7. _____   Total assets/Shareholders' equity

8. _____   Current assets/Current liabilities

9. _____   Market value of shares/Net income

Quiz Solutions

Quiz A		Quiz B	
1.	T	1.	d
2.	F	2.	h
3.	T	3.	c
4.	F	4.	e
5.	T	5.	i
6.	F	6.	a
7.	T	7.	g
8.	F	8.	b
9.	T	9.	f
10.	T		

MULTIPLE CHOICE

The Types of Errors That Can Occur

1. Which of the following is NOT a reason for problems occurring in the financial statements?
    a. Fraud
    b. Disagreement
    c. Errors
    d. Safeguards

    ANS: D

2. If rent for 2007 is paid in advance during 2006 but is mistakenly debited to Rent Expense in 2006,
    a. Net income for 2006 will be overstated
    b. There will be no error in 2006 net income
    c. Net income for 2006 will be understated
    d. The answer cannot be determined from the above information

    ANS: C

3. Recording $130 of insurance expense as advertising expense will result in
    a. An understatement of assets and an understatement of expenses
    b. An overstatement of assets and an overstatement of expenses
    c. An overstatement of assets and an understatement of expenses
    d. None of the above

    ANS: D

4. Recording the payment of an account payable twice will result in the
    a. Overstatement of total assets and total liabilities
    b. Understatement of total assets and total liabilities
    c. Overstatement of total assets and understatement of total liabilities
    d. Understatement of total assets and overstatement of total liabilities

    ANS: B

5. If an employee steals cash from a company and successfully covers up his/her actions by recording a fictitious debit to Prepaid Advertising and a credit to Cash, then
    a. Expenses will be understated
    b. Net income will be overstated
    c. Net income will be understated
    d. Net income will be stated correctly

    ANS: D

6. If an employee steals cash from a company and tries to cover up his/her actions by recording a fictitious debit to Prepaid Insurance and a credit to Cash, then
   a. Expenses will be understated
   b. Assets will be overstated
   c. Assets will be understated
   d. Assets will be stated correctly

   ANS: B

7. If an employee steals cash from a company and tries to cover up his/her actions by recording a fictitious debit to Insurance Expense and a credit to Cash, then
   a. Expenses will be overstated
   b. Expenses will be understated
   c. Cash will be overstated
   d. Cash will be understated

   ANS: A

8. If an employee steals inventory from a company and successfully covers up his/her actions by recording a fictitious debit to Accounts Payable and a credit to Cash, then
   a. Liabilities will be overstated
   b. Liabilities will be understated
   c. Assets will be overstated
   d. Assets will be understated

   ANS: B

9. Failure to record the expired amount of prepaid rent expense
   a. Overstates expenses
   b. Understates net income
   c. Overstates owners' equity
   d. Overstates liabilities

   ANS: C

10. Recording the collection of accounts receivable by debiting Cash and crediting Revenue
    a. Overstates cash
    b. Understates owners' equity
    c. Overstates assets
    d. Both a and c

    ANS: C

11. Recording Rent Expense as Wages Expense
    a. Overstates income
    b. Understates expenses
    c. Understates owners' equity
    d. None of the above

    ANS: D

12. Failure to record the used portion of supplies on hand during the month has what effect on the financial statements prepared at the end of the month?
    a. Overstates liabilities
    b. Understates net income
    c. Overstates assets
    d. Understates owners' equity

    ANS: C

13. Which one of the following errors causes net income to be overstated?
    a. Failure to record collection of an account receivable
    b. Failure to record depreciation expense
    c. Failure to accrue revenue earned but not billed
    d. Failure to record fees received in advance that are earned by the end of the period

    ANS: B

14. Which one of the following errors causes net income to be understated?
    a. Failure to record wages employees have earned but not yet been paid
    b. Failure to record depreciation expense
    c. Failure to record collection of accounts receivable
    d. Failure to record revenue earned but not billed

    ANS: D

15. A company purchased a two-year insurance policy on September 1, debiting Prepaid Insurance for the full amount. If no adjusting entry is made at the end of the year, how does this affect the year-end financial statements?
    a. Overstates revenue
    b. Overstates expenses
    c. Overstates assets
    d. Understates owners' equity

    ANS: C

16. If a company does NOT record accrued wages expense at the end of the year, how does this affect the year-end financial statements?
    a. Overstates revenue
    b. Overstates expenses
    c. Overstates assets
    d. Overstates owners' equity

    ANS: D

17. If the total amount for Rent Expense is inadvertently posted to Prepaid Rent at the end of the year, what will be the effect on the year-end financial statements?
    a. Assets will be understated.
    b. Revenues will be overstated.
    c. Revenues will be understated.
    d. Revenues will be correctly stated.

    ANS: D

18. If the total amount for Insurance Expense is inadvertently posted to Prepaid Insurance at the end of the year, what will be the effect on the year-end financial statements?
    a. Revenues will be overstated.
    b. Revenues will be understated.
    c. Owners' equity will be overstated.
    d. Owners' equity will be understated.

    ANS: C

19. If the total amount for Rent Expense is inadvertently posted to Prepaid Rent at the end of the year, what will be the effect on the year-end financial statements?
    a. Expenses will be overstated.
    b. Assets will be overstated.
    c. Revenues will be understated.
    d. Owners' equity will be understated.

    ANS: B

20. If the total amount for Insurance Expense is inadvertently posted to Prepaid Insurance at the end of the year, what will be the effect on the year-end financial statements?
    a. Expenses will be understated.
    b. Owners' equity will be overstated.
    c. Net income will be overstated.
    d. All of the above are true.

    ANS: D

21. A collection of an account receivable was erroneously recorded and posted as a debit to Cash and a credit to Consulting Fees Revenue. The journal entry to correct this error would be
    a. A debit to Cash and a credit to Accounts Receivable
    b. A debit to Accounts Receivable and a credit to Consulting Fees Revenue
    c. A debit to Consulting Fees Revenue and a credit to Unearned Consulting Fees
    d. A debit to Consulting Fees Revenue and a credit to Accounts Receivable

    ANS: D

22. Blake Co. provided $5,000 of consulting services to Simmons Co. for which it has not yet received payment. When Blake billed Simmons for the consulting services, Blake mistakenly journalized and posted the transaction as a $5,000 debit to Accounts Receivable and a $5,000 credit to Unearned Consulting Fees. The entry Blake needs to make to correct this error is debit
    a. Unearned Consulting Fees and credit Consulting Fees Earned for $5,000
    b. Unearned Consulting Fees and credit Accounts Receivable for $5,000
    c. Consulting Fees Earned and credit Accounts Receivable for $5,000
    d. Consulting Fees Earned and credit Unearned Consulting Fees for $5,000

    ANS: A

23. A purchase of $800 of supplies for cash was incorrectly journalized and posted as an $800 debit to Supplies Expense and an $800 credit to Cash. The entry to correct this error is
    a. An $800 debit to Supplies on Hand and an $800 credit to Cash
    b. An $800 debit to Supplies on Hand and an $800 credit to Supplies Expense
    c. An $800 debit to Cash and an $800 credit to Supplies on Hand
    d. An $800 debit to Accounts Receivable and an $800 credit to Supplies on Hand

    ANS: B

24. When an accountant prepares a trial balance that balances, management can be certain that
    a. All journal entries were made correctly
    b. Net income is stated correctly
    c. No fraudulent activities took place during the period
    d. Total debits equal total credits

    ANS: D

25. Which of the following errors in recording transactions will always cause the trial balance to be out of balance?
    a. Entering a credit as a debit
    b. Forgetting to record a transaction
    c. Recording a transaction twice
    d. Recording an amount in the wrong account

    ANS: A

26. Which of the following errors would NOT be detected by preparing a trial balance?
    a. Entering one or more amounts in the wrong accounts
    b. Entering a transaction more than once
    c. Failing to record a particular transaction
    d. All of the above

    ANS: D

27. The following errors were made in preparing a trial balance: $8,000 of inventory was not counted at the end of the year and therefore omitted from the inventory account on the trial balance; the $1,800 balance of Wages Payable was listed as a debit; and the $2,000 balance of Interest Revenue was listed as Dividend Revenue. The debit and credit totals of the trial balance would differ by
    a. $9,800
    b. $4,400
    c. $11,800
    d. $10,000

    ANS: B

28. The following errors were made in preparing a trial balance: $1,200 of Accounts Receivable were not counted at the end of the year and therefore omitted from Accounts Receivable on the trial balance; the $800 balance of Supplies on Hand was listed as a credit; and the $400 balance of Utilities Expense was listed as Advertising Expense. The debit and credit totals of the trial balance would differ by
    a. $2,400
    b. $2,000
    c. $1,200
    d. $2,800

    ANS: D

29. Estimates are used in many instances when recording a company's results of operations. Which of the following would NOT require an estimate to be made?
    a. Uncollectible accounts
    b. Contract percentage of completion
    c. Wages earned
    d. None of the above

    ANS: C

30. If two different accountants were to estimate the percentage of customers who will not pay their accounts (bad debts), they could arrive at different estimates. These differing estimates would affect the financial statements. Such differences in assessing estimates are due to
    a. Fraudulent financial reporting
    b. Errors in accounts and ledgers
    c. Disagreements in judgment
    d. Lack of internal controls

    ANS: C

31. All of the following are likely to be methods that could be used to conduct fraud, EXCEPT
    a. Overstating liabilities
    b. Not recording various expenses
    c. Creating fictitious invoices
    d. Overstating receivables

    ANS: A

Safeguards to Minimize Problems

32. Which of the following requires that all publicly traded corporations maintain an adequate system of internal controls?
    a. Foreign Corrupt Practices Act
    b. Securities Act of 1934
    c. Internal Revenue Code
    d. Sarbanes-Oxley Act

    ANS: A

33. Which of the following is NOT one of the major safeguards in the financial reporting process?
    a. The Internal Revenue Service
    b. The Securities and Exchange Commission
    c. Internal auditors
    d. External auditors

    ANS: A

34. Which of the following is NOT one of the major concerns most companies have when they are designing internal controls?
    a. The assets and records are safeguarded
    b. The Securities and Exchange Commission
    c. Management policies are followed
    d. The Foreign Corrupt Practices Act

    ANS: B

35. Which of the following is NOT one of the three basic categories of internal control?
    a. The accounting system
    b. The control environment
    c. The control procedures
    d. The auditing system

    ANS: D

36. Which of the following is NOT usually considered a component of a company's control environment?
    a. The organizational structure
    b. The audit committee
    c. The Foreign Corrupt Practices Act
    d. Management's philosophy and operating style

    ANS: C

37. Which of the following requires that audit committee members be financially literate?
    a. Securities Exchange Commission
    b. Sarbanes-Oxley Act
    c. Foreign Corrupt Practices Act
    d. American Institute of CPAs

    ANS: B

38. Which of the following are usually members of a company's audit committee?
    a. Securities and Exchange Commission members
    b. External auditors
    c. Internal auditors
    d. Members of the board of directors who are not officers of the company

    ANS: D

39. Which of the following is NOT one of the seven control objectives that an accounting system should contain?
    a. Valuation
    b. Classification
    c. Preciseness
    d. Validity

    ANS: C

40. Which of the following are the three functions that should be performed by separate departments or individuals?
    a. Authorization, purchasing, and custody
    b. Record keeping, validation, and classifying
    c. Record keeping, validation, and authorization
    d. Authorization, record keeping, and custody

    ANS: D

41. Which of the following are valid control procedures?
    a. Segregation of duties
    b. Adequate documents and records
    c. Independent checks on performance
    d. All of the above

    ANS: D

42. Which of the following is desirable in a good system of internal accounting control?
    a. All accounting personnel in a company should be certified public accountants.
    b. Appropriate forms, such as checks and sales invoices, should be prenumbered.
    c. To obtain the benefit of specialization, employees should not be rotated among jobs.
    d. Responsibility and authority for a given function should be shared among several employees.

    ANS: B

43. Which of the following is a poor internal accounting control feature?
    a. Division of work
    b. Combining accountability with custodianship
    c. Rotation of personnel
    d. Internal auditing

    ANS: B

44. The internal control structure of a company is a system of policies and procedures established to
    a. Safeguard assets
    b. Promote operational efficiency
    c. Ensure accurate accounting records
    d. All of the above

    ANS: D

45. Which of the following is NOT an objective of the accounting system?
    a. Make sure a company only records profitable transactions
    b. Make sure a company only records valid transactions
    c. Make sure a company values transactions properly
    d. Make sure a company records transactions in the proper time period

    ANS: A

Earnings Management

46. Which of the following items of the earnings management continuum is in the correct order?
    a. Strategic matching, change in methods or estimates with full disclosure, non-GAAP accounting
    b. Strategic matching, change in methods or estimates with little or no disclosure, fictitious transactions
    c. Change in methods or estimates with little or no disclosure, non-GAAP accounting, fictitious transactions
    d. Change in methods or estimates with full disclosure, non-GAAP accounting, fictitious transactions

    ANS: C

47. Most companies that engage in earnings management typically do NOT go beyond which of the following activities on the earnings management continuum?
    a. Strategic matching
    b. Change in methods or estimates with full disclosure
    c. Change in methods or estimates with little or no disclosure
    d. Non-GAAP accounting

    ANS: A

48. Earnings management through strategic matching is best exemplified by
    a. Changing the useful life of a depreciable asset
    b. Timing transactions such that large one-time gains and losses occur in the same quarter
    c. Changing the interest rate used in accounting for leases without describing the change in the notes to the financial statements
    d. Capitalizing as assets expenditures that have no future economic benefit

    ANS: B

49. Recording as an asset expenditures that have no future economic benefit is an example of
    a. Strategic matching
    b. Change in methods or estimates with full disclosure
    c. Non-GAAP accounting
    d. A fictitious transaction

    ANS: C

50. Which of the following typically involves the use of non-GAAP accounting?
    a. Strategic matching
    b. A change in accounting estimate that is fully disclosed
    c. Recording expenses as assets
    d. A change in accounting principle that is fully disclosed

    ANS: C

51. Excessive earnings management typically begins as a result of
    a. A regulatory investigation
    b. Pressure to meet the expectations of stakeholders
    c. A downturn in business
    d. A violation of generally accepted accounting principles

    ANS: C

52. The GAAP Oval best represents the
    a. Fact that only one true earnings number exists
    b. Flexibility managers have within GAAP to report one earnings number from among many possibilities
    c. Philosophy that earnings management within limits is ethical
    d. Fact that GAAP are not subject to interpretation

    ANS: B

53. Fraud is
    a. Deceptive concealment of transactions
    b. The creation of fictitious transactions
    c. Unintentional errors
    d. Both a and b

    ANS: D

Sarbanes-Oxley

54. The Sarbanes-Oxley Act establishes
    a. Independent oversight of auditors
    b. Constraints on auditors
    c. Constraints on company management
    d. All of the above

    ANS: D

55. The Public Company Accounting Oversight Board
    a. Establishes requirements for entry into the CPA profession
    b. Conducts inspections of accounting firms
    c. Reviews tax returns of public companies
    d. Enforces compliance with the Foreign Corrupt Practices Act

    ANS: B

56. The Public Company Accounting Oversight Board is NOT required to
    a. Establish standards relating to the preparation of audit reports for public companies
    b. Conduct inspections of accounting firms
    c. Register all public accounting firms that provide audits for public companies
    d. Enforce compliance with the Foreign Corrupt Practices Act

    ANS: D

The Role of Auditors in the Accounting Process

57. The internal audit manager reports directly to the
    a. Controller
    b. Chief financial officer
    c. Accounting committee
    d. Audit committee

    ANS: D

58. Which activity would internal auditors NOT typically perform in a large company?
    a. Evaluate internal controls
    b. Assist with increasing the efficiency of operations
    c. Prepare the primary financial statements
    d. Detect fraud

    ANS: C

59. External audits are performed by
    a. Certified internal auditors
    b. Certified public accountants
    c. Certified financial analysts
    d. Certified management accountants

    ANS: B

60. What is the most common professional designation for external auditors?
    a. Certified internal auditor
    b. Certified external auditor
    c. Certified professional accountant
    d. Certified public accountant

    ANS: D

61. Which statement best describes the role of external auditors in auditing a large public company?
    a. Examine the organization's accounting for a sample of business transactions to provide reasonable assurance that the financial statements are presented fairly
    b. Examine the organization's accounting for a sample of business transactions to guarantee that the financial statements are presented fairly
    c. Examine the organization's accounting for every business transaction to provide reasonable assurance that the financial statements are presented fairly
    d. Examine the organization's accounting for every business transaction to guarantee that the financial statements are presented fairly

    ANS: A

62. Which of the following is NOT a type of audit opinion that is issued by external auditors related to the financial statements of a client company?
    a.   Adverse opinion
    b.   Accurate opinion
    c.   Disclaimer of opinion
    d.   Qualified opinion

    ANS: B

63. Which of the following audit opinions is most frequently issued by external auditors relating to the financial statements of a client company?
    a.   Qualified opinion
    b.   Disclaimer of opinion
    c.   Adverse opinion
    d.   Unqualified opinion

    ANS: D

The Securities and Exchange Commission

64. When does the Securities and Exchange Commission (SEC) typically require a company to submit a registration statement to the SEC for approval?
    a.   When the company receives a qualified opinion from the external auditors
    b.   When the company receives a disclaimer of opinion from the external auditors
    c.   When the company issues new debt or stock securities to the public
    d.   When the company has experienced a major fraud

    ANS: C

65. What is the detailed report that companies file annually with the Securities and Exchange Commission?
    a.   Form 8-K
    b.   Form 10-K
    c.   Form 10-Q
    d.   Form S-16

    ANS: B

66. Which form must be filed quarterly by all publicly held corporations?
    a.   Form 10-K
    b.   Form 8-K
    c.   Form 10-Q
    d.   Form 8-Q

    ANS: C

PROBLEMS

1. Discuss the three types of problems that can occur in financial statements.

    ANS:

    1. Errors can occur when care is not taken in recording, posting, and summarizing accounting data. They are not intentional and are corrected when discovered.
    2. Disagreement occurs when different people arrive at different conclusions based on the same set of facts. Disagreements usually occur when judgment and estimates are required. The differences occur when those involved with producing the financial statements are motivated by differing incentives.
    3. Fraud occurs when intentional errors are made by management to manipulate the financial statements for their own purposes.

2. List the five major concerns that companies must keep in mind when designing their internal control system.

    ANS:

    1. Provide accurate accounting records and financial statements containing reliable data for business decisions.
    2. Safeguard the assets and records.
    3. Effectively and efficiently run their operations, without duplication of effort or waste.
    4. Follow management policies.
    5. Comply with the Foreign Corrupt Practices Act, which requires companies to maintain proper record-keeping systems and controls.

3. To be effective, an accounting system should contain adequate controls to ensure that seven control objectives are met. List those seven objectives.

    ANS:

    1. Validity
    2. Authorization
    3. Completeness
    4. Classification
    5. Timeliness
    6. Valuation
    7. Posting and summarization

4. Research has shown that numerous companies manage their earnings. A variety of earnings management techniques are available ranging from income smoothing to outright fraud.

    Define income smoothing and explain how it is implemented.

ANS: Income smoothing is the careful timing of the recognition of revenues and expenses in order to reduce the volatility of income. Managers of many companies seek to report gradual and continual increases in income in the belief that investors view an erratic earnings trend as being more risky than a smooth trend. These managers fear the economic consequences of lower earnings in the form of reduced stock prices, higher borrowing costs, or possible technical default as a result of noncompliance with debt covenants.

Income smoothing can be implemented in a number of ways. Large corporations with diverse operating units can match a large one-time loss for one operating unit with a large one-time gain of another operating unit to achieve the desired earnings result. Careful timing of the recognition of such gains and losses can eliminate much of the volatility in earnings. Other means of smoothing include deferring revenues from sales to a later period or accelerating the recognition of sales revenue to the current period. Prices of products also can be lowered to facilitate additional sales that otherwise might not have occurred.

Expenses can be used to smooth income as well. A purchaser can persuade a supplier to split a single purchase order into several orders with invoice dates in more than one accounting period. Bad debt expense, warranty expense, and other estimated expenses can be manipulated to reach a desired earnings goal. Oil and gas companies have particular flexibility in their choice of when to declare a dry well as unsuccessful thus timing needed reductions in income to suit their needs.

5. Internal earnings targets represent an important tool in motivating managers to increase sales efforts, control costs, and use resources more efficiently. Such internal targets also can cause managers to resort to extreme measures in order to meet goals established by upper management. Earnings management often appears in a variety of forms as a means of reaching these internal goals.

Earnings management also is associated with earnings-based internal bonus plans which are also a form of internal target.

Explain how earnings management is related to earnings-based internal bonus plans and how managers behave in response to such plans.

ANS: Academic research has shown that managers subject to an earnings-based bonus plan are indeed motivated to manage earnings. Managers are likely to manage earnings upward if they are close to the bonus threshold. Conversely, research has shown that managers are more likely to manage earnings downward if reported earnings are substantially in excess of the maximum bonus level, causing managers to defer these excess earnings for use in future periods when operating results may be less favorable.

Bonus plans typically provide a maximum amount that can be transferred to the bonus pool from which bonuses are paid. The maximum transfer usually is some percentage of earnings over a target earnings number, the target frequently being a percentage of shareholder equity or total assets. When earnings are below the target, no bonuses are awarded.

If actual earnings are above the upper bound, managers have an incentive to reduce reported earnings by deferring earnings. Failure to defer the earnings in excess of the upper bound would result in the loss of the bonus on the excess earnings. Alternatively, deferring the excess earnings increases expected future bonuses.

If actual earnings are between the target and the upper bound, managers will take steps to ensure that the current period's earnings are equal to the upper bound in an effort to maximize the amount received currently. If earnings are below the target, then managers may engage in "big bath" accounting and recognize as much expense as possible in the current period in order to avoid recognizing such expenses in the future.

6. Restoring public confidence in the financial reporting process requires that management ensure financial statement users of the steps taken to provide quality financial information. How does the Sarbanes-Oxley Act constrain management to achieve that public confidence?

    ANS:

    1. The CEO and CFO of each public company are required to prepare a statement to accompany the audit report to certify the appropriateness of the financial statements and disclosures.
    2. All public companies are required to develop and enforce an officer code of ethics.
    3. Loans to executive officers and directors are prohibited.
    4. Support a much stronger audit committee in each public company.

Name_____   **Section**_____

TRUE/FALSE

Circle T or F to indicate whether each of the following statements is true or false.

T F   1.   Fraudulent transactions recorded in a company's accounting records will cause the basic accounting equation to be out of balance.

T F   2.   Internal accountants in a large company only need a relatively limited knowledge of financial accounting and reporting principles because the company's financial statements typically are prepared by external CPAs.

T F   3.   A company's internal control structure refers to the policies and procedures established to provide reasonable assurance that specific entity objectives will be achieved.

T F   4.   Under an effective system of internal control, errors occur only as a result of fraud or dishonesty.

T F   5.   A company's accounting controls refer to the policies and procedures established to produce accurate and reliable financial data as well as to safeguard the company's assets.

T F   6.   Good internal accounting control requires that the same person should not have both the responsibility for a given function and the authority to perform that function.

T F   7.   Requiring employees to take vacations is an example of a good internal accounting control feature.

T F   8.   Good internal accounting control requires that the person handling cash should also make any related journal entries so that responsibility for cash can be assigned to one person.

T F   9.   A disclaimer of opinion means that the auditor believes the financial statements have not been presented fairly in accordance with GAAP.

T F   10. The major role of a company's internal audit staff is to issue an opinion on the fairness of management's financial statements so that users will have more confidence in them.

Chapter 6—Ensuring the Integrity of Financial Information—Quiz B

Name_____   Section_____

MATCHING

In the spaces provided, write the letter of the definition for each of the following terms.

   a. Report used to communicate audit findings to users of financial statements.
   b. Safeguards in the form of policies and procedures that provide management with reasonable assurance that the entity's objectives will be achieved.
   c. A voluntary organization of CPAs that sets professional requirements, conducts research, and publishes materials pertinent to accounting, auditing, management advisory services, and taxes.
   d. Precautions used to protect assets and records such as locks, vaults, passwords, security guards, etc.
   e. An agency organized in the 1930s because of financial reporting and stock market abuses.
   f. Independent CPAs who are retained by organizations to perform audits of financial statements.
   g. Provides a type of internal check on performance.
   h. Members of a client's board of directors who are responsible for dealing with the external and internal auditors.
   i. Procedures for continual internal verification of other controls.
   j. The actions, policies, and procedures that reflect the overall attitudes of top management, the directors, and the owners about control and its importance to the organization.

1. _____   Control environment

2. _____   Segregation of duties

3. _____   Independent checks

4. _____   Audit committee

5. _____   External auditors

6. _____   The Securities and Exchange Commission (SEC)

7. _____   Internal control structure

8. _____   Audit report

9. _____   American Institute of Certified Public Accountants (AICPA)

10. _____   Physical safeguards

Name_____   Section_____

TRUE/FALSE

Circle T or F to indicate whether each of the following statements is true or false.

T F 1. Managers subject to an earnings-based bonus plan typically manage earnings downward if the reported earnings are substantially in excess of the maximum bonus level.

T F 2. An earnings-based bonus plan has no effect on the planning of the nature and extent of the work of independent auditors.

T F 3. An independent auditor would not be concerned about an adjusting journal entry made by a client that turned a negative earnings number into a positive earnings number.

T F 4. The forecasts of financial analysts regarding the earnings of companies are independent and objective and are not influenced by the management of companies.

T F 5. A company with a large number of diverse operating units is well suited to earnings management.

T F 6. Company earnings are considered to be of higher quality when management chooses accounting measurement rules that recognize revenues sooner rather than later, but that delay the recognition of expenses.

T F 7. Most managers of publicly traded companies prefer an earnings trend line that rises very sharply.

T F 8. The Sarbanes-Oxley Act requires that every company's annual report contain an internal control report.

T F 9. Fraud is the deceptive concealment of transactions.

T F 10. The Sarbanes-Oxley Act requires that all public companies develop and enforce an officer code of ethics.

Quiz Solutions

Quiz A		Quiz B		Quiz C	
1.	F	1.	j	1.	T
2.	F	2.	g	2.	F
3.	T	3.	i	3.	F
4.	F	4.	h	4.	F
5.	T	5.	f	5.	T
6.	F	6.	e	6.	F
7.	T	7.	b	7.	F
8.	F	8.	a	8.	T
9.	F	9.	c	9.	T
10.	F	10.	d	10.	T

MULTIPLE CHOICE

Major Activities of a Business

1. The major activities of a business include all BUT which of the following?
   a. Financing activities
   b. Operating activities
   c. Investing activities
   d. Earning activities

   ANS: D

2. Which type of the major activities of a business is best described as those events that occur less frequently and are usually quite large?
   a. Financing activities
   b. Operating activities
   c. Investing activities
   d. Earning activities

   ANS: C

3. Which type of the major activities of a business is best described as those events that raise money by means other than operations?
   a. Financing activities
   b. Operating activities
   c. Investing activities
   d. Earning activities

   ANS: A

4. Buying inventory is an example of a(n)
   a. Operating activity
   b. Investing activity
   c. Financing activity
   d. Revenue activity

   ANS: A

5. Selling property, plant, and equipment is a(n)
   a. Operating activity
   b. Investing activity
   c. Financing activity
   d. Revenue activity

   ANS: B

6. Selling additional shares of stock is a(n)
   a. Operating activity
   b. Investing activity
   c. Financing activity
   d. Revenue activity

   ANS: C

Recognizing Revenue

7. Revenues are most often recognized when
   a. A sale takes place or a service is performed
   b. Cash is collected
   c. Inventory is purchased for resale
   d. Inventory is manufactured for resale

   ANS: A

8. The best measure of how much a firm marks up its inventory for resale is its
   a. Gross margin
   b. Cost of goods sold
   c. Income from operations
   d. Income before taxes

   ANS: A

Cash Collection

9. Edwards Company sells foods wholesale. On January 15, Edwards sold 200 cases of beans to
   Swoops Company for $4 per case with terms of 2/10, n/30. On January 25, Swoops Company
   paid Edwards the full amount due. Given these data, the entry to record the sale of beans on
   January 15 would include a
   a. Debit to Sales Revenue of $800
   b. Credit to Cash of $800
   c. Debit to Accounts Receivable of $800
   d. Credit to Sales Revenue of $784

   ANS: C

10. Edwards Company sells foods wholesale. On January 15, Edwards sold 200 cases of beans to
    Swoops Company for $4 per case with terms of 2/10, n/30. On January 25, Swoops Company
    paid Edwards the full amount due. Given these data, the entry to record the collection of cash on
    January 25 would include a
    a. Credit to Sales Discounts of $16
    b. Debit to Cash of $800
    c. Credit to Accounts Receivable of $800
    d. Credit to Cash of $784

    ANS: C

11. Jones Company, a customer, has been authorized to return $1,000 of goods purchased on account. The journal entry to record this transaction is
    a. Sales Returns and Allowances   1,000
       Accounts Receivable   1,000
    b. Sales   1,000
       Sales Returns and Allowances   1,000
    c. Sales Returns and Allowances   1,000
       Inventory   1,000
    d. Accounts Receivable   1,000
       Sales Returns and Allowances   1,000

    ANS: A

12. Under the perpetual inventory method, the entry required to record a sales return by a customer would consist of
    a. Only a debit to Sales Revenue and a credit to Accounts Receivable
    b. Only a debit to Sales Returns and Allowances and a credit to Accounts Receivable
    c. Debits to Sales Returns and Allowances and Inventory and credits to Accounts Receivable and Cost of Goods Sold
    d. Debits to Sales Returns and Allowances and Cost of Goods Sold and credits to Accounts Receivable and Inventory

    ANS: C

13. Which of the following accounts would normally be found on the income statement?
    a. Unearned Service Revenues
    b. Rent Payable
    c. Sales Returns and Allowances
    d. Cash

    ANS: C

14. Which of the following would best determine a small theft of inventory by employees?
    a. A physical count of inventory when using the periodic inventory method
    b. A physical count of inventory when using the perpetual inventory method
    c. An analysis of the gross margin percentage when using the periodic inventory method
    d. An analysis of the gross margin percentage when using the perpetual inventory method

    ANS: B

15. Sales Discounts is which type of account?
    a. Revenue
    b. Contra-revenue
    c. Expense
    d. Contra-expense

    ANS: B

16. The difference between gross sales and net sales is
    a.   Cost of goods sold
    b.   Selling and administrative expenses
    c.   Sales discounts and sales returns and allowances
    d.   Gross margin

    ANS: C

17. Which of the following is NOT a cash control procedure?
    a.   Separate the handling and recording of cash
    b.   Deposit all cash receipts daily
    c.   Make all cash disbursements by check
    d.   Invest excess cash in high-yielding securities

    ANS: D

18. Bleeker Company had the following account balances: Sales Revenue, $50,000; Sales Returns
    and Allowances, $1,200; Sales Discounts, $1,200; and Bad Debts, $200. Given these balances,
    the amount of net sales is
    a. $50,000
    b. $49,000
    c. $47,800
    d. $47,600

    ANS: D

19. Edwards Company sells foods wholesale. On January 15, Edwards sold 100 cases of beans to
    Swoops Company for $3 per case with terms of 2/10, n/30. On February 14, Swoops Company
    paid Edwards the full amount due. Given this information, the entry to record the collection of
    cash by Edwards Company on February 14 would include a debit to
    a.   Cash of $294
    b.   Accounts Receivable of $300
    c.   Cash of $300
    d.   Accounts Receivable of $294

    ANS: C

20. Edwards Company sells foods wholesale. On January 15, Edwards sold 100 cases of beans to
    Swoops Company for $3 per case with terms of 2/10, n/30. On January 25, Swoops Company
    paid Edwards the full amount due. Given this information, the entry to record the collection of
    cash by Edwards Company on January 25 would include a debit to
    a.   Cash of $294
    b.   Accounts Receivable of $300
    c.   Cash of $300
    d.   Accounts Receivable of $294

    ANS: A

21. Amy Company sold $8,000 of merchandise to Tory Turnbull with terms 2/10, n/30. If Tory paid for three-fourths of the merchandise within the discount period and one-fourth after the discount period, he paid a total of
    a. $7,840
    b. $7,880
    c. $7,920
    d. $7,960

    ANS: B

Direct Write-Off Method

22. Bad Debt Expense is classified as a(n)
    a. Cost of sales expense
    b. Administrative expense
    c. Other expense
    d. Selling expense

    ANS: D

23. The direct write-off method
    a. Complies with the matching principle
    b. Is acceptable from a theoretical point of view
    c. Is only acceptable if bad debts are small, insignificant amounts
    d. Is the primary method used to recognize Bad Debt Expense

    ANS: C

24. When the direct write-off method of recognizing bad debt expense is used, which of the following accounts would NOT be used?
    a. Bad Debt Expense
    b. Accounts Receivable
    c. Allowance for Bad Debts
    d. All of the above accounts are used in the direct write-off method

    ANS: C

25. The direct write-off method of accounting for bad debts
    a. Often fails to match bad debt losses with sales for the same period
    b. Is subject to a significant amount of estimation error
    c. Causes accounts receivable to appear on the balance sheet at their estimated net realizable value
    d. Requires that losses from bad debts be recorded in the period in which sales are made

    ANS: A

26. The direct write-off method
    a. Results in a better matching of costs with revenues than the allowance method
    b. Is more precise than the allowance method
    c. Is the only acceptable method allowed under generally accepted accounting principles
    d. Is used only by large companies

    ANS: B

27. When the direct write-off method of recognizing bad debt expense is used, the entry to write off a specific customer account would
    a. Increase net income
    b. Have no effect on net income
    c. Increase the accounts receivable balance and increase net income
    d. Decrease the accounts receivable balance and decrease net income

    ANS: D

28. For the month of December, the records of Scrooge Corporation show the following information:

Cash received on accounts receivable..	$45,000
Cash sales..	30,000
Accounts receivable, December 1..	80,000
Accounts receivable, December 31..	75,000
Accounts receivable written off...	2,000

    The corporation uses the direct write-off method in accounting for uncollectible accounts receivable. What are the gross sales for the month of December?
    a. $59,000
    b. $60,000
    c. $61,000
    d. $72,000

    ANS: D

The Allowance Method

29. When the allowance method of recognizing bad debt expense is used, the entry to record the write-off of a specific uncollectible account would decrease
    a. Allowance for Bad Debts
    b. Net income
    c. Net realizable value of accounts receivable
    d. Working capital

    ANS: A

30. When the allowance method of recognizing bad debt expense is used, the entries at the time of collection of a small account previously written off would
    a. Increase net income
    b. Increase Allowance for Bad Debts
    c. Decrease net income
    d. Decrease Allowance for Bad Debts

    ANS: B

31. Allowance for Bad Debts is an example of a(n)
    a. Expense account
    b. Contra account
    c. Adjunct account
    d. Control account

    ANS: B

32. When a specific customer's account is written off by a company using the allowance method, the effect on net income and the net realizable value of the accounts receivable is

Net Income	Net Realizable Value of Accounts Receivable
a. None	None
b. Decrease	Decrease
c. Increase	Increase
d. Decrease	None

    ANS: A

33. The two methods of accounting for bad debts are the direct write-off method and the allowance method. When comparing the two, which of the following is true?
    a. The direct write-off method is exact and also better illustrates the matching principle.
    b. The allowance method is less exact, but it better illustrates the matching principle.
    c. The direct write-off method is theoretically superior.
    d. The direct write-off method requires two separate entries to write off an uncollectible account.

    ANS: B

34. Using the allowance method, the journal entry required to adjust the accounting records when an amount is collected that had previously been written off as uncollectible would probably include a credit to
    a. Notes Receivable
    b. Bad Debt Expense
    c. Allowance for Bad Debts
    d. Cash

    ANS: C

35. When the allowance method is used to account for uncollectible accounts, the net amount of accounts receivable
    a. Increases when an account is written off as uncollectible
    b. Decreases when an account is written off as uncollectible
    c. Stays the same when an account is written off as uncollectible
    d. Is sometimes increased and sometimes decreased when an account is written off as uncollectible

    ANS: C

36. The journal entry

    Accounts Receivable.............................   xxx
        Allowance for Bad Debts...................   xxx

    would be made when
    a. A customer pays the account balance
    b. A customer defaults on the account
    c. A previously defaulted customer pays the outstanding balance
    d. Estimated uncollectible receivables are too low

    ANS: C

37. Based on the aging of its accounts receivable at December 31, Charman Company determined
    that the net realizable value of the receivables at that date is $304,000. Additional information is
    as follows:

    Accounts receivable at December 31 .... $384,000
    Allowance for bad debts at January 1 ....   51,200 (cr.)
    Accounts written off as uncollectible during the year   35,200

    Charman's Bad Debt Expense for the year ended December 31 is
    a. $32,000
    b. $38,400
    c. $48,000
    d. $64,000

    ANS: D

Estimating Uncollectible Accounts Receivable

38. In which of the following bad debt estimation methods is "matching" a principal concern?
    a. Percentage of sales method
    b. Percentage of receivables method
    c. Aging method
    d. Direct write-off method

    ANS: A

39. The existing balance in Allowance for Bad Debts is ignored when which estimation method is
    used?
    a. Percentage of receivables method
    b. Percentage of sales method
    c. Aging method
    d. All of the above

    ANS: B

40. The December 31 trial balance of Jedi Company included the following accounts:

Accounts Receivable	$ 10,000
Allowance for Bad Debts	800 (cr.)
Sales Revenue	130,000
Sales Returns and Allowances	5,000

If it is estimated that 1 percent of the net sales is uncollectible, the entry to record the estimate of bad debts would include a debit to Bad Debt Expense for
a. $400
b. $450
c. $1,200
d. $1,250

ANS: D

41. Deuce Company uses the allowance method to estimate losses from uncollectible receivables. Net sales for the year are $120,000, and the company estimates its bad debts as 1 percent of net sales. If there is already a $1,200 debit balance in Allowance for Bad Debts, how much should be recorded as Bad Debt Expense?
a. $1,200
b. $2,400
c. $24,000
d. No entry is required

ANS: A

42. Samson Corporation had sales of $1,000,000 during 2006, of which 60 percent were on credit. On December 31, 2006, Accounts Receivable totaled $80,000, and Allowance for Bad Debts had a credit balance of $1,200. Given this information, if uncollectible receivables are estimated to be 1/2 of 1 percent of credit sales, the adjusting entry to account for uncollectible receivables as of December 31, 2006, would include a
a. Debit to Bad Debt Expense of $3,000
b. Debit to Bad Debt Expense of $1,800
c. Credit to Bad Debt Expense of $3,000
d. Credit to Allowance for Bad Debts of $5,000

ANS: A

43. JR Corporation has a debit balance of $2,500 in Allowance for Bad Debts. If it estimates that 2 percent of the net sales of $1,000,000 will be uncollectible, it should debit
a. Allowance for Bad Debts for $20,000
b. Allowance for Bad Debts for $22,500
c. Bad Debt Expense for $22,500
d. Bad Debt Expense for $20,000

ANS: D

44. Samson Corporation had sales of $1,000,000 during 2006, of which 80 percent were on credit. On December 31, 2006, Accounts Receivable totaled $80,000 and Allowance for Bad Debts had a credit balance of $1,200. Given the preceding information, if uncollectible receivables are estimated to be 1/2 of 1 percent of credit sales, the adjusting entry to account for uncollectible receivables as of December 31, 2006, would include a
    a. Debit to Bad Debt Expense of $4,000
    b. Debit to Bad Debt Expense of $5,000
    c. Credit to Bad Debt Expense of $2,800
    d. Credit to Allowance for Bad Debts of $5,000

    ANS: A

45. Following are the account balances from the December 31 trial balance of Hark Company:

Accounts Receivable...	$ 20,000
Allowance for Bad Debts.....................................	800 (dr.)
Sales Revenue	135,000
Sales Returns and Allowances	5,000

    If 1 percent of the net sales is estimated to be uncollectible, the entry to record the estimate of bad debts would include a debit to Bad Debt Expense for
    a. $1,300
    b. $500
    c. $550
    d. $2,100

    ANS: A

46. Following are the account balances from the December 31 trial balance of Hark Company:

Accounts Receivable...	$ 20,000
Allowance for Bad Debts.....................................	800 (cr.)
Sales Revenue	135,000
Sales Returns and Allowances	5,000

    If 1 percent of the net sales is estimated to be uncollectible, the entry to record the estimate of bad debts would include a debit to Bad Debt Expense for
    a. $1,300
    b. $500
    c. $550
    d. $2,100

    ANS: A

47. Following are the account balances from the December 31 trial balance of Hark Company:

Accounts Receivable	$ 20,000
Allowance for Bad Debts	800 (cr.)
Sales Revenue	135,000
Sales Returns and Allowances	5,000

If 10 percent of the Accounts Receivable is estimated to be uncollectible, the entry to record the estimate of bad debts would include a debit to Bad Debt Expense for
a. $2,000
b. $1,920
c. $2,080
d. $1,200

ANS: D

48. Following are the account balances from the December 31 trial balance of Hark Company:

Accounts Receivable	$ 20,000
Allowance for Bad Debts	800 (dr.)
Sales Revenue	135,000
Sales Returns and Allowances	5,000

If 10 percent of the Accounts Receivable is estimated to be uncollectible, the entry to record the estimate of bad debts would include a debit to Bad Debt Expense for
a. $2,000
b. $2,080
c. $2,800
d. $1,200

ANS: C

49. A method of estimating bad debts that focuses on the balance sheet rather than the income statement is the allowance method based on
a. Direct write-off
b. Aging the accounts receivable
c. Credit sales
d. Specific accounts determined to be uncollectible

ANS: B

50. Samson Corporation had sales of $1,000,000 during 2006, of which 60 percent were on credit. On December 31, 2006, Accounts Receivable totaled $80,000, and Allowance for Bad Debts had a credit balance of $1,200. Given this information, if uncollectible receivables are estimated to be 3 percent of accounts receivable, the adjusting entry as of December 31, 2006, to account for bad debts would include a
a. Debit to Bad Debt Expense of $2,400
b. Debit to Bad Debt Expense of $3,000
c. Credit to Bad Debt Expense of $1,200
d. Credit to Allowance for Bad Debts of $1,200

ANS: D

51. You have just analyzed customers' accounts receivable through an "aging" process and have determined that $3,000 of the accounts receivable are probably uncollectible. Noting that your trial balance shows an Allowance for Bad Debts with a debit balance of $100, what is the correct adjusting entry?

    a. Bad Debt Expense 3,100
       Allowance for Bad Debts   3,100
    b. Allowance for Bad Debts 3,100
       Bad Debt Expense   3,100
    c. Allowance for Bad Debts 3,000
       Bad Debt Expense   3,000
    d. Bad Debt Expense 2,900
       Allowance for Bad Debts   2,900

    ANS: A

52. Samson Corporation had sales of $1,000,000 during 2006, of which 80 percent were on credit. On December 31, 2006, Accounts Receivable totaled $80,000 and Allowance for Bad Debts had a debit balance of $1,200. Given this information, if uncollectible receivables are estimated to be 3 percent of accounts receivable, the adjusting entry as of December 31, 2006, to account for bad debts would include a

    a. Debit to Bad Debt Expense of $1,200
    b. Debit to Bad Debt Expense of $2,400
    c. Debit to Bad Debt Expense of $3,600
    d. Credit to Allowance for Bad Debts of $2,400

    ANS: C

53. An analysis and aging of the accounts receivable of Kaiten Company at December 31 revealed the following data:

Accounts receivable	$475,000
Allowance for bad debts (before adjustment)	25,000 (cr.)
Accounts estimated to be uncollectible...	32,000

    The net realizable value of the accounts receivable at December 31 should be
    a. $475,000
    b. $443,000
    c. $450,000
    d. $443,000

    ANS: B

54. Ward Company uses the allowance method of accounting for bad debts. The following summary schedule was prepared from an aging of accounts receivable outstanding on December 31 of the current year.

No. of Days Outstanding	Amount	Probability of Collection
0–31 days	$500,000	0.98
31–60 days	200,000	0.90
Over 60 days	100,000	0.80

The following additional information is available for the current year:

Net credit sales for the year	$4,000,000
Allowance for bad debts:	
Balance, January 1	45,000 (cr.)
Balance before adjustment, December 31...............................	2,000 (cr.)

If Ward bases its estimate of bad debts on the aging of accounts receivable, Bad Debt Expense for the current year ending December 31 is
a. $47,000
b. $48,000
c. $50,000
d. $52,000

ANS: B

55. Based on the aging of its accounts receivable at December 31, Dudikoff Company determined that the net realizable value of the receivables at that date is $760,000. Additional information is as follows:

Accounts receivable at December 31..	$880,000
Allowance for bad debts at December 31 (unadjusted)	28,000 (cr.)

Dudikoff's Bad Debt Expense for the year ended December 31 is
a. $28,000
b. $80,000
c. $92,000
d. $148,000

ANS: C

56. Penn Inc. reported an allowance for bad debts of $30,000 (debit) at December 31, 2006, before performing an aging of accounts receivable. As a result of the aging, Penn Inc. determined that an estimated $52,000 of the December 31, 2006 accounts receivable would prove uncollectible. The adjusting entry required at December 31, 2006, would be

    a.   Bad Debt Expense 52,000
          Allowance for Bad Debts   52,000
    b.   Allowance for Bad Debts 52,000
          Accounts Receivable   52,000
    c.   Bad Debt Expense 82,000
          Allowance for Bad Debts   82,000
    d.   Allowance for Bad Debts 82,000
          Bad Debt Expense   82,000

ANS: C

57. Gordie Co. reported an Allowance for Bad Debts of $20,000 (credit) at December 31, 2006, before performing an aging of accounts receivable. As a result of the aging, Gordie determined that an estimated $28,000 of the December 31, 2006 accounts receivable would prove uncollectible. The adjusting entry required at December 31, 2006, would be

    a.   Bad Debt Expense 28,000
          Allowance for Bad Debts   28,000
    b.   Bad Debt Expense 20,000
          Accounts Receivable   20,000
    c.   Allowance for Bad Debts 8,000
          Bad Debt Expense   8,000
    d.   Bad Debt Expense 8,000
          Allowance for Bad Debts   8,000

ANS: D

Assessing How Well Companies Manage Their Receivables

58. In calculating a company's accounts receivable turnover ratio, which of the following sets of factors would be used?
    a.   Net income and average accounts receivable
    b.   Net sales and net income
    c.   Total accounts receivable and net sales
    d.   Net sales and average accounts receivable

ANS: D

59. Which of the following factors are used to compute the average collection period of accounts receivable?
    a. Inventory turnover and 365 days
    b. Net sales and average inventory
    c. Accounts receivable turnover and 365 days
    d. Average accounts receivable and cost of goods sold

    ANS: C

60. Dana Company's December 31, 2006 financial statements showed the following

Net sales (all credit sales)	$451,200
Average receivables	94,000
Cost of goods sold	450,200
Average inventory	150,000
Net income	75,200
Average total assets	940,000

    Given this information, Dana Company's accounts receivable turnover ratio for 2006 was
    a. 10
    b. 4.8
    c. 0.8
    d. 8

    ANS: B

61. If a company's accounts receivable turnover ratio is 8.0 times, cost of goods sold is $360,000, and net sales (all credit sales) are $480,000, then the average accounts receivable balance must have been
    a. $60,000
    b. $80,000
    c. $120,000
    d. $160,000

    ANS: A

62. On December 31, 2006, Seau Inc.'s financial statements showed the following:

Net sales revenue (all credit sales)	$150,000
Average accounts receivable	16,850
Cost of goods sold	90,000
Average inventory	12,000
Net income	10,500
Total assets	940,000

    Given this information and assuming a 365-day business year, what was Seau's average collection period (rounded) during 2006?
    a. 56 days
    b. 53 days
    c. 49 days
    d. 41 days

    ANS: D

63. On December 31, 2006, Seau Inc.'s financial statements showed the following:

Net sales revenue (all credit sales)..	$150,000
Average accounts receivable	16,850
Cost of goods sold	90,000
Average inventory	12,000
Net income...	10,500
Total assets..	940,000

Given this information and assuming a 365-day business year, what was Seau's accounts receivable turnover (rounded) during 2006?
a. 8.90
b. 12.5
c. 7.4
d. 6.3

ANS: A

64. The following information is available for Bridges Company:

Bridges Company
Partial Balance Sheet
December 31, 2007 and 2006

	2007	2006
Accounts receivable......................................	$500,000	$470,000
Allowance for bad debts	(25,000)	(20,000)
Net accounts receivable	$475,000	$450,000
Inventories at lower of cost or market	$600,000	$550,000

Bridges Company
Partial Income Statement
For the Years Ended December 31, 2007 and 2006

	2007	2006
Net credit sales...	$2,500,000	$2,200,000
Net cash sales..	500,000	400,000
Net sales...	$3,000,000	$2,600,000
Cost of goods sold	$2,000,000	$1,800,000
Selling, general, and administrative expenses	300,000	270,000
Other expenses...	50,000	30,000
Total operating expenses	$2,350,000	$2,100,000

The accounts receivable turnover for 2007 is computed as follows:
a. $2,350,000 ÷ $462,500
b. $2,500,000 ÷ $462,500
c. $2,500,000 ÷ $475,000
d. $3,000,000 ÷ $485,000

ANS: B

Recording Warranty and Service Costs Associated with a Sale

65. Estimated warranty costs associated with sales should be expensed to properly
    a. Recognize revenue
    b. Follow the historical cost concept
    c. Match revenues and expenses
    d. Satisfy SEC requirements

    ANS: C

66. The entry to record service expenses related to sales would include a
    a. Credit to Sales Revenue
    b. Debit to Sales Revenue
    c. Debit to Estimated Liability for Service
    d. Credit to Estimated Liability for Service

    ANS: D

67. The entry to record actual expenses incurred to perform service under warranty would include a
    a. Debit to Customer Service Expense
    b. Credit to Customer Service Expense
    c. Debit to Estimated Liability for Service
    d. Credit to Estimated Liability for Service

    ANS: C

EXPANDED MATERIAL

Reconciling the Bank Account

68. Bank statements provide information about all the following, EXCEPT
    a. Checks cleared during the period
    b. NSF checks
    c. Bank charges for the period
    d. Errors made by the company

    ANS: D

69. Which of the following items would be added to the book balance on a bank reconciliation?
    a. Outstanding checks
    b. A check written for $63 entered as $36 in the accounting records
    c. Interest paid by the bank
    d. Deposits in transit

    ANS: C

70. When reconciling a bank statement, direct deposits are
    a. Added to the balance per the books
    b. Added to the balance per the bank
    c. Subtracted from the balance per the books
    d. Subtracted from the balance per the bank

    ANS: A

71. Alco Corporation's accountant wrote a check to a supplier for $15,000. He then wrote himself a check for $5,000. For the first check he deducted $15,000 from the books, for the second check he wrote "void" in the check register. How would the accountant conceal his theft on the bank reconciliation?
    a. Overstate deposits in transit
    b. Overstate outstanding checks
    c. Understate outstanding checks
    d. Understate NSF checks

    ANS: B

72. In preparing a bank reconciliation, interest paid by the bank on the account is
    a. Added to the bank balance
    b. Subtracted from the bank balance
    c. Added to the book balance
    d. Subtracted from the book balance

    ANS: C

73. In preparing a monthly bank reconciliation, which of the following items would be added to the balance reported on the bank statement to arrive at the correct cash balance?
    a. Outstanding checks
    b. Bank service charge
    c. Deposits in transit
    d. A customer's note collected by the bank on behalf of the depositor

    ANS: C

74. Wiley Company's monthly bank statement showed an ending balance of $18,464. The bank reconciliation included a deposit in transit, $1,637; outstanding checks, $2,170; an NSF check, $788; a bank service charge, $25; and proceeds of a customer's note collected by the bank, $2,300. The correct cash balance at the end of the month is
    a. $20,231
    b. $20,101
    c. $18,744
    d. $17,931

    ANS: D

75. During the month, Wilson received a $1,200 check from Richard for the purchase of his 1994 Ford. Wilson deposited the check in his bank account. At the end of the month, Wilson received his monthly bank statement along with Richard's check returned and marked "NSF." What should Wilson do when reconciling his bank statement?
    a. Subtract $1,200 from the cash balance per the books
    b. Add $1,200 to the cash balance per the bank statement
    c. Subtract $1,200 from the cash balance per the bank statement
    d. Add $1,200 to the cash balance per the books

    ANS: A

76. During the current month, Barnabee wrote a check for $459.25, but recorded it on his books as a credit to Cash in the amount of $452.95. To reconcile the bank statement, he will need to
   a. Add $6.30 to the balance per the bank statement
   b. Subtract $6.30 from the balance per the bank statement
   c. Add $6.30 to the balance per the books
   d. Subtract $6.30 from the balance per the books

   ANS: D

77. During the current month, Jones wrote a check for $989.25, but recorded it on his books as a credit to Cash in the amount of $892.95. To reconcile the bank statement, he must
   a. Add $96.30 to the balance per the bank statement
   b. Subtract $96.30 from the balance per the bank statement
   c. Add $96.30 to the balance per the books
   d. Subtract $96.30 from the balance per the books

   ANS: D

78. At the end of the month, a company's cash account indicates a balance of $9,820. Upon receiving a bank statement, the following amounts are used in the bank reconciliation: deposit in transit, $2,400; outstanding checks, $926; bank service charge, $28; NSF check, $425; proceeds of a customer's note collected by the bank, $4,097. Given this information, what is the corrected cash balance?
   a. $13,464
   b. $11,993
   c. $14,392
   d. $11,294

   ANS: A

79. Thorpe Company has prepared the following partial bank reconciliation for January 2006:

Ending balance per bank statement	$22,000		Balance per books	$22,900
Deposit in transit	4,000		Interest earned	?
Outstanding checks	(3,000)		Service charge	(90)
			NSF check	(110)
Adjusted balance	$23,000			$23,000

   Given this information, how much interest was earned? (Assume there are no other adjustments.)
   a. $100
   b. $200
   c. $300
   d. None of the above

   ANS: C

80. Alii Company wrote a check for $990, but recorded it in the accounting records as $909. This error would require an adjustment on the bank reconciliation of
   a. Adding $81 to the balance per the bank statement
   b. Deducting $81 from the balance per the bank statement
   c. Adding $81 to the balance per the books
   d. Deducting $81 from the balance per the books

   ANS: D

81. Assume the following facts for Erich Company: the month-end bank statement shows a balance of $27,200; outstanding checks totaled $2,000; a deposit of $8,000 is in transit at month-end; and a check for $400 was erroneously charged against the account by the bank. What is the correct cash balance at the end of the month?
   a. $33,600
   b. $34,400
   c. $45,600
   d. $46,400

   ANS: A

82. In preparing its bank reconciliation for the month of February, Jesse Company has available the following information:

Balance per bank statement, February 28	$20,025
Deposit in transit, February 28	3,125
Outstanding checks, February 28	2,875
Check erroneously deducted by bank from Jesse's account, February 10	25
Bank service charges for February	25

   What is the corrected cash balance at February 28?
   a. $20,025
   b. $20,050
   c. $20,175
   d. $20,300

   ANS: D

Foreign Currency Transactions

83. When a U.S. company enters into a credit sales transaction denominated in a foreign currency, the transaction must be recorded in U.S. dollars. The exchange is measured at the exchange rate on the date of
   a. Collection
   b. Conversion
   c. Sale
   d. Record

   ANS: C

84. Fluctuations between the sale date and the settlement date of a foreign currency transaction are
   a. Not recognized
   b. Recognized as adjustments to Stockholders' Equity
   c. Recognized as exchange gains or losses
   d. Recognized as increases or decreases in Sales Revenue

   ANS: C

85. If the exchange rate between the U.S. dollar and a foreign currency increases between the sale date and the settlement date, the adjustment the U.S. company must make will include a
   a. Credit to Accounts Receivable
   b. Credit to Exchange Gains
   c. Debit to Sales Revenue
   d. Debit to Exchange Receivables

   ANS: A

86. A U.S. company makes a sale to a Mexican company for 10,000 pesos on June 15. The Mexican company will pay on August 1. The exchange rate on June 15 is 1 peso = $0.125 and on August 1 is 1 peso = $0.100. The average rate was 1 peso = $0.114. The U.S. company will record the sale on June 15 as
   a. $1,000
   b. $1,250
   c. $1,140
   d. None of the above

   ANS: B

87. A U.S. company makes a sale to a Mexican company for 10,000 pesos on June 15. The Mexican company will pay on August 1. The exchange rate on June 15 is 1 peso = $0.125 and on August 1 is 1 peso = $0.100. The average rate was 1 peso = $0.114. The U.S. company will receive cash on August 1 of
   a. $1,000
   b. $1,250
   c. $1,140
   d. None of the above

   ANS: A

88. A U.S. company makes a sale to a Mexican company for 10,000 pesos on June 15. The Mexican company will pay on August 1. The exchange rate on June 15 is 1 peso = $0.125 and on August 1 is 1 peso = $0.100. The average rate was 1 peso = $0.114. The U.S. company will record a foreign currency gain (loss) of
   a. $0
   b. ($250)
   c. ($110)
   d. $250

   ANS: B

PROBLEMS

1. The trial balance of Lozier Inc. shows a $52,000 outstanding balance in Accounts Receivable at the end of 2005. During 2006, 80 percent of the total credit sales of $2,600,000 was collected, and no receivables had been written off as uncollectible. The company estimated that 1 percent of the credit sales would be uncollectible. During 2007, the account of El Cajon Company, with a balance of $3,500, was judged to be uncollectible and written off. At the end of 2007, the amount previously written off was collected from El Cajon.

Prepare the necessary journal entries to record the following:

1. The credit sales during 2006.
2. The collection of cash from credit sales during 2006.
3. The bad debts expense for 2006.
4. The write-off of the El Cajon account in 2007.
5. The collection of the El Cajon account in 2007.

ANS:

1.	Accounts Receivable	2,600,000	
	Sales Revenue		2,600,000
2.	Cash	2,080,000	
	Accounts Receivable		2,080,000
3.	Bad Debt Expense	26,000	
	Allowance for Bad Debts		26,000
	[1% × $2,600,000]		
4.	Allowance for Bad Debts	3,500	
	Accounts Receivable—El Cajon		3,500
5.	Accounts Receivable—El Cajon	3,500	
	Allowance for Bad Debts		3,500
	Cash	3,500	
	Accounts Receivable—El Cajon		3,500

2. The following information was abstracted from the records of Sydney Corporation:

Accounts receivable, December 31, 2006	$ 580,000
Allowance for bad debt before adjustment, December 31, 2006	18,000 (dr.)
Sales (2006)	2,180,000
Sales discounts (2006)	18,000
Sales returns and allowances (2006)	27,000

Prepare the adjusting entry for Bad Debt Expense under each of the following assumptions:

1. Three percent of outstanding accounts receivable are uncollectible.
2. An aging schedule of the accounts shows that $22,300 of the accounts are uncollectible.

ANS:

1. Bad Debt Expense 35,400
       Allowance for Bad Debts 35,400
       [(3% × $580,000) + $18,000]

2. Bad Debt Expense 40,300
       Allowance for Bad Debts 40,300
       ($22,300 + $18,000)

3. The following information was abstracted from the 2006 financial statements of Alina Company:

    Sales... $747,000*
    Accounts receivable, December 31, 2006......................... 128,000
    Allowance for bad debts .... 1,220 (cr.)
    Sales discounts.. 18,000*
    Sales returns and allowances 12,400*
    * 30% related to credit sales

    Prepare the adjusting entry for Bad Debt Expense assuming 3 percent of current accounts receivable are uncollectible.

    ANS:

    Bad Debt Expense [(3% × $128,000) – $1,220]............... 2,620
       Allowance for Bad Debts.. 2,620

4. The following are summary financial data of the three most recent years for two companies.

	2006	2005	2004
Net sales (in millions)			
Ayala, Inc.	$ 7,400	$ 7,850	$ 7,960
Mendez, Inc.	14,650	13,200	12,850
Net accounts receivable (in millions)			
Ayala, Inc.	1,200	1,450	1,160
Mendez, Inc.	4,320	4,640	4,450

    1. Using the data above, compute the accounts receivable turnover and average collection period for each company for 2006 and 2005. (Round to two decimal places.)
    2. Which company appears to have a better credit collection policy? Explain why.

ANS:

1. Accounts receivable turnover

Ayala, Inc.	2006:	$7,400/[($1,200 + $1,450)/2]	= 5.59 times
	2005:	$7,850/[($1,450 + $1,160)/2]	= 6.02 times
Mendez, Inc.	2006:	$14,650/[($4,320 + $4,640)/2]	= 3.27 times
	2005:	$13,200/[($4,640 + $4,450)/2]	= 2.90 times

Average collection period

Ayala, Inc.	2006:	365/5.59 = 65.30 days
	2005:	365/6.02 = 60.63 days
Mendez, Inc.	2006:	365/3.27 = 111.62 days
	2005:	365/2.90 = 125.86 days

2. Ayala manages accounts receivable better. The turnover is higher and the number of days to collect receivables is shorter.

5. MacroTek has the following information from its records and from the May bank statement:

Cash balance per books..	$20,000
Ending cash balance per bank statement..................................	25,000
Deposits made, not received by bank.......................................	6,000
Checks written, not processed by bank....................................	10,000
Interest earned on bank account..	50
Bank service charge	70
Direct deposit by customer (on account receivable)................	1,020

Based on this information:

1. Prepare a bank reconciliation for May.
2. Prepare the necessary journal entry.

ANS:

1.

Balance per bank	$25,000	Balance per books	$20,000
+ Deposits in transit..........	6,000	+ Interest earned on account.....	50
−Outstanding checks........	(10,000)	+ Direct deposit	1,020
		−Service charge	(70)
Adjusted bank balance.....	$21,000	Adjusted book balance	$21,000

2.

Cash	1,000	
Bank Service Charge Expense.................................	70	
Interest Revenue		50
Accounts Receivable		1,020

6. The following information is available for Binford Company:

    1. The May 2006 bank statement showed the following:

Balance, May 1	$21,000.00
Canceled checks	13,904.20
Deposits	16,471.65
Interest earned by Binford	28.75
Balance, May 31	23,596.20

    2. Binford Company's cash accounts showed the following for May:

Balance, May 1	$20,971.25
Debits	22,700.40
Credits	22,886.34
Balance, May 31	20,785.31

    3. The bank service charge for May was $18.
    4. Outstanding checks totaled $9,100.14.
    5. Deposits in transit totaled $8,000.00.
    6. The bank statement reveals that Binford Company's account has been reduced by $100. The company had deposited a $100 check from one of its customers, which was subsequently returned to Binford's bank and marked "Not Sufficient Funds."
    7. The bank collected an $1,800 note for Binford Company. The company was not aware of the collection until receiving the bank statement.

    Prepare a:

    1. Bank reconciliation for May 31, 2006.
    2. The necessary journal entry.

    ANS:

    1.

    Binford Company
    Bank Reconciliation
    May 31, 2006

Balance per bank	$23,596.20	Balance per books	$20,785.31
Add: Deposits in transit	8,000.00	Add: Note collected	1,800.00
		Interest earned	28.75
Less: Outstanding checks	(9,100.14)	Less: Service charge	(18.00)
		NSF check	(100.00)
Corrected bank balance	$22,496.06		$22,496.06

    2.

Cash	1,710.75	
Bank Service Charge Expense	18.00	
Accounts Receivable	100.00	
Notes Receivable		1,800.00
Interest Revenue		28.75

7. A U.S. company entered into a sales transaction with a Japanese company on September 15 for 200,000 yen. The U.S. company prepares quarterly financial statements. The Japanese company will pay for the sale on November 20. The exchange rates were as follows:

	1 Yen
September 15	$0.0125
September 30	0.0109
November 20	0.0114

Prepare the appropriate journal entries to record the sale, the quarterly adjustment, and the collection.

ANS:

September 15:	Accounts Receivable	2,500	
	Sales Revenue		2,500

September 30:	Foreign Exchange Loss	320	
	Accounts Receivable		320

November 20:	Cash	2,280	
	Accounts Receivable		2,180
	Foreign Exchange Gain		100

Chapter 7—Selling a Product or a Service—Quiz A

Name_____   **Section**_____

TRUE/FALSE

Circle T or F to indicate whether each of the following statements is true or false.

T   F   1.   An account receivable is an unconditional written promise to pay a specific amount of money on or before a certain date.

T   F   2.   The direct write-off method of accounting for uncollectible receivables is more theoretically appropriate than is the allowance method.

T   F   3.   Allowance for Bad Debts normally has a credit balance.

T   F   4.   Accounts receivable are to be reported at their net realizable value.

T   F   5.   The direct write-off method for uncollectible accounts provides for the matching of current revenues with related expenses.

T   F   6.   The use of the direct write-off method is acceptable under generally accepted accounting principles.

T   F   7.   Bad debt expense is normally reported as an offset to sales in the income statement.

T   F   8.   The entry to write off an uncollectible account under the allowance method is a debit to Bad Debt Expense and a credit to Accounts Receivable.

T   F   9.   The method of estimating uncollectibles based on the accounts receivable balance emphasizes the determination of the net realizable value of the receivables.

T   F   10.   When estimating collectibility based on an analysis of the accounts receivable balance, any existing balance in the allowance for bad debts is considered.

Chapter 7—Selling a Product or a Service—Quiz B

Name_____   **Section**_____

MATCHING

In the spaces provided, write the letter of the definition for each of the following terms.

    a. Transactions and events that involve the purchase and sale of Property, Plant, and Equipment and other assets not generally held for resale.

    b. A reduction in the selling price that is allowed if payment is received within a specified period.

    c. A contra-revenue account in which the return of, or allowance for reduction in the price of, merchandise previously sold is recorded.

    d. The recording of actual losses from uncollectible accounts as expenses during the period in which accounts receivable are determined to be uncollectible.

    e. The recording of estimated losses due to uncollectible accounts as expenses during the period in which the sales occurred.

    f. A contra account, deducted from Accounts Receivable, that shows the estimated losses from uncollectible accounts.

    g. A measure used to indicate how fast a company collects its receivables.

    h. A measure of the average number of days it takes to collect a credit sale.

    i. The process of systematically comparing the cash balance as reported by the bank with the cash balance on the company's books and explaining any differences.

    j. A deduction from the bank balance for checks written that have not yet cleared the bank.

1. _____ Direct write-off method

2. _____ Allowance for bad debts

3. _____ Accounts receivable turnover

4. _____ Investing activities

5. _____ Average collection period

6. _____ Sales returns and allowances

7. _____ Bank reconciliation

8. _____ Outstanding checks

9. _____ Sales discount

10. _____ Allowance method

Quiz Solutions

Quiz A	Quiz B
1. F	1. d
2. F	2. f
3. T	3. g
4. T	4. a
5. F	5. h
6. F	6. c
7. F	7. i
8. F	8. j
9. T	9. b
10. T	10. e

MULTIPLE CHOICE

Inventory and Cost of Goods Sold

1. Items that are either manufactured or purchased for resale in the normal course of business are called
   a. Supplies
   b. Inventory
   c. Purchases
   d. Materials

   ANS: B

2. Which of the following is an inventory account for a retailer?
   a. Raw Materials
   b. Work-in-Process
   c. Finished Goods
   d. Merchandise

   ANS: D

3. Inventory costs include all of the following, EXCEPT
   a. Selling costs
   b. Production costs
   c. Purchase costs
   d. Freight costs

   ANS: A

4. Which of the following would NOT be included in ending inventory?
   a. Goods shipped to customers, F.O.B. shipping point
   b. Goods purchased from suppliers, F.O.B. destination
   c. Goods held on consignment
   d. Goods out on consignment

   ANS: C

5. Inventory accounting is most complex in
   a. Merchandising companies
   b. Service companies
   c. Manufacturing companies
   d. Wholesale companies

   ANS: C

6. When products are sold, their costs are removed from inventory and reported on the income statement as an expense called
   a. Operating expenses
   b. Cost of goods sold
   c. Cost of goods manufactured
   d. Inventory expenses

   ANS: B

7. Which of the following is NOT an inventory in a manufacturing company?
   a. Raw materials
   b. Finished goods
   c. Work-in-process
   d. Merchandise

   ANS: D

8. The cost of finished goods inventory includes all BUT which of the following?
   a. Advertising costs
   b. Manufacturing overhead costs
   c. Labor costs
   d. Raw material costs

   ANS: A

9. If the shipping terms indicate that the seller owns the goods until delivered to the buyer, this arrangement is known as
   a. Goods in transit
   b. FOB shipping point
   c. FOB destination
   d. FOB carrier

   ANS: C

10. If the shipping terms indicate that the buyer owns the goods upon shipment from the seller, this arrangement is known as
    a. Goods in transit
    b. FOB shipping point
    c. FOB destination
    d. FOB carrier

    ANS: B

11. Cost of goods sold is equal to the cost of inventory on hand at the
    a. End of a period plus net purchases minus the cost of inventory on hand at the beginning of a period
    b. Beginning of a period minus net purchases plus the cost of inventory on hand at the end of a period
    c. Beginning of a period plus net sales minus the cost of inventory on hand at the end of a period
    d. Beginning of a period minus the cost of inventory on hand at the end of a period plus net purchases

    ANS: D

12. If goods shipped FOB destination are in transit at the end of the year, they should be included in the inventory balance of the
    a. Seller
    b. Common carrier
    c. Buyer
    d. Bank

    ANS: A

13. Inventory sold with terms FOB shipping point, freight prepaid, represents a situation in which the
    a. Buyer agreed to bear the transportation cost and paid the seller, who then paid the carrier
    b. Buyer agreed to bear the transportation cost, but the seller paid the carrier
    c. Seller agreed to bear the transportation cost and paid the carrier
    d. Seller agreed to bear the transportation cost, but the buyer paid the carrier

    ANS: B

14. Merchandise shipped FOB shipping point on the last day of the year should probably be included in
    a. The buyer's inventory balance
    b. The seller's inventory balance
    c. Neither the buyer's nor seller's inventory balance
    d. Both the buyer's and the seller's inventory balances

    ANS: A

Accounting for Inventory Purchases and Sales

15. When the periodic inventory method is used, the entry to record a return of defective merchandise to a supplier would include a credit to
    a. Accounts Payable
    b. Inventory
    c. Purchase Returns and Allowances
    d. Cash

    ANS: C

16. When a company uses the perpetual inventory method, purchase returns are recorded by
    a. Debiting Purchase Returns and Allowances
    b. Crediting Purchase Returns and Allowances
    c. Crediting Accounts Payable
    d. Crediting Inventory

    ANS: D

17. A firm that used the periodic inventory method returned defective merchandise costing $2,000 to one of its suppliers. The entry to record this transaction would include a credit to
    a. Accounts Receivable
    b. Inventory
    c. Purchase Returns and Allowances
    d. Accounts Payable

    ANS: C

18. A firm using the periodic inventory method returned defective merchandise costing $2,000 to one of its suppliers. The entry to record this transaction would include a debit to
    a. Accounts Receivable
    b. Inventory
    c. Purchase Returns and Allowances
    d. Accounts Payable

    ANS: D

19. Which of the following accounts would be found on the income statement?
    a. Unearned Fees
    b. Wages Payable
    c. Freight-In
    d. Cash

    ANS: C

20. Which of the following statements is true under the periodic inventory method?
    a. Freight-In is subtracted from purchases in order to derive net purchases.
    b. Freight-In is added to purchases in order to derive net purchases.
    c. Freight-In is used only with the perpetual inventory method, not with the periodic inventory method.
    d. Freight-In is neither subtracted nor added to purchases in order to derive net purchases.

    ANS: B

21. ACE Manufacturing pays a freight bill of $54 to United Trucking Company for merchandise purchased from Jackson Sales, terms FOB shipping point. When recording the payment with the periodic inventory method, ACE would debit the $54 cost of the freight to
    a. Purchases
    b. Freight-In
    c. Prepaid Freight
    d. Freight-Out

    ANS: B

22. ACE Manufacturing pays a freight bill of $54 to United Trucking Company for merchandise purchased from Jackson Sales, terms FOB shipping point. When recording the payment with the perpetual inventory method, ACE would debit the $54 cost of the freight to
    a. Inventory
    b. Freight-In
    c. Prepaid Freight
    d. Freight-Out

    ANS: A

23. Which of the following accounts is NOT used in the calculation of cost of goods sold in a retail business?
    a. Purchases
    b. Freight-In
    c. Depreciation Expense
    d. Beginning Inventory

    ANS: C

24. Which of the following accounts is NOT a contra account?
    a. Sales Returns and Allowances
    b. Sales Discounts
    c. Purchase Discounts
    d. Purchases

    ANS: D

25. A firm that uses the perpetual inventory method purchased $1,000 of inventory on terms 2/10, n/30. The journal entry to record this transaction would include a debit to
    a. Purchases
    b. Purchase Discounts
    c. Inventory
    d. Accounts Payable

    ANS: C

26. A firm using the periodic inventory method purchased $2,000 of inventory on terms 2/10, n/30. The journal entry to record this transaction would include a debit to
    a. Purchases
    b. Purchase Discounts
    c. Inventory
    d. Accounts Payable

    ANS: A

27. Company D makes the following entry in its accounting records:

Inventory	200	
Cost of Goods Sold		200

    This entry would be made when
    a. Merchandise is sold and the periodic inventory method is used
    b. Merchandise is sold and the perpetual inventory method is used
    c. Merchandise is returned and the perpetual inventory method is used
    d. Merchandise is returned and the periodic inventory method is used

    ANS: C

28. The perpetual method of accounting for inventory
    a. Requires that a physical count of inventory be taken before the cost of goods sold can be determined with any reasonable degree of accuracy
    b. Is likely to be less expensive to maintain than a periodic inventory method
    c. Is not as helpful as a periodic method in providing management with timely reports about inventory quantities and costs
    d. Allows management to better estimate inventory losses from pilferage than does a periodic inventory method

    ANS: D

29. Which of the following is NOT true of the perpetual inventory method?
    a. Purchases are recorded as debits to the inventory account.
    b. The entry to record a sale includes a debit to Cost of Goods Sold and a credit to Inventory.
    c. After a physical inventory count, Inventory is credited for any missing inventory.
    d. Purchase returns are recorded by debiting Accounts Payable and crediting Purchase Returns and Allowances.

    ANS: D

30. The entry (or entries) required to record a sales return by a customer when using the perpetual inventory method would consist of
    a. A debit to Sales Revenue and a credit to Accounts Receivable
    b. A debit to Sales Returns and Allowances and a credit to Accounts Receivable
    c. Debits to Sales Returns and Allowances and Inventory and credits to Accounts Receivable and Cost of Goods Sold
    d. Debits to Sales Returns and Allowances and Cost of Goods Sold and credits to Accounts Receivable and Inventory

    ANS: C

31. Which of the following accounts would NOT normally have a debit balance?
    a. Sales Discounts
    b. Cost of Goods Sold
    c. Purchase Discounts
    d. Freight-In

    ANS: C

32. Under the periodic inventory method, if merchandise is sold for cash on December 31 and is recorded as a sale but is not shipped (and thus is included in the ending inventory count), the financial statements will
    a. Overstate assets
    b. Understate net income
    c. Understate liabilities
    d. Understate assets

    ANS: A

33. A firm using the perpetual inventory method returned defective merchandise costing $2,000 to one of its suppliers. The entry to record this transaction will include a debit to
    a. Accounts Receivable
    b. Inventory
    c. Purchase Returns and Allowances
    d. Accounts Payable

    ANS: D

34. A firm using the perpetual inventory method returned defective merchandise costing $2,000 to one of its suppliers. The entry to record this transaction will include a credit to
    a. Accounts Receivable
    b. Inventory
    c. Purchase Returns and Allowances
    d. Accounts Payable

    ANS: B

35. If a company sold merchandise for a profit, the accounting equation would show a(n)
    a. Net increase in assets and increase in revenues
    b. Net increase in assets and decrease in liabilities
    c. Net decrease in assets and increase in revenues
    d. Increase in liabilities and increase in revenues

    ANS: A

36. Which of the following is NOT true of the perpetual inventory method?
    a. It requires that a physical count of inventory be taken before the cost of goods sold can be approximated.
    b. It requires adjustments to inventory after every purchase and sales transaction.
    c. It is more helpful than the periodic inventory method in providing management with timely reports about inventory quantities and costs.
    d. It allows management to estimate inventory losses from theft and spoilage better than does the periodic inventory method.

    ANS: A

37. ABC Company purchased inventory on account with credit terms of 2/10, n/30. It paid the amount owed within 10 days and recorded the following entry:

Account A...	800	
Account B		784
Account C		16

    Given this entry, what would be the nature of Account C?
    a. Current liability
    b. Long-term liability
    c. Discount on Purchases
    d. Retained Earnings

    ANS: C

38. Wyoming Sheep Company uses a perpetual inventory system. Wyoming purchased sheep from Big L Ranch at a cost of $19,500, payable at time of delivery. The entry to record the delivery would be

   a. Purchases............................ 19,500
         Accounts Payable   19,500
   b. Inventory 19,500
         Accounts Payable   19,500
   c. Purchases............................ 19,500
         Cash.....................................   19,500
   d. Inventory 19,500
         Cash.....................................   19,500

   ANS: D

39. Garfunkle Company had the following four transactions during January 2006:

   Jan. 3   Purchased 200 hair dryers from Hot Aire Corporation for $30 each, terms n/30.
        5   Sold 50 hair dryers purchased on January 3 for $50 each, terms n/30.
      15   Returned five of the hair dryers purchased on January 3 because they were defective.
      22   A customer returned two hair dryers purchased on January 5 because they were defective.

   Given this information, with the perpetual inventory method, the entry to record the January 5 transaction would include
   a. A debit to Cost of Goods Sold of $1,500
   b. A debit to Accounts Receivable of $2,500
   c. A credit to Inventory of $1,500
   d. All of the above

   ANS: D

40. The entry to close Cost of Goods Sold when the perpetual inventory method is used includes a
   a. Credit to Purchase Returns and Allowances
   b. Debit to Purchase Discounts
   c. Debit to Purchases
   d. Debit to Retained Earnings

   ANS: D

41. Garfunkle Company had the following four transactions during January 2006:

Jan. 3   Purchased 200 hair dryers from Hot Aire Corporation for $30 each, terms n/30.
    5   Sold 50 hair dryers purchased on January 3 for $50 each, terms n/30.
  15   Returned five of the hair dryers purchased on January 3 because they were defective.
  22   A customer returned two hair dryers purchased on January 5 because they were defective.

Given this information, with the perpetual inventory method, the entry to record the January 15 transaction would include a
a. Debit to Purchases of $150
b. Credit to Purchases of $150
c. Credit to Inventory of $150
d. Credit to Purchase Returns and Allowances of $150

ANS: C

42. Lindsey Corporation had the following account balances:

Sales revenue	$100,000
Beginning inventory	20,000
Purchases	40,000
Sales discounts	2,000
Purchase discounts	1,500
Freight-in	500
Ending inventory	15,000
Purchase returns and allowances	1,000

Given this information, the gross margin is
a. $43,000
b. $45,000
c. $53,000
d. $55,000

ANS: D

43. Lindsey Corporation had the following account balances:

Sales revenue	$100,000
Beginning inventory	20,000
Purchases	40,000
Sales discounts	2,000
Purchase discounts	1,500
Freight-in	500
Ending inventory	15,000
Purchase returns and allowances	1,000

Given this information, and assuming that Lindsey's total operating expenses (exclusive of cost of goods sold) are $20,000, pretax income is
a. $23,000
b. $55,000
c. $57,000
d. $35,000

ANS: D

44. If a firm's beginning inventory is $35,000, goods purchased during the period cost $130,000, and the cost of goods sold is $150,000, what is the ending inventory?
a. $15,000
b. $25,000
c. $20,000
d. $45,000

ANS: A

45. With the perpetual inventory method, which of the following entries would be made when inventory costing $3,600 is sold for $5,000?

a. Inventory 5,000
      Accounts Payable 5,000
b. Cost of Goods Sold 3,600
      Inventory 3,600
c. Purchases 5,000
      Accounts Receivable 5,000
d. Inventory 3,600
   Cost of Goods Sold 5,000
      Accounts Payable 3,600
      Purchases 5,000

ANS: B

46. If cost of goods sold is $12,000 and the ending inventory balance is $6,000, the
a. Beginning inventory is $18,000
b. Net income is $6,000
c. Cost of goods available for sale is $18,000
d. Purchases are $6,000

ANS: C

47. If a firm's beginning inventory is $35,000, purchases are $160,000, and the cost of goods sold is $150,000, what is its ending inventory?
   a. $165,000
   b. $130,000
   c. $45,000
   d. $15,000

   ANS: C

Closing Entries (Periodic Inventory System)

48. Which of the following accounts would be debited when making closing entries?
   a. Cost of Goods Sold
   b. Purchases
   c. Sales Discounts
   d. Purchase Returns and Allowances

   ANS: D

49. An entry is made to close Purchases and Purchase Discounts as:

Account A...	35,000	
Account B...	1,600	
Account C...		36,600

   Based on this entry, total (gross) purchases for the year were
   a. $35,000
   b. $1,600
   c. $36,600
   d. Undeterminable, given the preceding information

   ANS: C

50. Chyna Corporation has the following income statement for the year ended December 31, 2006:

Sales revenue		$100,000
Cost of goods sold:		
Beginning inventory	$12,000	
Purchases (net)...	48,000	
Cost of goods available for sale.............................	$60,000	
Cost of ending inventory...	12,000	
Cost of goods sold		48,000
Gross margin..		$ 52,000
Expenses..		30,000
Net income...		$ 22,000

   Given this information, if ending inventory was $10,000 instead of $12,000, net income would be
   a. $18,000
   b. $22,000
   c. $20,000
   d. None of the above

   ANS: C

Counting Inventory and Calculating Cost of Goods Sold

51. For external reporting purposes, inventory shrinkage is usually combined with
     a. Merchandise inventory
     b. Gross profit
     c. Cost of goods sold
     d. Operating expenses

     ANS: C

52. If the ending inventory is overstated, net income for the same period will be
     a. Unaffected
     b. Overstated
     c. Understated
     d. Cannot be determined from information given

     ANS: B

53. A physical count would be necessary at the end of the accounting period under which inventory system?
     a. Periodic inventory system
     b. Perpetual inventory system
     c. Both periodic and perpetual inventory systems
     d. Neither periodic nor perpetual inventory systems

     ANS: C

54. Under which inventory system would a company NOT be able to specifically determine the amount of inventory lost or stolen?
     a. Periodic inventory system
     b. Perpetual inventory system
     c. Both periodic and perpetual inventory systems
     d. Neither periodic nor perpetual inventory systems

     ANS: A

55. The inventory shrinkage account is
     a. Reduced to a zero balance in the closing process
     b. A permanent (real) account
     c. A balance sheet account
     d. Used only with the periodic inventory method

     ANS: A

56. If expenses are overstated on the income statement, net income
     a. Will be unaffected
     b. Will be overstated
     c. Will be understated
     d. Cannot be determined from the above information

     ANS: C

57. When the current year's ending inventory amount is overstated, the
    a. Current year's cost of goods sold is overstated
    b. Current year's total assets are understated
    c. Current year's net income is overstated
    d. Next year's income is overstated

    ANS: C

58. If the ending inventory balance is understated, net income of the same period will be
    a. Overstated
    b. Understated
    c. Unaffected
    d. Cannot be determined from the above information

    ANS: B

59. An overstatement of ending inventory in period 1 would result in income of period 2 being
    a. Overstated
    b. Understated
    c. Correctly stated
    d. Cannot be determined from the information given

    ANS: B

60. Which of the following will result if the current year's ending inventory amount is understated in the cost of goods sold calculation?
    a. Cost of goods sold will be overstated
    b. Total assets will be overstated
    c. Net income will be overstated
    d. Both a and c

    ANS: A

61. If ending inventory on December 31, 2005, is overstated by $30,000, what is the effect on net income for 2006?
    a. Net income is overstated by $30,000.
    b. Net income is understated by $30,000.
    c. Net income is overstated by $60,000.
    d. The answer cannot be determined from the information given.

    ANS: B

62. Following are the account balances from Connery Company's income statement:

Inventory, January 1, 2006	$34,000
Purchases	50,000
Purchase returns and allowances	5,000
Purchase discounts	4,000
Freight-in	6,000
Inventory, December 31, 2006	15,000
Freight-out	8,000

Given this information, the cost of goods sold during 2006 is
a. $51,000
b. $46,000
c. $56,000
d. $66,000

ANS: D

63. Following are the account balances from Samuel Company's income statement:

Inventory, January 1, 2006	$25,000
Purchases	35,000
Purchase returns and allowances	2,000
Purchase discounts	4,000
Freight-in	5,000
Inventory, December 31, 2006	10,000
Freight-out	6,000

Given this information, the cost of merchandise available for sale during 2006 is
a. $65,000
b. $59,000
c. $69,000
d. $61,000

ANS: B

64. From the following information, determine the amount of freight-in.

Beginning inventory	$20,000
Purchases	40,000
Purchase returns and allowances	3,000
Purchase discounts	4,000
Freight-in	?
Cost of goods available for sale	55,000
Ending inventory	?
Cost of goods sold	22,000

a. $3,000
b. $4,000
c. $2,000
d. $1,000

ANS: C

65. From the following information, determine the amount of ending inventory.

Beginning inventory	$20,000
Purchases	40,000
Purchase returns and allowances	3,000
Purchase discounts	4,000
Freight-in	?
Cost of goods available for sale	55,000
Ending inventory	?
Cost of goods sold	23,000

   a. $23,000
   b. $32,000
   c. $33,000
   d. $22,000

ANS: B

66. The following information was obtained from the accounts of Wychoff Company:

Inventory, January 1	$30,000
Purchases	45,000
Purchase returns and allowances	5,000
Purchase discounts	4,000
Freight-in	5,000
Inventory, December 31	10,000
Freight-out	6,000

Given this information, the cost of goods sold during the year is
   a. $46,000
   b. $41,000
   c. $51,000
   d. $61,000

ANS: D

67. The following information was obtained from the accounts of Dees Company:

Beginning inventory	$30,000
Purchases	40,000
Purchase returns and allowances	2,000
Purchase discounts	4,000
Freight-in	5,000
Ending inventory	10,000
Freight-out	6,000

Given this information, the cost of goods available for sale is
   a. $65,000
   b. $59,000
   c. $69,000
   d. $61,000

ANS: C

68. Agassi Company is a wholesale electronics distributor. On December 31, 2006, it prepared the following partial income statement:

Gross sales		$500,400
Sales discounts		400
Net sales		$500,000
Cost of goods sold:		
Beginning inventory	$200,000	
Net purchases	300,000	

Given this information, if the ending inventory balance was $210,000, what would be its gross margin?
a. $290,000
b. $300,000
c. $310,000
d. $210,000

ANS: D

69. Montgomery Corporation has the following account balances:

Sales revenue	$100,000
Beginning inventory	22,000
Purchases	40,000
Sales discounts	2,000
Purchase discounts	1,500
Freight-in	500
Ending inventory	15,000
Purchase returns and allowances	1,000

Given this information, total cost of goods available for sale is
a. $60,000
b. $57,000
c. $58,000
d. $62,000

ANS: A

70. The net sales figure of XYZ Company in 2006 was $300,000. If the cost of goods available for sale was $280,000 and gross margin was 35 percent of net sales, ending inventory must have been
a. $70,000
b. $85,000
c. $195,000
d. $105,000

ANS: B

Inventory Cost Flow Assumptions

71. Which inventory cost flow assumption is most often used by businesses that sell a limited number of high-priced items?
    a. Average cost
    b. FIFO
    c. Specific identification
    d. LIFO

    ANS: C

72. Which inventory cost flow assumption matches current costs against current revenues?
    a. Average cost
    b. FIFO
    c. Specific identification
    d. LIFO

    ANS: D

73. Which inventory cost flow assumption best reflects the current value of inventory on the balance sheet?
    a. Average cost
    b. FIFO
    c. Specific identification
    d. LIFO

    ANS: B

74. Which inventory cost flow assumption will provide the same amounts for ending inventory and cost of goods sold under both the periodic and perpetual inventory systems?
    a. FIFO
    b. LIFO
    c. Average cost
    d. NIFO

    ANS: A

75. Which of the following would be true if inventory costs were increasing?
    a. LIFO would result in lower net income and lower ending inventory amounts than would FIFO.
    b. FIFO would result in lower net income and higher ending inventory amounts than would LIFO.
    c. LIFO would result in a lower net income amount but a higher ending inventory amount than would FIFO.
    d. None of the above would be true.

    ANS: A

76. Which of the following will occur when inventory costs are decreasing?
    a. LIFO will result in lower net income and lower ending inventory than will FIFO.
    b. FIFO will result in lower net income and lower ending inventory than will LIFO.
    c. LIFO will result in a lower net income but a higher ending inventory than will FIFO.
    d. FIFO will result in a lower net income but a higher ending inventory than will LIFO.

    ANS: B

77. During an inflationary period, which inventory costing alternative usually results in a firm paying the lowest income taxes?
    a. FIFO
    b. LIFO
    c. Average cost
    d. Average

    ANS: B

78. When average cost inventory costing is used under the periodic inventory method,
    a. The average cost is computed only at the end of the accounting period
    b. The average cost computation ignores the beginning inventory amount
    c. A series of average costs is computed
    d. A new average cost is computed after each purchase of inventory

    ANS: A

79. When average cost inventory costing is used under the perpetual inventory method, a new average cost is computed after
    a. Each sales transaction
    b. Each purchase transaction
    c. Each sales and purchase transaction
    d. None of the above

    ANS: B

80. During a period of continuing inflation, which inventory cost flow alternative usually results in the highest reported net income?
    a. FIFO
    b. LIFO
    c. Average cost
    d. All of the above result in the same reported net income

    ANS: A

81. When Inventory on a trial balance reflects the inventory that was on hand at the beginning of the period, which of the following inventory costing alternatives is being employed?
    a. Average cost
    b. Periodic
    c. Perpetual LIFO
    d. Perpetual FIFO

    ANS: B

82. When ending inventory is overstated in period 1, net income in period 2 will be
    a. Understated
    b. Overstated
    c. Stated correctly
    d. None of the above

    ANS: A

83. Purchases and sales during a recent period for Casora Inc. were:

Purchases During the Period				Sales During the Period			
1st purchase	700	units × $2		1st sale	400	units × $ 7	
2nd purchase	1,000	units × $3		2nd sale	750	units × $ 8	
3rd purchase	500	units × $4		3rd sale	500	units × $ 9	
4th purchase	500	units × $5		4th sale	500	units × $10	
	2,700	units			2,150	units	

    Beginning inventory was 100 units at $1 each. Given this information, what is the ending inventory if the periodic FIFO costing alternative is used?
    a. $400
    b. $500
    c. $1,250
    d. $3,100

    ANS: D

84. Purchases and sales during a recent period for Casora Inc. were:

Purchases During the Period				Sales During the Period			
1st purchase	500	units × $2		1st sale	600	units × $ 7	
2nd purchase	1,000	units × $3		2nd sale	750	units × $ 8	
3rd purchase	500	units × $4		3rd sale	500	units × $ 9	
4th purchase	500	units × $5		4th sale	500	units × $10	
	2,500	units			2,350	units	

    Beginning inventory was 100 units at $2 each. Given this information, what is the ending inventory if the periodic LIFO costing alternative is used?
    a. $400
    b. $500
    c. $1,250
    d. $3,100

    ANS: B

85. Purchases and sales during a recent period for Casora Inc. were

Purchases During the Period			**Sales During the Period**		
1st purchase	500	units × $2	1st sale	600	units × $ 7
2nd purchase	1,000	units × $3	2nd sale	750	units × $ 8
3rd purchase	500	units × $4	3rd sale	500	units × $ 9
4th purchase	500	units × $5	4th sale	500	units × $10
	2,500	units		2,350	units

Beginning inventory was 100 units at $1 each. Given this information, what is the average cost per unit available for sale during the year if the periodic inventory method is used (rounded to the nearest cent)?
    a. $2.61
    b. $3.10
    c. $3.53
    d. $3.31

ANS: D

86. The following information is available for Waggoner Corporation for the month of June:

Beginning inventory	8 units × $20 = $160
Purchased, June 3	5 units × $22 = $110
Purchased, June 5	7 units × $24 = $168
Sold, June 9	9 units
Purchased, June 15	8 units × $26 = $208
Sold, June 19	6 units

Given this information, the average (periodic) ending inventory balance is approximately
    a. $277
    b. $300
    c. $297
    d. $308

ANS: B

87. The following information is available for Waggoner Corporation for the month of June:

Beginning inventory	8 units × $20 = $160
Purchased, June 3	5 units × $22 = $110
Purchased, June 5	7 units × $24 = $168
Sold, June 9	9 units
Purchased, June 15	8 units × $26 = $208
Sold, June 19	6 units

Given this information, the perpetual LIFO ending inventory balance is
    a. $252
    b. $240
    c. $278
    d. $297

ANS: C

88. Iliescu Sporting Goods had the following inventory records for one line of skis for the month of January:

Beginning inventory	70 pairs × $100 per pair = $7,000
Sales, Jan. 1 – Jan. 7	50 pairs
Purchase, Jan. 8	46 pairs × $104 per pair = $4,784
Sales, Jan. 9 – Jan. 16	59 pairs
Purchase, Jan. 17	62 pairs × $110 per pair = $6,820
Sales, Jan. 18 – Jan. 29	56 pairs
Purchase, Jan. 30	18 pairs × $112 per pair = $2,016

Assuming the perpetual FIFO inventory method is used, what is the cost of Iliescu's ending inventory?
a. $3,000
b. $3,446
c. $3,276
d. $3,546

ANS: B

89. Iliescu Sporting Goods had the following inventory records for one line of skis for the month of January:

Beginning inventory	70 pairs × $100 per pair = $7,000
Sales, Jan. 1 – Jan. 7	50 pairs
Purchase, Jan. 8	46 pairs × $104 per pair = $4,784
Sales, Jan. 9 – Jan. 16	59 pairs
Purchase, Jan. 17	62 pairs × $110 per pair = $6,820
Sales, Jan. 18 – Jan. 29	56 pairs
Purchase, Jan. 30	18 pairs × $112 per pair = $2,016

Assuming the perpetual LIFO inventory method is used, what is the cost of Iliescu's ending inventory?
a. $3,546
b. $3,376
c. $3,268
d. $3,124

ANS: B

90. Iliescu Sporting Goods had the following inventory records for one line of skis for the month of January:

Beginning inventory	70 pairs × $100 per pair = $7,000
Sales, Jan. 1 – Jan. 7	50 pairs
Purchase, Jan. 8	46 pairs × $104 per pair = $4,784
Sales, Jan. 9 – Jan. 16	59 pairs
Purchase, Jan. 17	62 pairs × $110 per pair = $6,820
Sales, Jan. 18 – Jan. 29	56 pairs
Purchase, Jan. 30	18 pairs × $112 per pair = $2,016

Assuming the perpetual LIFO inventory method is used, what is Iliescu's cost of goods sold?
a. $16,986
b. $17,244
c. $17,328
d. $17,174

ANS: B

91. Warren Clothing Store sells jeans. During January 2006, its inventory records of one brand of designer jeans were as follows:

Beginning inventory	10 pairs × $22 = $220
January 6 purchase	4 pairs × $25 = $100
January 10 sale	5 pairs
January 15 purchase	7 pairs × $30 = $210
January 20 sale	10 pairs
January 25 purchase	4 pairs × $30 = $120

Using this information, periodic FIFO cost of goods sold is
a. $330
b. $300
c. $430
d. $350

ANS: D

92. Warren Clothing Store sells jeans. During January 2006, its inventory records of one brand of designer jeans were as follows:

Beginning inventory	10 pairs × $22 = $220
January 6 purchase	4 pairs × $25 = $100
January 10 sale	5 pairs
January 15 purchase	7 pairs × $30 = $210
January 20 sale	10 pairs
January 25 purchase	4 pairs × $30 = $120

Using this information, periodic LIFO cost of goods sold is
a. $430
b. $360
c. $330
d. $300

ANS: A

93. Warren Clothing Store sells jeans. During January 2006, its inventory records of one brand of designer jeans were as follows:

Beginning inventory	10 pairs × $22 = $220
January 6 purchase	4 pairs × $25 = $100
January 10 sale	5 pairs
January 15 purchase	7 pairs × $30 = $210
January 20 sale	10 pairs
January 25 purchase	4 pairs × $30 = $120

Using this information, average cost of goods sold is
a. $450
b. $390
c. $375
d. $330

ANS: B

94. Warren Clothing Store sells jeans. During January 2006, its inventory records of one brand of designer jeans were as follows:

Beginning inventory	10 pairs × $22 = $220
January 6 purchase	4 pairs × $25 = $100
January 10 sale	5 pairs
January 15 purchase	7 pairs × $30 = $210
January 20 sale	10 pairs
January 25 purchase	4 pairs × $30 = $120

Using this information, perpetual LIFO cost of goods sold is
a. $430
b. $375
c. $398
d. $403

ANS: C

95. Martin Inc. is a wholesaler of office supplies. The activity for supply number 47519 during October is shown below:

Date	Balance/Transaction	Units	Cost
Oct. 1	Inventory	2,000	$36.00
7	Purchase	3,000	37.20
12	Sales	3,600	
21	Purchase	4,800	38.00
22	Sales	3,800	
29	Purchase	1,600	38.60

If Martin Inc. uses a FIFO periodic inventory system, the ending inventory of supply number 47519 at October 31 is reported as
a. $152,960
b. $152,288
c. $150,160
d. $150,080

ANS: A

96. Martin Inc. is a wholesaler of office supplies. The activity for supply number 47519 during October is shown below:

Date	Balance/Transaction	Units	Cost
Oct. 1	Inventory	2,000	$36.00
7	Purchase	3,000	37.20
12	Sales	3,600	
21	Purchase	4,800	38.00
22	Sales	3,800	
29	Purchase	1,600	38.60

If Martin Inc. uses a LIFO periodic inventory system, the ending inventory of supply number 47519 at October 31 is reported as
a. $152,960
b. $150,160
c. $150,080
d. $146,400

ANS: D

97. Martin Inc. is a wholesaler of office supplies. The activity for supply number 47519 during October is shown below:

Date	Balance/Transaction	Units	Cost
Oct. 1	Inventory	2,000	$36.00
7	Purchase	3,000	37.20
12	Sales	3,600	
21	Purchase	4,800	38.00
22	Sales	3,800	
29	Purchase	1,600	38.60

If Martin Inc. uses a periodic average cost inventory system, the ending inventory of supply number 47519 at October 31 is reported as (round the average cost to the nearest cent)
a. $152,232
b. $150,160
c. $150,080
d. $146,400

ANS: C

98. With LIFO, cost of goods sold is $195,000, and ending inventory is $45,000. If FIFO ending inventory is $65,000, how much is FIFO cost of goods sold?
a. $215,000
b. $195,000
c. $175,000
d. $65,000

ANS: C

Assessing How Well Companies Manage Their Inventories

99. Which of the following factors are used in calculating a company's inventory turnover?
     a.   Cost of goods sold and average working capital
     b.   Average accounts receivable and net sales
     c.   Net sales and average inventory
     d.   Average inventory and cost of goods sold

     ANS: D

100. Monica Mills Co. began the year with $100,000 in inventory and ends the year with $300,000.
     Purchases during the year amounted to $1,660,000. The number of days' sales in inventory for
     the year was
     a.   43.98
     b.   8.30
     c.   7.30
     d.   50.00

     ANS: D

101. Andromeda, Inc., purchased $100,000 of inventory during the year and had average receivables
     and payables of $46,575 and $21,918, respectively. The number of days' purchases in accounts
     payable was approximately
     a.   60
     b.   170
     c.   80
     d.   128

     ANS: C

102. During the current calendar year, Franco Corporation purchased $330,000 of inventory. The
     beginning inventory balance was $42,000, and the inventory balance at year-end was $60,000.
     The inventory turnover for the current year was
     a.   5.20 times
     b.   5.50 times
     c.   6.12 times
     d.   7.86 times

     ANS: C

103. The following information was taken from the records of Kane Company for 2006:

Beginning inventory	$ 54,000
Ending inventory	60,000
Net credit sales	576,000
Cost of goods sold	324,000
Net income	45,000

Given this information, Kane's inventory turnover for 2006 is
a. 5.68
b. 5.40
c. 10.11
d. 1.33

ANS: A

104. The December 31, 2006 balance sheet and income statement for Santana Company are presented below:

Santana Company
Balance Sheet
December 31, 2006

Assets		Liabilities and Stockholders' Equity	
Cash	$ 96,000	Accounts payable	$ 243,000
Accounts receivable	560,000	Income taxes payable	67,000
Inventory	234,000	Salaries payable	46,000
Plant and equipment	770,000	Bonds payable	760,000
Intangible assets	40,000	Common stock	340,000
		Retained earnings	244,000
		Total liabilities and	
Total assets	$1,700,000	stockholders' equity	$1,700,000

Santana Company
Income Statement
For the Year Ended December 31, 2006

Net sales revenue	$1,800,000
Cost of goods sold	945,000
Gross margin	$ 855,000
Operating expenses (including $40,000 of bond interest)	567,000
Income before taxes	$ 288,000
Income taxes	115,000
Net income	$ 173,000

Additional information:
Total assets (12/31/05)	$2,400,000
Inventory (12/31/05)	238,500
Total stockholders' equity (12/31/05)	616,000

Given this information, Santana's inventory turnover during 2006 was
a.   4
b.   5
c.   7
d.   8

ANS: A

105.   The following information is available for Brown Company:

Cost of goods sold for 2006	$1,200,000
Inventories at December 31, 2005	350,000
Inventories at December 31, 2006	310,000

Assuming that a business year consists of 360 days, the number of days' sales in inventory for 2006 was
a.   49.5
b.   93
c.   100
d.   105

ANS: C

106.   The following information is available for Lendo Company:

Lendo Company
Partial Balance Sheet
December 31, 2006 and 2005

	2006	2005
Accounts receivable	$500,000	$470,000
Allowance for uncollectible accounts	(25,000)	(20,000)
Net accounts receivable	$475,000	$450,000
Inventories at lower of cost or market	$600,000	$550,000

Lendo Company
Partial Income Statement
For the Years Ended December 31, 2006 and 2005

	2006	2005
Net credit sales	$2,500,000	$2,200,000
Net cash sales	500,000	400,000
Net sales	$3,000,000	$2,600,000
Cost of goods sold	$2,000,000	$1,800,000
Selling, general, and administrative expenses	300,000	270,000
Other expenses	50,000	30,000
Total operating expenses	$2,350,000	$2,100,000

Lendo's inventory turnover for 2006 is computed by
a. $2,000,000/$600,000
b. $2,350,000/$600,000
c. $2,000,000/$575,000
d. $3,000,000/$575,000

ANS: C

EXPANDED MATERIAL

Further Coverage of Inventory Errors

107. An understatement of purchases results in cost of goods sold being
a. Overstated
b. Understated
c. Stated correctly
d. None of the above

ANS: B

108. Under the periodic inventory method, if an inventory purchase has been made and recorded but has not yet arrived (and thus is not counted), the financial statements will
a. Overstate assets
b. Overstate net income
c. Understate net income
d. Understate revenues

ANS: C

109. The misclassification of Freight-In as an operating expense will result in
a. An overstatement of cost of goods sold
b. An overstatement of gross margin
c. An overstatement of net income
d. None of the above

ANS: B

Complications of the Perpetual Method with LIFO and Average

110. Under certain methods of inventory cost flow assumption, the amount of cost of goods sold can be affected by when the sale occurs. Which of the following methods is NOT affected by when the sale occurs?
a. LIFO
b. FIFO
c. Average cost
d. None of the above

ANS: B

111.   Under which system must a determination of the "last in" units be evaluated at the time of each
        individual sale?
        a.   Perpetual system
        b.   Periodic system
        c.   Both perpetual and periodic systems
        d.   Neither periodic nor perpetual

        ANS: A

Reporting Inventory at Amounts Below Cost

112.   The ceiling, or the maximum market amount at which inventory can be carried on the books, is
        equal to
        a.   Current replacement cost
        b.   Net realizable value
        c.   Historical cost
        d.   Selling price

        ANS: B

113.   The floor, or the minimum market amount at which inventory can be carried on the books, is
        equal to
        a.   Selling price less estimated selling costs
        b.   Current replacement cost
        c.   Net realizable value less normal profit margin
        d.   Historical cost

        ANS: C

114.   Inventories are carried in the accounting records at cost, EXCEPT when
        a.   The inventory is damaged
        b.   The market value of the inventory falls below its acquisition cost
        c.   Either a or b occurs
        d.   The market price rises above cost

        ANS: C

115.   Inventory is usually carried in the accounting records at
        a.   Lower of cost or market
        b.   Market
        c.   Cost
        d.   Selling price

        ANS: A

116.   Inventory valued at lower of cost or market can never be recorded at amounts below its
        a.   Net realizable value
        b.   Net realizable value minus a normal profit margin
        c.   Sales price
        d.   Ceiling

        ANS: B

117. Tena Company has the following information related to its two products:

	Original Cost	Replacement Cost	Ceiling	Floor
Product A	$12	$ 9	$10	$ 8
Product B	15	16	18	14

The net realizable value of product B is
a. $15
b. $16
c. $18
d. $14

ANS: C

118. Tena Company has the following information related to its two products:

	Original Cost	Replacement Cost	Ceiling	Floor
Product A	$12	$ 9	$10	$ 8
Product B	15	16	18	14

Assuming that the lower of cost or market rule is applied to individual products, the amount at which product A should be valued is
a. $12
b. $9
c. $10
d. $8

ANS: B

119. Commodity X sells for $12.00; selling expenses are $2.40; and normal profit is $3.00. If the cost of Commodity X is $7.80 and the replacement cost is $6.00, the lower of cost or market is
a. $5.40
b. $6.00
c. $6.60
d. $7.80

ANS: C

120. A firm is writing its inventory down to the lower of cost or market. It has determined the following per unit costs and market prices for its product:

Original cost..	$52
Sales price..	60
Selling cost...	10
Normal profit	9
Replacement cost	39

Given these data, the firm should value its inventory at a per-unit cost of
a. $52
b. $50
c. $41
d. $39

ANS: C

Method of Estimating Inventories

121. Which of the following statements is true of the gross margin method of estimating the dollar amount of ending inventory?
a. It is helpful in estimating inventory when a fire burns the warehouse.
b. It uses the current gross margin percentage in its calculation.
c. It is a method of estimating ending inventory that can be used only in retail firms.
d. All the above statements are true.

ANS: A

122. The use of the gross profit method assumes
a. The amount of gross profit is the same as in prior years
b. Sales and cost of goods sold have not changed from previous years
c. Inventory values have not increased from previous years
d. The relationship between selling price and cost of goods sold is similar to prior years

ANS: D

123. The gross profit method of estimating inventory would NOT be useful when
a. A periodic system is in use and inventories are required for interim statements
b. Inventories have been destroyed or lost by fire, theft, or other casualty, and the specific data required for inventory valuation are not available
c. There is a significant change in the mix of products being sold
d. The relationship between gross profit and sales remains stable over time

ANS: C

124. A firm had a beginning inventory balance of $1,000, net purchases of $35,000, and sales of $40,000. Its gross margin percentage was 25 percent. Using the gross margin method, the ending inventory balance is
    a. $1,000
    b. $7,000
    c. $6,000
    d. $10,000

    ANS: C

125. Collins Company is a wholesale electronics distributor. On December 31, 2006, it prepared the following partial income statement:

Gross sales		$600,400
Sales discounts		400
Net sales		$600,000
Cost of goods sold:		
Beginning inventory	$200,000	
Net purchases	300,000	

    Given this information, if Collins Company's gross margin is 25 percent of net sales, what is the estimated ending inventory balance?
    a. $150,000
    b. $75,000
    c. $25,000
    d. $50,000

    ANS: D

126. Penn Company needs an estimate of its ending inventory balance. The following information is available:

Sales revenue	$180,000
Beginning inventory	45,000
Net purchases	100,000
Gross margin percentage	30%

    Given this information, when using the gross margin estimation method, ending inventory is approximately
    a. $1,000
    b. $9,000
    c. $19,000
    d. $11,650

    ANS: C

127. The following information is available for the Segura Company for the three months ended June 30:

Inventory, April 1	$1,200,000
Purchases	4,500,000
Freight-in	300,000
Sales	6,400,000

    The gross margin was 25 percent of sales. What is the estimated inventory balance at June 30?
    a. $880,000
    b. $933,000
    c. $1,200,000
    d. $1,500,000

    ANS: C

128. On August 31, a flood at Crawford Company's only warehouse caused severe damage to its entire inventory. Based on recent history, Crawford has a gross profit of 25 percent of net sales. The following information is available from Crawford's records for the 10 months ended August 31:

Inventory, January 1	$ 520,000
Purchases	4,120,000
Purchase returns	60,000
Sales	6,000,000
Sales discounts	400,000

    A physical inventory disclosed usable damaged goods which Crawford estimates can be sold to a jobber for $70,000. Using the gross profit method, the estimated cost of goods sold for the 10 months ended August 31 should be
    a. $680,000
    b. $3,830,000
    c. $3,900,000
    d. $4,200,000

    ANS: D

129. The following information appears in Gordon Company's records for the year ended December 31:

Inventory, January 1	$ 325,000
Purchases	1,150,000
Purchase returns	40,000
Freight-in	30,000
Sales	1,700,000
Sales discounts	10,000
Sales returns	15,000

On December 31, a physical inventory revealed that the ending inventory was only $210,000. Gordon's gross profit on net sales has remained constant at 30 percent in recent years. Gordon suspects that some inventory may have been pilfered by one of the company's employees. At December 31, what is the estimated cost of missing inventory?
a. $75,000
b. $82,500
c. $210,000
d. $292,500

ANS: B

130. The following information is available for Mizo Company for its most recent year:

Net sales	$3,600,000
Freight-in	90,000
Purchase discounts	50,000
Ending inventory	280,000

The gross margin is 40 percent of net sales. What is the cost of goods available for sale?
a. $1,680,000
b. $1,920,000
c. $2,400,000
d. $2,440,000

ANS: D

PROBLEMS

1. Compute the missing numbers for the following three partial income statements:

	Dexter Company	Essex Company	Faldo Company
Beginning inventory	$32,500	$12,700	(5)$_____
Purchases	53,000	(3)_____	123,000
Purchase returns and allowances	(1)_____	800	5,100
Goods available for sale	83,800	(4)_____	174,200
Ending inventory	(2)_____	11,500	43,400
Cost of goods sold	66,500	33,600	(6)_____

ANS:

1. $1,700
2. $17,300
3. $33,200
4. $45,100
5. $56,300
6. $130,800

2. Prepare journal entries to record the following four transactions for Labatt Company using the perpetual inventory method. (Omit explanations for the entries.)

   1. June 1—purchased on account inventory costing $15,000 terms 2/10, n/30.
   2. June 9—returned inventory costing $1,500 that was purchased on June 1.
   3. June 10—paid for the merchandise purchased on June 1.
   4. June 15—sold one-half of its inventory for $12,000 cash. (Assume the inventory purchased on June 1 was the company's only inventory.)

   ANS:

June	1	Inventory..	15,000	
		Accounts Payable.................................		15,000
	9	Accounts Payable.....................................	1,500	
		Inventory...		1,500
	10	Accounts Payable.....................................	13,500	
		Inventory...		270
		Cash		13,230
	15	Cash	12,000	
		Sales Revenue		12,000
		Cost of Goods Sold	6,615	
		Inventory...		6,615

   [($15,000 – $1,500 – $270) × 0.50 = $6,615]

3. Prepare journal entries to record the following four transactions for Labatt Company using the periodic inventory method. (Omit explanations for the entries.)

   1. June 1—purchased on account inventory costing $15,000 terms 2/10, n/30.
   2. June 9—returned inventory costing $1,500 that was purchased on June 1.
   3. June 10—paid for the merchandise purchased on June 1.
   4. June 15—sold one-half of its inventory for $12,000 cash. (Assume the inventory purchased on June 1 was the company's only inventory.)

ANS:

June	1	Purchases	15,000	
		Accounts Payable...................................		15,000
	9	Accounts Payable.....................................	1,500	
		Purchase Returns and Allowances.........		1,500
	10	Accounts Payable.....................................	13,500	
		Purchase Discounts.............................		270
		Cash		13,230
	15	Cash	12,000	
		Sales Revenue......................................		12,000

4. The following data are available for Toltec Company:

	Year 1	Year 2
Beginning inventory...	$ 90,000	$ 60,000
Purchases	150,000	180,000
Cost of goods available for sale	240,000	240,000
Ending inventory...	60,000	50,000
Cost of goods sold..	180,000	190,000

Based on these data, answer the following three independent questions:

1. If ending inventory in year 1 is understated by $5,000 (it is recorded as $55,000),
    how much is cost of goods sold in year 1?
2. Assuming the same error as in (1), how much is total cost of goods sold for the two
    years combined?
3. If beginning inventory in year 2 is understated by $15,000 (it is recorded as
    $45,000), how much is cost of goods sold in year 2?

ANS:

	(1)	(2)		(3)
		Year 1	Year 2	
Beginning inventory..................	$ 90,000	$ 90,000	$ 55,000	$ 45,000
Purchases	150,000	150,000	180,000	180,000
Cost of goods available for sale .	$240,000	$240,000	$235,000	$225,000
Ending inventory........................	55,000	55,000	50,000	50,000
Cost of goods sold.....................	$185,000	$185,000	$185,000	$175,000
			$370,000	

5. Compute the missing numbers in the following income statements:

	Year 1	Year 2
Sales revenue	$ 25,000	(4)$_____
Beginning inventory	6,200	(5)_____
Purchases	15,300	21,000
Purchase returns and allowances	500	300
Ending inventory	(1)_____	(6)_____
Cost of goods sold	(2)_____	16,000
Gross margin	7,000	17,500
Expenses	3,800	(7)_____
Net income (or loss)	(3)_____	9,800

ANS:

1. $3,000
2. $18,000
3. $3,200
4. $33,500
5. $3,000
6. $7,700
7. $7,700

6. The following account balances were included in the ledger of Muldar Company as of December 31, 2006. Using these accounts, prepare in good form an income statement for the year ending December 31, 2006. (Muldar Company uses the periodic inventory method.)

Cash	$ 14,300
Freight-in	800
Inventory, January 1, 2006	15,000
Prepaid insurance	7,900
Purchases	72,000
Sales revenue	150,000
Selling expenses	34,200
Purchase returns and allowances	1,500
General and administrative expenses	40,500
Inventory, December 31, 2006	18,100
Sales discounts	1,500

ANS:

Muldar Company
Income Statement
For the Year Ended December 31, 2006

Sales revenue			$150,000
Less sales discounts			(1,500)
Net sales revenue			$148,500
Cost of goods sold:			
Beginning inventory		$15,000	
Purchases	$72,000		
Freight-in	800		
Purchase returns and allowances	(1,500)		
Net purchases....................................		71,300	
Cost of goods available for sale..........		$86,300	
Less ending inventory........................		(18,100)	
Cost of goods sold			68,200
Gross margin.......................................			$ 80,300
Operating expenses:			
Selling expenses................................		$34,200	
General and administrative expenses..		40,500	
Total operating expenses			74,700
Net income...			$ 5,600

7. Jahn Company had the following balances in its general ledger at December 31, 2006:

Inventory (as of January 1, 2006)	$240,000
Purchases	440,000
Purchase returns and allowances	5,000

For the year 2006, Jahn Company's electronic sales registers showed a total cost of goods sold of $480,000. Assuming that a physical count of inventory on December 31, 2006, revealed inventory on hand costing $185,000, complete the following:

1. Prepare the journal entries needed to adjust the inventory records and close the related purchases accounts, assuming the periodic inventory method is used.
2. Prepare any entries necessary to adjust the inventory records and close the appropriate accounts, assuming the perpetual inventory method is used, but that the information preceding beginning inventory, purchases, and purchase returns and allowances is known.

ANS:

1. Inventory... 435,000
    Purchase Returns and Allowances.......................... 5,000
        Purchases 440,000
            To close the purchases accounts.

    Cost of Goods Sold... 490,000
        Inventory... 490,000
            To record the Cost of Goods Sold and adjust
            Inventory to $185,000 balance.

2. Inventory Shrinkage... 10,000
        Inventory... 10,000
            To adjust the inventory balance for the
            shortage revealed in the physical count
            ($240,000 + $440,000 – $5,000 – $480,000 =
            $195,000; $195,000 – $185,000 = $10,000).

Cost of goods sold has already been determined under the perpetual method. No entry is needed to record cost of goods sold.

8. The following data are available for Ali Company for the first two quarters of the current year:

	1st Quarter	2nd Quarter
Sales...	$ 50,000	$ 60,000
Beginning inventory...	3,000	(5)_____
Purchases	10,000	(6)_____
Purchase discounts...	(1)_____	200
Cost of goods available for sale	11,900	16,000
Ending inventory..	(2)_____	5,000
Cost of goods sold..	7,000	(7)_____
Gross margin...	(3)_____	(8)_____
Selling expenses...	(4)_____	20,000
Administrative expenses	12,000	(9)_____
Net income..	15,000	18,000

Compute the missing income statement amounts.

ANS:

1. $3,000 + $10,000 – $11,900 = $1,100
2. $11,900 – $7,000 = $4,900
3. $50,000 – $7,000 = $43,000
4. $43,000 – $12,000 – $15,000 = $16,000
5. $4,900 (from ending inventory, 1st quarter)
6. $16,000 + $200 – $4,900 = $11,300
7. $16,000 – $5,000 = $11,000
8. $60,000 – $11,000 = $49,000
9. $49,000 – $20,000 – $18,000 = $11,000

9. Ling Company's inventory records for the current year are as follows:

	Number of Units	Cost per Unit	Total Cost
Beginning inventory	2,200	$3.00	$ 6,600
First purchase	3,000	$2.90	8,700
Second purchase	3,500	$2.80	9,800
Third purchase	2,800	$2.70	7,560
Fourth purchase	2,500	$2.60	6,500
Goods available for sale	14,000		$39,160
Units sold during the year	9,000		

Compute the cost of ending inventory using the following inventory costing methods:
1. FIFO
2. LIFO
3. Average cost

ANS:

1. FIFO   2,500   × $2.60   = $ 6,500
           2,500   ×   2.70   =   6,750
                                            $13,250

2. LIFO   2,200   × $3.00   = $ 6,600
           2,800   ×   2.90   =   8,120
                                            $14,720

3. Average cost ($39,160/14,000) = $2.797 per unit × 5,000 units = $13,985

10. The financial statements of Alphonso, Inc., reflect the following data:

Sales	$1,000,000	Beginning inventory	$80,100
Cost of goods sold	250,000	Ending inventory	84,170
Beginning accounts receivable	420,000	Beginning accounts payable	69,000
Ending accounts receivable	403,045	Ending accounts payable	70,216

You are analyzing the company's statements to determine how much of the company's operating cycle must be financed through external financing.

1. Determine the length of the company's operating cycle.
2. Determine the number of days the company will need external financing.
3. Identify the means of obtaining the necessary external financing.

ANS:

1. Inventory turnover   = Cost of goods sold ÷ Average inventory
                                            = \$250,000 ÷ [(\$80,100 + \$84,170)/2]
                                            = 3.04

    Number of days' sales in inventory = 365 ÷ 3.04 = 120 days

    Accounts receivable turnover   = Sales ÷ Average accounts receivable
                                            = \$1,000,000 ÷ [(\$420,000 + \$403,045)/2]
                                            = 2.43

    Average collection period = 365 ÷ 2.43 = 150 days

    Operating cycle   = 120 days + 150 days = <u>270 days</u>

2. | Cost of goods sold | \$250,000 |
    |---|---|
    | Add: Increase in inventory | 4,070 |
    | Purchases | \$254,070 |

    Number of days' purchases
    in accounts payable   = 365 days ÷ (Purchases/Average accounts payable)
                                            = 365 ÷ [\$254,070/(\$69,000 + \$70,216/2)]
                                              = 365 ÷ 3.65
                                              = 100 days

Operating cycle	270 days
Less: Number of days' purchases in accounts payable	<u>100 days</u>
Number of days company will need external financing	<u>170 days</u>

3. a. Borrowing
    b. Issuing additional shares of stock
    c. Charging interest on its credit card sales

11. Feldman Company has the following inventory information for the current year:

Item	Quantity	Unit Cost	Replacement Cost	Net Realizable Value	Floor
1A	100	$34	$36	$45	$41
2A	150	16	13	19	14
3A	50	25	20	21	18
4A	200	41	36	35	34

Determine the total inventory cost to appear on Feldman's balance sheet under the lower of cost or market rule assuming:

1. The rule is applied to inventory as a whole.
2. The rule is applied on an item-by-item basis.

ANS:

Item	Qty.	Original Cost			Market Value			LCM
1A	100	100 × $34	=	$ 3,400	100 × $41	=	$ 4,100	$ 3,400
2A	150	150 × 16	=	2,400	150 × 14	=	2,100	2,100
3A	50	50 × 25	=	1,250	50 × 20	=	1,000	1,000
4A	200	200 × 41	=	8,200	200 × 35	=	7,000	7,000
				$15,250			$14,200	$13,500

1. $14,200
2. $13,500

12. Hughes Medical Supply, a retail business, had net sales of $46,200 during January. Purchases of merchandise during the month amounted to $21,350, of which $13,700 had been paid for by the end of January. The merchandise purchased had a retail sales value of $29,500. On January 1, inventory on hand cost $13,090 and had a retail sales value of $19,700. Traditionally, Hughes' gross margin percentage has been 30 percent.

Use the gross margin estimation method to determine the cost of Hughes' inventory at the end of January.

ANS:

Sales revenue		$46,200
Cost of goods sold..		
Beginning inventory..	$13,090	
Purchases	21,350	
Goods available for sale...	$34,440	
Less: Ending inventory	2,100	
Cost of goods sold...		32,340
Gross margin (0.30 × $46,200)		$13,860
Ending inventory at cost	$ 2,100	

Name_____   Section_____

TRUE/FALSE

Circle T or F to indicate whether each of the following statements is true or false.

T   F   1.   Sales Discounts normally has a credit balance.

T   F   2.   Credit terms of 2/10, n/30 mean that a 2 percent discount is allowed if payment is made within 10 days.

T   F   3.   Purchase Discounts is a contra-revenue account.

T   F   4.   The perpetual inventory method usually provides better control over inventory than does the periodic method.

T   F   5.   There is usually no cost of goods sold account when the perpetual inventory method is used.

T   F   6.   Purchases is an account that is not used with the periodic inventory method.

T   F   7.   The balance in Freight-In has the effect of increasing cost of goods sold.

T   F   8.   Purchase Returns and Allowances is an account that is used only with the perpetual inventory method.

T   F   9.   Closing entries will bring the inventory balance to zero.

T   F   10. Purchase Discounts is brought to a zero balance (closed) with a credit entry.

Name_____   **Section**_____

MATCHING

In the spaces provided, write the letter of the term for each of the following definitions:

    a. LIFO
    b. Periodic inventory method
    c. Specific identification
    d. Cost of goods sold
    e. Inventory turnover ratio
    f. Gross margin
    g. Perpetual inventory method
    h. FIFO
    i. Average cost
    j. Purchase discount

1. _____ A perpetual inventory cost flow alternative whereby the cost of goods sold and the cost of ending inventory are determined by using an average cost of all merchandise on hand after each purchase.

2. _____ The cost incurred to purchase the merchandise sold during a period.

3. _____ A system of accounting for inventory in which cost of goods sold is determined and inventory is adjusted at the end of the accounting period, not when merchandise is purchased or sold.

4. _____ An inventory cost flow alternative whereby the first goods purchased are assumed to be the first goods sold so that the ending inventory consists of the most recently purchased goods.

5. _____ A reduction in the purchase price allowed if payment is made within a specified period.

6. _____ A measure of the efficiency with which inventory is managed; computed by dividing cost of goods sold by average inventory for a period.

7. _____ A system of accounting for inventory whereby detailed records of the number of units and the cost of each purchase and sales transaction are prepared throughout the period.

8. _____ A method of valuing inventory and determining cost of goods sold whereby the actual costs of specific inventory items are assigned to them.

9. _____ An inventory cost flow alternative whereby the last goods purchased are assumed to be the first goods sold so that the ending inventory consists of the first goods purchased.

10. _____ The excess of net sales revenues over the cost of goods sold.

Name_____   Section_____

MULTIPLE CHOICE

Pro Throw

Pro Throw is a wholesaler of sporting goods. The activity for NCAA-sanctioned footballs during July is shown below:

Date	Balance/Transaction	Units	Cost
July 1	Inventory	1,000	$36.00
3	Purchase	1,500	37.20
4	Sales	1,800	
16	Purchase	2,400	38.00
25	Sales	1,900	
28	Purchase	800	38.60

1. Refer to Pro Throw above. If Pro Throw uses a FIFO periodic inventory system, the ending inventory of footballs at July 31 is reported as
    a. $73,200
    b. $75,040
    c. $75,080
    d. $76,480

2. Refer to Pro Throw above. If Pro Throw uses an average cost periodic inventory system, the ending inventory of footballs at July 31 is reported as (unit cost rounded to the nearest penny)
    a. $73,200
    b. $75,040
    c. $75,080
    d. $76,480

3. Commodity X sells for $13.00; selling expenses are $2.40; and normal profit is $3.00. If the cost of Commodity X is $7.50 and the replacement cost is $6.00, then the lower of cost or market is
    a. $5.40
    b. $4.50
    c. $7.60
    d. $7.50

4. The following information appears in Cobra Co.'s records for the year ended December 31:

Inventory, January 1	$ 650,000
Net purchases	2,280,000
Sales	3,500,000

On December 31, a physical inventory revealed that the ending inventory was only $420,000. Cobra's gross profit on net sales has remained constant at 40 percent in recent years. Cobra suspects that some inventory may have been stolen. What is the estimated cost of missing inventory at December 31?
a. $410,000
b. $180,000
c. $1,530,000
d. $880,000

5. The following information is available for Ripple Company for the year ended December 31:

Net sales	$2,500,000
Ending inventory	500,000

The gross margin is 30 percent of net sales. What is the cost of goods that are available for sale during the year?
a. $1,250,000
b. $1,500,000
c. $2,250,000
d. $1,750,000

Quiz Solutions

Quiz A	Quiz B	Quiz C
1. F	1. i	1. d
2. T	2. d	2. b
3. F	3. b	3. d
4. T	4. h	4. a
5. F	5. j	5. c
6. F	6. e	
7. T	7. g	
8. F	8. c	
9. F	9. a	
10. F	10. f	

MULTIPLE CHOICE

Employee Compensation

1. To properly recognize the expense associated with compensated absences, a company should
   a. Expense these obligations in the period the employee is absent
   b. Estimate and expense these obligations when a new employee is hired
   c. Estimate and expense these obligations in the period that the employee earns those days
   d. Not recognize any expense for compensated absences

   ANS: C

2. Which of the following is NOT true regarding taxes deducted from an employee's earnings?
   a. These items are expenses to the employer.
   b. These items are liabilities that must be paid to federal and state governments.
   c. These items are credited within the entry to record wage or salary expense.
   d. The employer serves as an agent for the governments for collecting these taxes.

   ANS: A

3. Which of the following taxes is NOT included in the payroll tax expense of the employer?
   a. State unemployment taxes
   b. Federal unemployment taxes
   c. FICA taxes
   d. Federal income taxes

   ANS: D

4. Which of the following payroll taxes are paid by the employer?
   a. FICA taxes
   b. Federal unemployment taxes
   c. State unemployment taxes
   d. All the above

   ANS: D

5. Which of the following taxes must be paid by both the employee and the employer?
   a. Social security tax (FICA)
   b. State unemployment tax
   c. State withholding tax
   d. Federal unemployment tax

   ANS: A

6. Which of the following would probably be classified as a current liability?
   a. Accumulated depreciation on equipment
   b. Payroll taxes payable
   c. Lease obligation
   d. Pension liability

   ANS: B

7. The entry to recognize the estimated expense related to sick days would include a
   a. Credit to Salaries Expense
   b. Credit to Cash
   c. Credit to Sick Days Payable
   d. Debit to Sick Days Payable

   ANS: C

8. The entry to record sick days taken by an employee would include a
   a. Credit to Salaries Expense
   b. Debit to Cash
   c. Credit to Sick Days Payable
   d. Debit to Sick Days Payable

   ANS: D

9. When managers are compensated based on the achievement of certain objectives, the company is said to be paying a(n)
   a. Incentive
   b. Bonus
   c. Salary
   d. Post-retirement benefit

   ANS: B

10. When the right to purchase stock in the future is used as a substitute for a cash bonus, the company is granting
    a. Post-retirement benefits
    b. Compensated absences
    c. Stock options
    d. Post-employment benefits

    ANS: C

11. A severance package would best be termed a
    a. Post-retirement benefit
    b. Compensated absence
    c. Stock option
    d. Post-employment benefit

    ANS: D

12. The gross pay for all employees is debited to
    a. Salaries Payable
    b. Salaries Expense
    c. Payroll Tax Expense
    d. Cash

    ANS: B

13. Which accounting principle requires that the expense associated with compensated absences be accounted for in the period in which it is earned by the employee?
    a. Revenue recognition principle
    b. Expense recognition principle
    c. Matching principle
    d. Economic entity principle

    ANS: C

14. Which of the following are the two methods used to account for employee stock options?
    a. Fair value and book value
    b. Intrinsic value and realizable value
    c. Book value and realizable value
    d. Fair value and intrinsic value

    ANS: D

15. Which method of accounting for employee stock options usually results in no expense being recognized?
    a. Intrinsic value method
    b. Recognition method
    c. Fair value method
    d. Book value method

    ANS: A

16. Which method of accounting for stock options results in compensation expense being recognized for almost all stock option plans?
    a. Intrinsic value method
    b. Recognition method
    c. Fair value method
    d. Book value method

    ANS: C

17. Which type of pension plan requires a company to place a certain amount of money into a pension fund each year on behalf of the employees?
    a. Defined benefit plan
    b. Defined payment plan
    c. Defined contribution plan
    d. Defined employee plan

    ANS: C

18. Which type of pension plan promises employees a certain monthly cash amount after they retire?
    a. Defined benefit plan
    b. Defined payment plan
    c. Defined contribution plan
    d. Defined employee plan

    ANS: A

19. Which of the following is NOT a component of pension expense?
    a. Interest cost
    b. Pension payment
    c. Service cost
    d. Return on pension fund assets

    ANS: B

20. A pension fund is "underfunded" when the
    a. Market value of the pension fund assets is greater than the estimated pension liability
    b. Pension expense is greater than the annual payment to the pension fund
    c. Pension expense is less than the annual payment to the pension fund
    d. Market value of the pension fund assets is less than the estimated pension liability

    ANS: D

21. During the first week of January, Joel Mayer earned $200. Assume that FICA taxes are 7.65 percent of wages up to $50,000; state unemployment tax is 5.0 percent of wages up to $13,000; and federal unemployment tax is 0.8 percent of wages up to $13,000. Assume that Joel has voluntary withholdings of $10 (in addition to taxes) and that federal and state income tax withholdings are $18 and $6, respectively. What amount is the check, net of all deductions, that Joel received for the week's pay?
    a. $150.70
    b. $141.70
    c. $140.10
    d. $155.20

    ANS: A

22. During the month of July, Joel Mayer earned $2,000. Joel has been on the payroll all year at a salary of $2,000 per month. Salaries are paid at the end of each month. Assume that FICA taxes are 7.65 percent of wages up to $50,000; state unemployment tax is 5.0 percent of wages up to $13,000; and federal unemployment tax is 0.8 percent of wages up to $13,000. Assume that Joel has voluntary withholdings of $75 (in addition to taxes) and that federal and state income tax withholdings are $300 and $100, respectively. What amount is the check, net of all deductions, that Joel received for his July pay?
    a. $1,372
    b. $1,256
    c. $1,314
    d. $1,525

    ANS: A

23. During the first week of January, Joel Mayer earned $200. Assume that FICA taxes are 7.65 percent of wages up to $50,000; state unemployment tax is 5.0 percent of wages up to $13,000; and federal unemployment tax is 0.8 percent of wages up to $13,000. Assume that Joel has voluntary withholdings of $10 (in addition to taxes) and that federal and state income tax withholdings are $18 and $6, respectively. What is the employer's payroll tax expense for the week, assuming that Joel Mayer is the only employee?
   a. $6.32
   b. $26.90
   c. $10.00
   d. $19.05

   ANS: B

24. During the month of July, Joel Mayer earned $2,000. Joel has been on the payroll all year at a salary of $2,000 per month. Salaries are paid at the end of each month. Assume that FICA taxes are 7.65 percent of wages up to $50,000; state unemployment tax is 5.0 percent of wages up to $13,000; and federal unemployment tax is 0.8 percent of wages up to $13,000. Assume that Joel has voluntary withholdings of $75 (in addition to taxes) and that federal and state income tax withholdings are $300 and $100, respectively. What is the employer's payroll tax expense for the month of July, assuming that Joel Mayer is the only employee?
   a. $58
   b. $211
   c. $75
   d. $611

   ANS: B

Taxes

25. Unger Sporting Goods Company sold a pair of skis for cash. It recorded the sale as:

Account A	210	
Account B		200
Account C		10

   Given this entry, what would be the nature of Account C?
   a. Account C is a current liability.
   b. Account C is a long-term liability.
   c. Account C is a revenue.
   d. Account C is an asset.

   ANS: A

26. Sales Taxes Payable is normally classified as a(n)
   a. Current liability
   b. Long-term liability
   c. Asset
   d. Expense

   ANS: A

27. Property Taxes Payable would typically appear on the balance sheet as a
    a. Deferred liability
    b. Contra liability
    c. Current liability
    d. Long-term liability

    ANS: C

28. Property taxes are usually assessed by county or city governments based on a company's
    a. Owners' equity
    b. Cash-basis net income
    c. Accrual-basis net income
    d. Land, buildings, and other assets

    ANS: D

29. Income taxes shown on the income statement are based on
    a. Net income
    b. Gross margin
    c. Income before taxes
    d. Sales

    ANS: C

30. Deferred income taxes arise from
    a. Differences between accounting standards and IRS rules
    b. The postponement of tax payments due to cash shortage
    c. A special tax created by the IRS
    d. A net loss

    ANS: A

31. The period covered by the assessment of property taxes usually covers a
    a. Calendar year
    b. Fiscal year
    c. Budgeted year
    d. Taxable year

    ANS: B

32. Which of the following is NOT a legal liability?
    a. Accounts Payable
    b. Pension Benefit Obligation
    c. Sales Tax Payable
    d. Deferred Tax Liability

    ANS: D

33. Marino, Inc. makes a sale and collects a total of $214, which includes a 7 percent sales tax. The amount credited to Sales Revenue is
    a. $214
    b. $199
    c. $229
    d. $200

    ANS: D

34. Marino, Inc. makes a sale and collects a total of $214, which includes a 7 percent sales tax. The amount credited to Sales Tax Payable is
    a. $14
    b. $15
    c. $16
    d. None of the above

    ANS: A

Contingencies

35. Which of the following types of contingency would NOT be disclosed on the financial statements until it has been resolved?
    a. A lawsuit against our company and it is probable that we will lose
    b. A lawsuit against our company and it is reasonably possible we will lose
    c. A lawsuit we have filed against a competitor and it is probable that we will win
    d. All of the above must be disclosed on the financial statements

    ANS: C

36. A contingent liability is recorded by making the appropriate journal entry if the likelihood of a loss from a contingency is
    a. Remote
    b. Reasonably possible
    c. Probable
    d. Negligible

    ANS: C

37. A footnote disclosure only is required if the likelihood of a loss due to a contingency is
    a. Remote
    b. Reasonably possible
    c. Probable
    d. Negligible

    ANS: B

38. What makes environmental liabilities unique among contingent liabilities?
    a. It is more difficult to estimate the costs.
    b. It is more difficult to estimate the likelihood of a loss.
    c. A company need not disclose environmental liabilities.
    d. All of the above are true of environmental liabilities.

    ANS: A

39. Which of the following is the appropriate disclosure in the financial statements for a contingent gain?
     a.   Under "other revenues and gains"
     b.   Under "extraordinary gains"
     c.   Under "unrealized gains"
     d.   None of the above

     ANS: D

40. No disclosure is required for contingent liabilities that are
     a.   Probable
     b.   Remote
     c.   Possible
     d.   Reasonably possible

     ANS: B

Capitalize versus Expense

41. Which of the following expenditures should be expensed in the year incurred?
     a.   Equipment
     b.   Targeted advertising
     c.   Prepaid rent
     d.   Research and development

     ANS: D

42. The required recording of research and development expenditures has which of the following effects on the financial statements?
     a.   Understatement of research and development expense
     b.   Understatement of research and development assets
     c.   Overstatement of research and development assets
     d.   None of the above

     ANS: D

43. Which of the following is the required treatment of research and development costs under international accounting rules?
     a.   Research and development costs are expensed as incurred.
     b.   Research and development costs are capitalized.
     c.   Research costs are expensed and development costs are capitalized.
     d.   Research costs are capitalized and development costs are expensed.

     ANS: C

44. Which of the following types of advertising is typically capitalized?
     a.   Specialty catalogs
     b.   Radio
     c.   Television
     d.   Newspaper

     ANS: A

45. On December 31, the trial balance of Cubico Company included the following accounts with debit balances:

Prepaid Advertising	$1,500
Advertising Expense	5,400

If it is determined that the cost of advertising applicable to future periods is $3,300, the correct adjusting entry would
a. Debit Advertising Expense $3,300; credit Prepaid Advertising $3,300
b. Debit Prepaid Advertising $1,800; credit Advertising Expense $1,800
c. Debit Advertising Expense $1,800; credit Prepaid Advertising $1,800
d. Debit Prepaid Advertising $3,300; credit Advertising Expense $3,300

ANS: B

Summarizing Operations on an Income Statement

46. Items incurred or earned from activities peripheral to normal operations are classified as
a. Extraordinary gains and losses
b. Other revenues and expenses
c. Discontinued operations
d. Operating gains and losses

ANS: B

47. Which of the following is NOT a criterion for qualifying as an extraordinary item?
a. Material in amount
b. Infrequent in occurrence
c. Unusual in nature
d. Peripheral to normal operations

ANS: D

48. Which of the following are reported on the income statement along with their tax effects?
a. Other revenues
b. Extraordinary items
c. Operating expenses
d. Other expenses

ANS: B

49. Earnings per share is NOT calculated on which of the following amounts?
a. Net income
b. Extraordinary items
c. Other revenue and gains
d. Income before extraordinary items

ANS: C

50. Which of the following items would NOT be classified in the "Other Revenues and Expenses" section of the income statement?
    a. Dividends on investments
    b. Gain on sale of buildings
    c. Interest expense
    d. Property tax expense

    ANS: D

51. Which of the following items would be classified in the "Other Revenues and Expenses" section of the income statement?
    a. Loss due to flood
    b. Loss on sale of land
    c. Administrative salaries expense
    d. Income tax expense

    ANS: B

52. Earnings per share is equal to
    a. Total revenues divided by total shares of capital stock
    b. Net income divided by total shares of capital stock
    c. Total expenses divided by total shares of capital stock
    d. Net income divided by newly issued shares of capital stock

    ANS: B

53. Which of the following items should be reported as an extraordinary item?
    a. Gains or losses from major foreign currency revaluations
    b. The effects of a strike
    c. Earthquake damage
    d. Gain or loss on disposal of a business segment

    ANS: C

54. Which of the following events would be considered an extraordinary item?
    a. An airline experienced a significant loss due to a strike by employees of the company who provide its aircraft maintenance.
    b. A food cannery was faced with a large loss of inventory of canned soups due to government condemnation because of possible botulism contamination; the company had never experienced a similar situation in its history.
    c. A company, located on an island which has experienced severe flooding three times in the past 25 years, was subjected to a heavy loss of physical plant due to flooding.
    d. A medical corporation was required to pay a patient damages equal to three times its average net income. The corporation had experienced suits of this nature in the past, but the amount of the losses had never exceeded 5 percent of the corporation's average net income.

    ANS: B

55. Under which of the following conditions would hurricane damage be considered an extraordinary item for financial reporting purposes?
    a. Under any circumstance, hurricane damage should be classified as an extraordinary item
    b. Only if hurricanes are unusual in nature and infrequent in occurrence in the geographic area
    c. Only if hurricanes are normal in the geographic area but do not occur frequently
    d. Only if hurricanes occur frequently in the geographic area but have been insured against

    ANS: B

56. Romulus Corporation incurred the following losses during 2006:

    - Loss of $150,000 was incurred in the abandonment of equipment.
    - Accounts receivable of $30,000 were written off as uncollectible.
    - Several factories were shut down during a strike at a cost of $240,000.
    - Loss of $100,000 was sustained as a result of flood damage, an unusual and infrequent occurrence.

    Ignoring income taxes, what amount of loss should Romulus report as extraordinary on its annual income statement?
    a. $100,000
    b. $150,000
    c. $270,000
    d. $520,000

    ANS: A

57. On November 1, Salvo Sporting Supplies, a calendar-year company, sold inventory that cost $300 for $450. The customer signed a four-month, 15 percent note in payment. On December 31, Salvo should
    a. Debit Interest Receivable for $67.50
    b. Debit Interest Revenue for $67.50
    c. Credit Interest Revenue for $11.25
    d. Credit Interest Receivable for $3.75

    ANS: C

58. During the year, Perez Company earned revenues of $113,625 and incurred $98,000 for various operating expenses. There are 1,250 shares of stock outstanding. Earnings per share is
    a. $12.50
    b. $12.80
    c. $8.80
    d. $8.50

    ANS: A

59. Assante Corporation reported the following data for the period: earnings per share, $2.40; retained earnings, $27,000; revenues, $75,000; capital stock, $15,000; expenses, $63,000. Given the above information, how many shares of stock are outstanding?
   a. 9,000
   b. 5,000
   c. 4,000
   d. 3,500

   ANS: B

60. The following information was taken from the records of Elton Corporation for the period ending December 31, 2006:

Advertising expense	$1,200
Equipment	800
Depreciation expense	50
Accounts receivable	1,500
Notes payable	6,000
Retained earnings	8,420
Utilities expense	1,335
Revenues	4,865
Dividends	975
Interest receivable	125
Rent expense	660

   Assuming that 6,000 shares of stock are outstanding, earnings per share is approximately
   a. $1.40
   b. $0.40
   c. $0.27
   d. $0.23

   ANS: C

61. The following information is from Olmos Corp.'s records at December 31, 2006:

Advertising expense	$15,220
Income tax expense	14,125
Accounts payable	13,450
Dividends paid	9,800
Retained earnings (12/01/03)	57,860
Consulting fees revenue	97,675
Rent expense	12,760
Supplies expense	10,450

   If Olmos has 2,000 shares of stock outstanding, earnings per share is approximately
   a. $34.62
   b. $22.56
   c. $16.94
   d. $15.59

   ANS: B

62. Diluted earnings per share includes stock transactions that might occur in the future such as
    a. Sale of additional shares of stock
    b. Exercise of stock options
    c. Declaration of dividends
    d. All of the above

    ANS: B

PROBLEMS

1. Amy Tan earns $4,500 per month as the only employee of a small shop. FICA taxes on her salary are 7.65 percent of the first $50,000. Federal income taxes are withheld at the rate of 30 percent and state income taxes at the rate of 7 percent. Her employer is subject to 0.8 percent FUTA tax and 3.0 percent SUTA tax.

   Prepare the journal entries to be made by her employer for the month of January. (Round to the nearest dollar.)

   ANS:

Jan. 31	Salaries Expense...	4,500	
	Federal Withholding Taxes Payable............		1,350
	State Withholding Taxes Payable................		315
	FICA Taxes Payable (employee).................		344*
	Cash (or Wages Payable)............................		2,491
31	Payroll Tax Expense..	515	
	FICA Taxes Payable (employer)		344*
	Federal Unemployment Taxes Payable		36*
	State Unemployment Taxes Payable		135
	Rounded		

2. Goldberg Company's accounting records contained the following information for a current year:

Pension service cost............	$ 142,500	Pension obligation,	
Pension fund assets,		year-end	$1,653,000
year-end	1,757,550		
Pension related interest		Return on pension fund	
cost for the year.................	152,000	assets for the year........	190,000

1. Indicate what pension amount Goldberg will report in its balance sheet at year-end.
2. Compute the amount of pension expense shown on the income statement for the year.

ANS:

1. Pension fund assets and pension obligation are offset against each other to show a net pension asset or net pension obligation.

   $1,757,500 – $1,653,000 = <u>$104,500 net pension asset</u>

2.
Pension service cost..	$142,500
Pension related interest...	152,000
Return on fund assets..	(190,000)
Pension expense..	$104,500

3. Gribble's fiscal year is the calendar year. During the month of July 2006, the following tax related events occurred at Gribble:

- Received a property tax summary from the county government for the period July 1, 2005, through June 30, 2006. The property tax for that period was $7,500. This bill was prepaid on December 30, 2005.
- Sales of $100,000 were made during the month. The sales tax rate is 6 percent, and the sales tax liability was recorded as sales were recorded.
- Income before taxes for the second quarter (ended on June 30, 2006) was $70,000, and the income tax rate is 30 percent.

Prepare journal entries to record:
1. The proper amount of property tax expense to June 30, 2006.
2. The payment of the sales tax collected during June.
3. The recognition of the income taxes for the second quarter.

ANS:

1.	Property Tax Expense...	3,750	
	Prepaid Property Taxes.....................................		3,750
2.	Sales Tax Payable	6,000	
	Cash		6,000
3.	Income Tax Expense...	21,000	
	Income Taxes Payable		21,000

4. Indicate the appropriate accounting treatment for each independent situation shown below:

    1. Assante Corporation is the defendant in an age-discrimination lawsuit for $10 million. The company's lawyers believe there is a 95 percent probability that Assante will lose the case and that the loss will more than likely be $9 million.
    2. Otay, Inc. has been accused of violating several federal regulatory laws. If found guilty, the company will incur significant fines and penalties. The company's attorneys feel the accusations are baseless and that there is only a 5 percent chance that the company will be found guilty.
    3. Grammar Company is being accused of fraudulent reporting. The company's lawyers believe there is a 45 percent chance of losing the case.
    4. Ortiz Corporation is suing another company for patent infringement. The attorneys for Ortiz feel there is an 80 percent chance that they will win the case and that the court will award them a $5 million judgment.

    ANS:

    1. A 95 percent probability is likely to be interpreted as probable. The liability and associated loss should be formally recorded in the accounting records, and a footnote disclosure should be made as well.
    2. A 5 percent chance is likely to be interpreted as remote. No information need be disclosed in the notes to the financial statements.
    3. A 45 percent probability falls somewhere between remote and probable. This would typically be interpreted as reasonably possible. If so, a footnote disclosure is appropriate.
    4. Gain contingencies are not recognized.

5. Indicate whether the following independent expenditures should be capitalized or expensed. Explain your answers.

    1. Cruz Company spent $500,000 on new equipment. The equipment has an estimated useful life of 12 years.
    2. Carver Corporation spent $5 million researching a new production process. The company expects to reduce operating costs significantly when the result of the research is implemented next year.
    3. Kids Klothes, Inc. has spent $2 million creating a targeted advertising campaign that will motivate regular customers of the company's on-line service to buy new clothes.
    4. Hype.com is paying $400,000 for newspaper advertising on its new product line. The company expects the ad will generate increased sales for the next two years.

    ANS:

    1. Capitalize. This is a depreciable asset whose service will help generate future revenues over its useful life.
    2. Expense. Research and development costs are expensed as incurred.
    3. Capitalize. This is targeted advertising directed at specific past customers.
    4. Expense. This is advertising pertaining to a new product and not directed at specific past customers.

6. Kline Corporation has taken the following information from the accounting records on December 31, 2006. Prepare an income statement for the year ended December 31, 2006. Assume that there are 50,000 shares of capital stock outstanding.

Gross sales revenue	$1,721,500
Income tax expense	48,000
Insurance expense (general and administrative)	950
Automobile expense (selling)	1,750
Miscellaneous selling expense	6,600
Payroll tax expense (selling)	1,550
Rent expense (selling)	9,000
Sales salaries expense	150,000
Cost of goods sold	1,270,500
Interest expense	23,000
Interest revenue	6,500
Advertising and promotion expense	80,000
Sales returns and allowances	6,000
Office supplies expense	5,550
Administrative salaries expense	70,000
Earthquake loss (net of taxes)	20,000

ANS:

Kline Corporation
Income Statement
For the Year Ended December 31, 2006

Gross sales revenue..	$1,721,500	
Less: Sales returns and allowances...........................	6,000	
Net sales revenue		$1,715,500
Less: Cost of goods sold		1,270,500
Gross margin..		$ 445,000
Expenses		
Selling expenses:		
Sales salaries expense	$ 150,000	
Advertising and promotion expense	80,000	
Automobile expense	1,750	
Rent expense..	9,000	
Payroll tax expense	1,550	
Miscellaneous selling expenses	6,600	
Total selling expenses...	$ 248,900	
General and administrative expenses:		
Administrative salaries expense............................	$ 70,000	
Office supplies expense	5,550	
Insurance expense...	950	
Total general and administrative expenses.............	$ 76,500	
Total selling, general, and administrative expenses....		325,400
Operating income..		$ 119,600
Other expenses and revenues:		
Interest revenue..	$ 6,500	
Interest expense	(23,000)	(16,500)
Income before taxes..		$ 103,100
Income tax expense...		48,000
Income before extraordinary items		$ 55,100
Earthquake loss (net of taxes)...................................		20,000
Net income...		$ 35,100
Earnings per share:		
Before extraordinary items		$ 1.10
Extraordinary loss...		0.40
Net income		$ 0.70

Chapter 9—Completing the Operating Cycle—Quiz A

Name_____   Section_____

TRUE/FALSE

Circle T or F to indicate whether each of the following statements is true or false.

T F 1. Taxes deducted from an employee's salary represent an expense for the employer.

T F 2. The portion of FICA taxes paid by the employee represents an expense of the employer.

T F 3. Sales taxes are borne by customers but remitted by the seller.

T F 4. Federal unemployment taxes are borne by employees but remitted by the employer.

T F 5. When a retailer collects a sales tax from a customer, the retailer accounts for the tax collected as sales revenue.

T F 6. FICA taxes are usually paid in equal amounts by both employers and employees.

T F 7. Sales taxes collected from customers are usually shown on the balance sheet as a liability when collected.

T F 8. Property taxes are often assessed for calendar years.

T F 9. Income taxes are based on the amount of net sales.

T F 10. Deferred taxes arise from differences between accounting rules and IRS regulations.

Name_____   Section_____

MATCHING

In the spaces provided, write the letter of the term for each of the following definitions:

    a.   Defined contribution plan
    b.   Income taxes payable
    c.   Accrued expenses
    d.   Social security taxes (FICA)
    e.   Extraordinary items
    f.   Other revenues and expenses
    g.   Contingency
    h.   Sales taxes payable
    i.   Prepaid expenses
    j.   Compensated absences

1. _____ The value of vacation and such days earned during the year.

2. _____ Taxes imposed on employee and employer; used mainly to provide retirement benefits.

3. _____ Expenses that have been incurred, but not yet paid.

4. _____ An uncertain circumstance involving a potential gain or loss that will not be resolved until some future event occurs.

5. _____ Nonoperating gains and losses that are unusual in nature, infrequent in occurrence, and material in amount.

6. _____ The amount expected to be paid to the federal and state governments based on taxable income.

7. _____ Items that are paid in advance of being incurred.

8. _____ Requires that a company place a certain amount of money into a pension fund each year for its employees.

9. _____ Money collected from customers that must be remitted to local governments and other taxing authorities.

10. _____ Items incurred or earned from activities that are outside the normal operations of a firm.

Quiz Solutions

Quiz A

1. F
2. F
3. T
4. F
5. F
6. T
7. T
8. F
9. F
10. T

Quiz B

1. j
2. d
3. c
4. g
5. e
6. b
7. i
8. a
9. h
10. f

MULTIPLE CHOICE

Nature of Operating Assets

1. Which of the following is NOT a current asset?
   a. Marketable Securities
   b. Cash
   c. Accounts Receivable
   d. Property, Plant, and Equipment

   ANS: D

2. The caption "property, plant, and equipment" generally includes
   a. Assets purchased for sale
   b. Depreciable assets
   c. Current assets
   d. Assets that have no future service potential

   ANS: B

3. The category of long-term assets includes
   a. Land
   b. Goodwill
   c. Equipment
   d. All of the above

   ANS: D

4. Assets that are not acquired for resale, but used by a business to generate revenues are
   a. Land
   b. Goodwill
   c. Inventory
   d. Both a and b

   ANS: D

5. An asset that does not have physical substance is
   a. Land
   b. Goodwill
   c. Equipment
   d. Supplies

   ANS: B

6. The major difference between an expenditure that is capitalized and one that is expensed is usually
    a. The length of time of the benefits from the expenditure
    b. The amount of the expenditure
    c. Whether or not the expenditure was approved by management
    d. Whether the expenditure involves inventory

    ANS: A

Deciding Whether to Acquire a Long-Term Operating Asset

7. The process of comparing the cost of an asset to the value of expected cash inflows, after adjusting for the time value of money, is called
    a. Acquisition analysis
    b. Present value analysis
    c. Capital budgeting
    d. Long-term asset budgeting

    ANS: C

8. To properly evaluate the purchase of a long-term asset, the expected future cash flows must be adjusted for
    a. Property taxes
    b. Interest
    c. Time value of money
    d. Future revenues

    ANS: C

Accounting for Acquisition of Property, Plant, and Equipment

9. Freight costs incurred when an operating asset is purchased should generally be
    a. Expensed in the period incurred
    b. Deducted from the accumulated depreciation account
    c. Added to the cost of the new asset
    d. Not recorded in the accounts

    ANS: C

10. The party who owns an asset that is rented to another is referred to as the
    a. Lessor
    b. Mortgagee
    c. Lessee
    d. Principal

    ANS: A

11. Which of the following is NOT a consideration in classifying a lease?
    a. Value of the asset on the lessor's books
    b. Economic life of the asset
    c. Present value of the lease payments
    d. Whether the lease is cancelable

    ANS: A

12. A noncancelable lease should be recorded as a capital lease if
    a. The present value of the lease payments is 75 percent or more of the fair market value of the leased asset
    b. Title to the asset transfers to the lessee by the end of the lease term
    c. The lessee is given an option to purchase the asset at its fair market value
    d. Any one of the above criteria is met

    ANS: B

13. Furniture with a list price of $3,000 is purchased on account for $2,500. Which of the following entries properly records this transaction?
    a. Furniture..................................... 2,500
          Cash... 2,500
    b. Furniture..................................... 3,000
          Accounts Payable 3,000
    c. Furniture..................................... 2,500
          Accounts Payable 2,500
    d. Furniture..................................... 3,000
          Cash... 3,000

    ANS: C

14. How would a company classify a two-year lease that requires monthly rental payments of $1,000 and also requires that the company must move out of the building, or negotiate a new lease when the current one ends?
    a. Capital lease
    b. Sales lease
    c. Operating lease
    d. Buy-back lease

    ANS: C

15. Leased assets are capitalized at
    a. Their historical cost
    b. The future value of the future lease payments
    c. The sum of the future lease payments
    d. The present value of the future lease payments

    ANS: D

16. How many of the criteria for determining whether a lease should be classified as an operating lease or a capital lease must a noncancelable lease meet to be recorded as a capital lease?
    a. 1
    b. 2
    c. 3
    d. 4

    ANS: A

17. Which of the following is NOT a reason for leasing rather than purchasing an asset?
    a. Avoiding a significant cash outlay for a down payment
    b. Avoiding the risks of obsolescence
    c. Avoiding the recognition of additional debt on the balance sheet
    d. None of the above

    ANS: D

18. Which of the following is NOT a capitalizable cost on a self-constructed asset?
    a. Total materials used
    b. Total labor costs incurred
    c. Total company overhead
    d. Interest associated with money borrowed to finance the construction project

    ANS: C

19. The cost assigned to the individual assets acquired in a basket purchase is based on their relative
    a. Historical costs
    b. Fair market values
    c. Book values
    d. Depreciable costs

    ANS: B

20. Boone Company purchased a piece of machinery by paying $5,000 cash. In addition to the purchase price, the company incurred $100 freight charges. The machine has an estimated useful life of five years and will require $125 for insurance over that period. Boone Company would record the cost of the machine at
    a. $5,000
    b. $5,100
    c. $5,125
    d. $5,225

    ANS: B

21. Radner Shipping purchased a truck and a trailer for $54,000. An appraisal has set the fair market values of the truck and the trailer at $19,000 and $38,000, respectively. At what amount should Radner record the truck?
    a. $18,000
    b. $19,000
    c. $36,000
    d. $38,000

    ANS: A

22. Henner Corporation made a basket purchase of three pieces of machinery for $24,000. The fair market values of the machinery were determined to be as follows:

Machine A	$ 4,500
Machine B...	9,000
Machine C...	13,500

What cost should Henner record for Machine C?
a. $13,500
b. $10,500
c. $9,000
d. $12,000

ANS: D

23. Land and a building were purchased for a sum of $100,000. If appraisals set the value of the land at $70,000 and the building at $35,000, the building will be recorded at
a. $30,000
b. $33,333
c. $40,000
d. $66,666

ANS: B

24. On January 1, 2006, Alberta Company purchased land and a building for $800,000. At the time of the purchase, it was estimated that the building had a market value of $500,000. On January 5, Alberta installed a fence around the property at a cost of $5,000. Given this information, the journal entry to record the purchase of the land and building would include a debit to Land for
a. $305,000
b. $300,000
c. $295,000
d. $500,000

ANS: B

25. On January 1, 2006, Alberta Company purchased land and a building for $800,000. At the time of the purchase, it was estimated that the building had a market value of $500,000. On January 5, Alberta installed a fence around the property at a cost of $5,000. Given this information, the entry to record the cost of the fence would include a
a. Debit to Land for $5,000
b. Debit to Fence Expense for $5,000
c. Credit to Land for $5,000
d. Debit to Land Improvements for $5,000

ANS: D

26. A company leases an asset for a seven-year period under a capital lease and agrees to pay an annual rental of $15,000. The initial entry to record this transaction, assuming the present value of the lease payments is $84,000, would include a
    a. Debit to Lease Expense for $15,000
    b. Debit to Lease Expense for $12,000
    c. Debit to Lease Asset for $84,000
    d. Credit to Lease Liability for $12,000

    ANS: C

27. Assume a company enters into a capital lease on January 1, 2006, to acquire the use of a machine for five years. The present value of the lease payments is $60,000, and the interest rate is 12 percent. If annual rental payments of $18,000 are due at the end of each year, the journal entry to record the first annual payment on December 31, 2006, would include a debit to
    a. Lease Expense, $18,000
    b. Interest Expense, $7,200 and Lease Expense, $10,800
    c. Interest Expense, $7,200 and Lease Liability, $10,800
    d. Interest Expense, $9,000 and Lease Liability, $9,000

    ANS: C

28. Assume that a company leases a truck for a five-year period under a capital lease and agrees to pay an annual rental of $8,000 at the end of each year. If the present value of the lease payments is $29,600, the entry to record the leasing transaction would include
    a. A debit to Lease Expense of $29,600
    b. A debit to Leased Truck of $29,600
    c. A debit to Leased Truck of $40,000
    d. A credit to Rent Payable of $8,000

    ANS: B

29. On January 1, 2006, Eugene Inc. entered into a capital lease to acquire the use of a computer for five years. The present value of the lease payments is $42,500, the applicable interest rate is 10 percent, and payments of $12,000 are due at the end of each year. The entry to record the first $12,000 payment on December 31, 2006, will include a debit to
    a. Lease Expense for $12,000
    b. Interest Expense for $12,000
    c. Leased Computer for $42,500
    d. Lease Liability for $7,750

    ANS: D

Calculating and Recording Depreciation Expense

30. The undepreciated cost of an asset is referred to as the
    a. Salvage value
    b. Book value
    c. Market value
    d. Sales value

    ANS: B

31. How is Accumulated Depreciation classified?
    a. Equity
    b. Liability
    c. Contra-asset
    d. Expense

    ANS: C

32. A depreciable asset's book value can never be less than its
    a. Historical cost
    b. Fair market value
    c. Capitalized cost
    d. Salvage value

    ANS: D

33. The accumulated depreciation account is credited when
    a. An asset is traded for a similar asset
    b. A new asset is purchased
    c. The depreciation expense for the year is recorded
    d. An asset is traded for a dissimilar asset

    ANS: C

34. Which of the following assets is NOT usually depreciated, depleted, or amortized?
    a. Furniture
    b. Mineral deposits
    c. Land
    d. Patents

    ANS: C

35. Depreciation can best be described as a method of
    a. Accumulating funds for the replacement of assets
    b. Reducing the carrying cost of assets to current market values
    c. Deriving tax benefits
    d. Allocating the costs of assets over their useful lives

    ANS: D

36. Another name for residual value is
    a. Book value
    b. Salvage value
    c. Carrying value
    d. Current value

    ANS: B

37. The book value of an asset is the
   a. Original cost of the asset
   b. Market value of the asset
   c. Total of all expenses associated with the asset
   d. Acquisition cost of the asset less any accumulated depreciation on the asset

   ANS: D

38. When the cost of equipment is divided by its estimated useful life, the result is referred to as
   a. Book value
   b. Accumulated depreciation
   c. Carrying value
   d. Depreciation expense

   ANS: D

39. In order to calculate periodic depreciation expense, which of the following need NOT be known about an asset?
   a. Its acquisition cost
   b. Its estimated salvage value
   c. The amount of the cash down payment
   d. Its estimated useful life

   ANS: C

40. On January 1, 2006, Powers Press purchased equipment at a cost of $6,300. The equipment had an estimated useful life of three years or 15,000 hours. The equipment will have a $600 salvage value at the end of its life. The depreciation expense for the year ending December 31, 2006, using the straight-line method would be
   a. $1,900
   b. $1,883
   c. $475
   d. $471

   ANS: A

41. On January 1, 2006, Powers Press purchased equipment at a cost of $6,300. The equipment had an estimated useful life of three years or 15,000 hours. The equipment will have a $600 salvage value at the end of its life. The equipment was used 3,250 hours in 2006. The depreciation expense for the year ending December 31, 2006, using the units-of-production method would be
   a. $1,900
   b. $1,235
   c. $3,250
   d. $1,365

   ANS: B

42. Rapid Deliveries purchased a delivery truck on July 1, 2006, at a cost of $11,200. The truck has an estimated useful life of four years or 40,000 miles and a salvage value of $800. If the truck was driven 5,200 miles during 2006, the depreciation expense for 2006 under the units-of-production method would be
    a. $1,300
    b. $1,352
    c. $1,456
    d. $728

    ANS: B

43. Spears Corporation bought a machine on January 1, 2005. In purchasing the machine, the company paid $50,000 cash and signed an interest-bearing note for $100,000. The estimated useful life of the machine is five years, after which time the salvage value is expected to be $15,000. The machine is expected to produce 67,500 widgets during its useful life. Given this information, if 10,000 widgets are produced in 2006, how much depreciation should be recorded in 2006, assuming that Spears Corporation uses the units-of-production depreciation method?
    a. $22,222
    b. $20,000
    c. $30,000
    d. $40,000

    ANS: B

44. Coppola Company purchased a machine on January 1, 2005, for $20,000 cash. In addition, Coppola paid $4,000 to have the machine delivered and installed. The estimated useful life of the machine is four years, after which time it is expected to have a salvage value of $8,000. It is also estimated that the machine will produce 200,000 units of product during its useful life. Assuming that the straight-line depreciation method is used, what will be the machine's book value on December 31, 2007?
    a. $8,000
    b. $12,000
    c. $16,000
    d. $14,000

    ANS: B

45. Wings Manufacturing Company purchased a new machine on July 1, 2005. It was expected to produce 200,000 units of product over its estimated useful life of eight years. Total cost of the machine was $600,000, and salvage value was estimated to be $60,000. Actual units produced by the machine in 2005 and 2006 are shown below:

2005	16,000 units
2006	30,000 units

    Wings reports on a calendar-year basis and uses the units-of-production method of depreciation. The amount of depreciation expense for this machine in 2006 would be
    a. $124,200
    b. $90,000
    c. $81,000
    d. $74,520

    ANS: C

Repairing and Improving Property, Plant, and Equipment

46. Which of the following is NOT a criterion for a capital expenditure?
    a. It must be significant in amount.
    b. It should benefit several periods.
    c. It should increase the productive life or capacity of an asset.
    d. None of the above

    ANS: D

47. Which of the following is a criterion for a capital expenditure?
    a. It must be significant in amount.
    b. It should benefit several periods.
    c. It should increase the productive life or capacity of an asset.
    d. All of the above

    ANS: D

48. An expenditure for the repair of an asset must be capitalized if it
    a. Maintains an asset in working order
    b. Requires prior approval by management
    c. Exceeds a fixed percentage of the asset's book value
    d. Benefits the company over several periods

    ANS: D

49. If a truck's engine is overhauled for $8,000, the journal entry would normally include a debit to
    a. Truck
    b. Notes Payable
    c. Depreciation
    d. Cash

    ANS: A

50. On January 1, 2004, Wayne's Waffle House purchased a freezer for $45,000. The freezer had an estimated useful life of 10 years and an estimated residual value of $3,000 at the time of purchase. Wayne spent $10,000 on January 1, 2006, to replace the freezer motor. This replacement increased the freezer's life by five years and the residual value by $2,000. Assuming that straight-line depreciation is used, what will be the depreciation expense for 2006?
    a. $3,200
    b. $3,585
    c. $8,320
    d. $3,431

    ANS: A

51. Giovanni Company purchased a tooling machine in 1996 for $120,000. The machine was being depreciated by the straight-line method over an estimated useful life of 20 years, with no salvage value. At the beginning of 2006, after 10 years of use, Giovanni paid $20,000 to overhaul the machine. Because of this improvement, the machine's estimated useful life would be extended an additional five years. What would be the depreciation expense recorded for the above machine in 2006?
    a. $4,000
    b. $5,333
    c. $6,000
    d. $7,333

    ANS: B

Recording Impairments of Asset Value

52. The entry to record an impairment loss on equipment would include which of the following?
    a. Credit to Loss on Impairment of Equipment
    b. Credit to Equipment Impairment
    c. Debit to Accumulated Depreciation—Equipment
    d. Debit to Cash

    ANS: C

53. The entry to record a gain on the increase in value of land would include which of the following?
    a. Credit to Gain on Land Increase
    b. Debit to Land
    c. Credit to Non-Impairment of Land
    d. None of these

    ANS: D

54. Occasionally, events occur that change an asset's value after purchase. Which of the following is true regarding these changes in value?
    a. Reductions in asset value are recognized.
    b. Increases in asset value are recognized.
    c. Both decreases and increases are recognized.
    d. Neither decreases nor increases are recognized.

    ANS: A

55. Under U.S. accounting rules (generally accepted accounting principles), an asset is impaired when the asset's
    a. Fair value is less than the book value
    b. Future cash inflows are less than the book value
    c. Market value is less than the book value
    d. Cost is less than the book value

    ANS: B

56. Once an asset has been determined to be impaired, the amount of impairment is measured as the asset's
    a. Book value minus the fair value
    b. Future cash inflows minus the book value
    c. Cost minus the book value
    d. Cost minus the fair value

    ANS: A

57. If an asset value recovers after an impairment loss has been recognized for the asset, what amount of restoration of that loss is recognized?
    a. The difference between the original loss and the new value
    b. The difference between the original cost and the new value
    c. The difference between the value recognized at the impairment and the new value
    d. None of the recovered value is recognized

    ANS: D

58. Xeno Corporation purchased a building for $400,000. The current book value of the building is $200,000, and the fair value is $180,000. The sum of future cash flows from the building is $160,000. The amount of impairment loss that should be recognized is
    a. $0
    b. $20,000
    c. $40,000
    d. $120,000

    ANS: B

59. Tanner Company purchased a building during 2004 for $600,000. From 2004 to 2006, $240,000 of depreciation was recorded. The current fair value is $350,000, and the sum of future cash flows from the building is $370,000. The amount of impairment that should be recognized is
    a. $0
    b. $10,000
    c. $20,000
    d. $30,000

    ANS: A

Disposal of Property, Plant, and Equipment

60. Which of the following is necessary when recording the disposal of a piece of equipment?
    a. Update the depreciation expense on the equipment to the date of sale
    b. Remove the equipment and related accumulated depreciation balances from the accounts
    c. Record any gain or loss on the disposal
    d. All the above are necessary

    ANS: D

61. On January 1, 2005, Kinnear Company purchased equipment at a cost of $20,000. The equipment has an estimated useful life of five years and a salvage value of $2,000. Kinnear Company uses the straight-line depreciation method for all its assets. Given this information, if Kinnear Company sells the equipment for $13,600 on December 31, 2006, it will have a(n)
   a. $2,000 loss
   b. $2,000 gain
   c. $800 loss
   d. $800 gain

   ANS: D

62. On January 1, 2005, Kinnear Company purchased equipment at a cost of $20,000. The equipment has an estimated useful life of five years and a salvage value of $2,000. Kinnear Company uses the straight-line depreciation method for all its assets. Given this information, if Kinnear Company scraps the equipment on December 31, 2006, it will have a loss of
   a. $18,000
   b. $0
   c. $12,800
   d. $5,600

   ANS: C

63. What is the gain or loss on the sale of an asset that originally cost $6,000, has accumulated depreciation of $2,500, and is sold for $3,000?
   a. $500 loss
   b. $1,500 loss
   c. $500 gain
   d. $3,000 loss

   ANS: A

64. A truck that cost $8,000 and was expected to last five years was scrapped after three years. If the truck was being depreciated on a straight-line basis (with no salvage value), the loss recognized on disposal would be
   a. $8,000
   b. $3,200
   c. $4,000
   d. $4,800

   ANS: B

65. A truck that cost $8,000 and was expected to last five years was scrapped after three years. If the truck was being depreciated on a straight-line basis (with no salvage value), the book value of the truck at the time of disposal was
   a. $8,000
   b. $4,800
   c. $2,000
   d. $3,200

   ANS: D

66. Suvari Company purchased a machine on November 1, 1997, for $148,000. At the time of acquisition, the machine was estimated to have a useful life of 10 years and a salvage value of $4,000. Suvari recorded monthly depreciation using the straight-line method. On July 1, 2006, the machine was sold for $13,000. What should be the loss recognized from the sale of the machine?
    a. $4,000
    b. $5,000
    c. $10,200
    d. $13,000

    ANS: C

Accounting for Intangible Assets

67. The balance sheet category "intangible assets" includes
    a.   Patents, trademarks, and franchises
    b.   Equipment, land, and buildings
    c.   Investments, receivables, and customer lists
    d.   Goodwill, inventory, and furnishings

    ANS: A

68. Which of the following accounts is generally NOT classified as an intangible asset?
    a.   Acquired customer lists
    b.   Goodwill
    c.   Equipment
    d.   Franchises

    ANS: C

69. Intangible assets are usually amortized using the
    a.   Straight-line method
    b.   Units-of-production method
    c.   Declining-balance method
    d.   Sum-of-the-years'-digits method

    ANS: A

70. Franchises are classified as
    a.   An expense
    b.   A current asset
    c.   An intangible asset
    d.   Property, plant, and equipment

    ANS: C

71. Which of the following is considered to be an intangible asset?
    a.   A gold mine
    b.   A copyright
    c.   Land improvement
    d.   Building

    ANS: B

72. Which of the following assets would normally involve a straight-line method of cost allocation?
    a. An oil well
    b. Land
    c. A timber tract
    d. Patent

    ANS: D

73. On March 3, 2006, Binford Tools acquired the following assets from Mace Hardware for $360,000:

	Book Value	Fair Market Value
Accounts Receivable	$ 58,000	$ 33,000
Inventory..	92,000	76,000
Equipment..	139,000	182,000
Patent	13,000	8,000

    How much goodwill should Binford record for this acquisition?
    a. $61,000
    b. $58,000
    c. $39,000
    d. $0

    ANS: A

74. The periodic allocation to expense of an intangible asset's cost is
    a. Amortization
    b. Depletion
    c. Depreciation
    d. Allocation

    ANS: A

75. Which intangible assets are amortized over their useful lives?
    a. Broadcast licenses
    b. Goodwill
    c. Patents
    d. All of the above

    ANS: C

76. The exclusive right to use a certain name or symbol is called a
    a. Franchise
    b. Patent
    c. Trademark
    d. Copyright

    ANS: C

EXPANDED MATERIAL

Accelerated Depreciation Methods

77. In order to calculate the third year's depreciation on an asset using the sum-of-the-years'-digits method, which of the following must be known about the asset?
    a. Its acquisition cost
    b. Its estimated salvage value
    c. Its estimated useful life
    d. All the above must be known

    ANS: D

78. Which of the following methods will always produce more depreciation expense in the early years of an asset's useful life than in the later years?
    a. Straight-line method
    b. Sum-of-the-years'-digits method
    c. Units-of-production method
    d. All of the above

    ANS: B

79. The sum-of-the-years'-digits method of depreciation is being used for a machine with a five-year estimated useful life. Which fraction would be applied to the cost to be depreciated in the second year?
    a. 4/5
    b. 2/5
    c. 4/15
    d. 2/15

    ANS: C

80. Which depreciation formula does NOT include salvage value?
    a. Productive-output method
    b. Straight-line method
    c. Sum-of-the-years'-digits method
    d. Double-declining-balance method

    ANS: D

81. On January 1, 2005, Heather Locks Corporation purchased drilling equipment for $11,500. The equipment has an estimated useful life of four years and a salvage value of $200. Given this information, if Heather uses the double-declining-balance method of depreciation and sells the equipment on December 31, 2006, for $3,000, it will have a(n)
    a. $2,750 loss
    b. $1,800 loss
    c. $1,562 gain
    d. $125 gain

    ANS: D

82. Soupy Soaps purchased a machine on January 1, 2006, for $18,000 cash. The machine has an estimated useful life of four years and a salvage value of $4,700. Soupy uses the double-declining-balance method of depreciation for all its assets. What will be the depreciation expense for 2006?
   a. $9,750
   b. $9,000
   c. $6,650
   d. $4,500

   ANS: B

83. Soupy Soaps purchased a machine on January 1, 2006, for $18,000 cash. The machine has an estimated useful life of four years and a salvage value of $4,700. Soupy uses the double-declining-balance method of depreciation for all its assets. What will be the machine's book value as of December 31, 2007?
   a. $5,100
   b. $4,700
   c. $4,500
   d. $4,300

   ANS: B

84. Spears Corporation bought a machine on January 1, 2005. In purchasing the machine, the company paid $50,000 cash and signed an interest-bearing note for $100,000. The estimated useful life of the machine is five years, after which time the salvage value is expected to be $15,000. The company uses the sum-of-the-years'-digits depreciation method. Given this information, how much depreciation expense would be recorded for the year ending December 31, 2006?
   a. $45,000
   b. $40,000
   c. $36,000
   d. $34,000

   ANS: C

85. On September 1, 2006, Tan Party Supplies purchased catering equipment for $4,680. The equipment is estimated to have a useful life of eight years and no salvage value. If Tan selected the sum-of-the-years'-digits method, what will be the depreciation expense for 2006?
   a. $1,040
   b. $347
   c. $260
   d. $130

   ANS: B

86. On September 1, 2006, Tan Party Supplies purchased catering equipment for $4,680. The equipment is estimated to have a useful life of eight years and no salvage value. Assuming that the sum-of-the-years'-digits method is used, what will be the depreciation expense for 2007?
      a. $1,040
      b. $1,008
      c. $997
      d. $910

      ANS: C

87. Ferrott Company purchased a machine that was installed and placed in service on January 2, 2005, at a total cost of $480,000. Salvage value was estimated at $80,000. The machine is being depreciated over 10 years by the double-declining-balance method. For the year 2006, Ferrott should record depreciation expense of
      a. $64,000
      b. $76,800
      c. $80,000
      d. $96,000

      ANS: B

88. On January 1, 2003, McMahan Company purchased equipment at a cost of $420,000. The equipment was estimated to have a useful life of five years and a salvage value of $60,000. McMahan uses the sum-of-the-years'-digits method of depreciation. What should the accumulated depreciation be at December 31, 2006?
      a. $240,000
      b. $280,000
      c. $336,000
      d. $360,000

      ANS: C

89. On January 1, 2004, Mena Co. purchased a new machine for $2,500,000. The machine has an estimated useful life of five years and a salvage value of $250,000. Mena uses the sum-of-the-years'-digits method of depreciation. The amount of depreciation expense for 2006 is
      a. $450,000
      b. $600,000
      c. $666,667
      d. $750,000

      ANS: A

90. On January 1, 2004, Mena Co. purchased a new machine for $2,500,000. The machine has an estimated useful life of five years and a salvage value of $250,000. Mena uses the double-declining-balance method of depreciation. The amount of depreciation expense for 2006 is
      a. $600,000
      b. $360,000
      c. $540,000
      d. $324,000

      ANS: B

A Comparison of Depreciation Methods

91. Four widely used methods of allocating the cost of equipment over its useful life are
    a. Depreciation, allocation, amortization, and depletion
    b. Straight-line, units-of-production, declining-balance, and sum-of-the-years'-digits
    c. FIFO, LIFO, weighted average, and specific identification
    d. None of the above

    ANS: B

92. The straight-line depreciation method usually provides for a higher amount of depreciation expense during the last year of an asset's life than does
    a. The sum-of-the-years'-digits method
    b. The 200% declining-balance method
    c. The 150% declining-balance method
    d. All of the above

    ANS: D

93. Which depreciation method usually allows the highest amount of net income to be reported during the first year an asset is owned?
    a. Straight-line method
    b. Double-declining-balance method
    c. Sum-of-the-years'-digits method
    d. Either b or c

    ANS: A

94. Which of the following depreciation methods cannot depreciate an asset below its salvage value?
    a. Straight-line method
    b. Units-of-production method
    c. Sum-of-the-years'-digits method
    d. All of the above

    ANS: D

95. Which of the following methods applies a declining depreciation rate each period to an asset's constant value?
    a. Straight-line method
    b. Units-of-production method
    c. Double-declining-balance method
    d. Sum-of-the-years'-digits method

    ANS: D

96. Which of the following depreciation methods most closely approximates the method used to deplete the cost of natural resources?
    a. Straight-line method
    b. Double-declining-balance method
    c. Sum-of-the-years'-digits method
    d. Units-of-production method

    ANS: D

97. Which of the following depreciation methods initially ignores salvage value in its calculation?
   a. Straight-line
   b. Sum-of-the-years'-digits
   c. Declining-balance
   d. Units-of-production

   ANS: C

98. Which of the following depreciation methods applies a uniform depreciation rate each period to an asset's book value?
   a. Straight-line
   b. Units-of-production
   c. Declining-balance
   d. Sum-of-the-years'-digits

   ANS: C

99. Unitas Company purchased a new $20,000 truck on January 1, 2006. The truck was expected to last four years and have no salvage value. During 2007, Unitas' depreciation expense on the truck was $6,000. Which of the following depreciation methods is Unitas Company using to depreciate the truck?
   a. Sum-of-the-years'-digits
   b. Double-declining-balance
   c. 150% declining-balance
   d. Straight-line

   ANS: A

Changes in Depreciation Estimates

100. If the estimate of an asset's useful life is changed, then
   a. Depreciation expense for all past periods must be recalculated
   b. There is no change in the amount of depreciation expense recorded for future years
   c. Only the depreciation expense in the remaining years is changed
   d. None of the above is true

   ANS: C

101. Shanahan Construction purchased a crane on January 1, 2004, for $102,750. At the time of purchase, the crane was estimated to have a useful life of six years and a residual value of $6,750. In 2006, Shanahan determined that the crane had a total useful life of seven years and a residual value of $4,500. If Shanahan uses the straight-line method of depreciation, what will be the 2006 depreciation expense for the crane?
   a. $16,000
   b. $13,250
   c. $9,464
   d. $8,000

   ANS: B

102. A truck that cost $8,000 was originally being depreciated over four years using the straight-line method with no salvage value. At the beginning of year 2, it was decided that the truck would last five more years. Given this information, the second year's depreciation would be
  a. $2,000
  b. $1,200
  c. $1,500
  d. $2,500

  ANS: B

103. Norton Company owns a machine that was bought on January 2, 2003, for $376,000. The machine was estimated to have a useful life of five years and a salvage value of $24,000. Norton uses the sum-of-the-years'-digits method of depreciation. At the beginning of 2006, Norton determined that the useful life of the machine should have been four years and the salvage value $35,200. For the year 2006, Norton should record depreciation expense on this machine of
  a. $19,200
  b. $44,400
  c. $59,200
  d. $70,400

  ANS: C

PROBLEMS

1. Saria Supply Printing Company, a calendar-year corporation, purchased a new scale for $165,000 on April 1, 2006. Additional costs of the scale included sales tax of 5 percent, freight-in of $5,800, and installation costs of $5,100. The scale has a useful life of five years with no salvage value.

  1. Compute the amount at which the scale should be recorded as an asset.
  2. Compute the depreciation expense for 2006 and 2007 using the straight-line depreciation method.

  ANS:

  1. $165,000 + $8,250 + $5,800 + $5,100 = $184,150

  2. 2006 .... $ 27,622.50
      2007 ....   36,830.00

2. On January 1, 2006, Versachi Industries, a calendar-year corporation, leased an airplane under a seven-year, noncancelable lease agreement that requires Versachi to pay the lessor $30,000 at the end of each year. The first payment is due December 31, 2006. The present value of the lease payments is $150,990, assuming an interest rate of 9 percent. At the end of the seven-year lease term, the airplane will be returned to the lessor unless Versachi chooses to purchase the airplane at its appraised market value. At January 1, 2006, the airplane has an estimated economic life of 10 years and a fair market value of $190,000.

1. Determine whether the airplane lease is an operating or a capital lease and explain your classification.
2. Without regard to your answer to (1), assume the lease is a capital lease and interest for 2006 is $13,600. Give the journal entries to record the lease at January 1 and the first payment at December 31, 2006.

ANS:

1. The airplane lease is an operating lease (a simple rental agreement) because it does not meet any of the four criteria for classification as a capital lease.

   a. Title to the airplane will not be transferred to the lessee.
   b. There is no bargain purchase option.
   c. The lease term is less than 75 percent of the asset's economic life (7 years/10 years = 70 percent).
   d. The present value of the lease payments is less than 90 percent of the asset's market value at the beginning of the lease term ($150,990/$190,000 = 79.5 percent).

2. Jan. 1   Leased Airplane.................................   150,990
               Lease Liability...............................   150,990

    Dec. 31   Lease Liability.................................   16,400
              Interest Expense   13,600
                 Cash...   30,000

3. Dilfer Corporation purchased equipment, a building, and land for $500,000 ($100,000 in cash and $400,000 in notes). After the purchase, the property was appraised. Fair market values were determined to be $120,000 for the equipment, $270,000 for the building, and $210,000 for the land.

Prepare the entry to record the purchase of this property by Dilfer Corporation.

ANS:

Equipment..	100,000	
Building	225,000	
Land	175,000	
Cash		100,000
Notes Payable		400,000

Allocation of basket purchase price:

Asset	FMV	Allocation	Cost
Equipment	$120,000	20% × $500,000	$100,000
Building	270,000	45% × $500,000	225,000
Land	210,000	35% × $500,000	175,000
	$600,000		$500,000

4. Saria Supply Company, a calendar-year corporation, purchased a new scale for $165,000 on April 1, 2006. Additional costs of the scale included sales tax of 5 percent, freight-in of $5,800, and installation costs of $5,100. The scale has a useful life of five years with no salvage value.

1. Compute the amount at which the scale should be recorded as an asset.
2. Compute the depreciation expense for 2006 and 2007 for each of the following depreciation methods:

   a. Double-declining-balance
   b. Sum-of-the-years'-digits

ANS:

1. $165,000 + $8,250 + $5,800 + $5,100 = $184,150

2.

	Double-Declining-Balance	Sum-of-the-Years'-Digits
2006	$55,245	$46,037.50
2007	51,562	52,175.83

5. On January 1, 2005, Milner Company purchased a machine for $115,000. The machine cost
    $1,000 to deliver and $4,000 to install. At the end of 10 years, Milner expects to sell the machine
    for $10,000. Compute depreciation expense for 2005 and 2006 using the following methods:

    1. Double-declining-balance
    2. 150% declining-balance
    3. Sum-of-the-years'-digits

    ANS:

    1. Double-declining-balance

2005:	$120,000 × 20% =	$24,000
2006:	($120,000 – $24,000) × 20% =	$19,200

    2. 150% declining-balance

2005:	$120,000 × 15% =	$18,000
2006:	($120,000 – $18,000) × 15% =	$15,300

    3. Sum-of-the-years'-digits: [10(11)/2] = 55

2005:	$110,000 × 10/55 =	$20,000
2006:	$110,000 × 9/55 =	$18,000

6. On May 1, 2005, Dominquez Inc. purchased equipment at a cost of $280,000. The equipment has
    an estimated salvage value of $12,000 and is being depreciated over an estimated life of six years.
    The company's policy is to recognize depreciation to the nearest whole month.

    Compute the depreciation expense (rounded to the nearest whole dollar) on this equipment for the
    years ended December 31, 2005 and 2006, using:

    1. Double-declining-balance
    2. Sum-of-the-years'-digits
    3. Straight-line

ANS:

1. Double-declining-balance

2005:	$280,000 × 33 1/3% × 8/12 =	$62,222
2006:	($280,000 – $62,222) × 33 1/3% =	$72,593

2. Sum-of-the-years'-digits: [6(7)/2] = 21

2005:	$268,000 × 6/21 × 8/12 =	$51,048
2006:	$268,000 × 6/21 × 4/12 =	$25,524
	$268,000 × 5/21 × 8/12 =	42,540
		$68,064

3. Straight-line

2005:	$268,000/6 × 8/12 =	$29,778
2006:	$268,000/6 =	$44,667

7. Mini Computers purchased a delivery truck four years ago for $30,000. Currently, the accumulated depreciation on the truck is $14,000. Prepare journal entries to show the sale of the truck assuming:

1. The truck is sold for $17,000.
2. The truck is sold for $14,000.
3. The truck is scrapped.

ANS:

1.	Cash...	17,000	
	Accumulated Depreciation—Delivery Truck.........	14,000	
	Delivery Truck...		30,000
	Gain on Sale of Delivery Truck.........................		1,000
2.	Cash...	14,000	
	Accumulated Depreciation—Delivery Truck.........	14,000	
	Loss on Sale of Delivery Truck............................	2,000	
	Delivery Truck..		30,000
3.	Accumulated Depreciation—Delivery Truck.........	14,000	
	Loss on Disposal of Delivery Truck......................	16,000	
	Delivery Truck..		30,000

8. In 1996, Young Company purchased land and a building at a cost of $1,000,000, $300,000 was allocated to land and $700,000 to the building. On December 31, 2005, the accounting records showed the following:

Land	$300,000
Building	700,000
Accumulated Depreciation—Building	400,000

During 2006, it is determined that the building is on the site of a toxic waste dump and the future cash flows associated with the land and building are less than the recorded total book value for these two assets. The fair value of the land and building is $100,000, of which $30,000 is land. Make any journal entries necessary to record the asset impairment.

ANS:

Loss on Impairment of Land and Building	500,000	
Accumulated Depreciation—Building	400,000	
Land ($300,000 – $30,000)		270,000
Building ($700,000 – $70,000)		630,000

9. On July 1, 2005, Macro Inc. purchased a franchise to operate a Blended Coffee Corner at a cost of $180,000. Assuming that Macro amortizes franchises over a 10-year period, prepare journal entries to record:

1. The purchase of the franchise on July 1, 2005.
2. The amortization of the franchise on December 31, 2005.
3. The amortization of the franchise on December 31, 2006.

ANS:

1.	Franchise	180,000	
	Cash		180,000
2.	Amortization Expense—Franchise	9,000	
	Franchise		9,000
	($180,000/10 = $18,000/2 for half year)		
3.	Amortization Expense—Franchise	18,000	
	Franchise		18,000
	($180,000/10)		

Chapter 10—Investments in Property, Plant, Equipment & in Intangible Assets—Quiz A

Name_____   Section_____

TRUE/FALSE

Circle T or F to indicate whether each of the following statements is true or false.

T F 1. The process of allocating the costs of intangible assets over their useful lives is called amortization.

T F 2. Delivery charges paid on a purchased asset are usually not included in the cost of the asset.

T F 3. Throughout its useful life, the book value of an asset is equal to its cost minus its accumulated depreciation.

T F 4. An expenditure to pay for changing the oil on a delivery truck would normally be expensed.

T F 5. Capitalized expenditures usually result in decreased depreciation expenses in future years.

T F 6. For most assets, book values do not equal market values.

T F 7. If an ordinary expenditure is erroneously recorded as a capital expenditure, net income in the year of the expenditure will be understated.

T F 8. If an asset is sold for less than its book value, a loss should be recognized.

T F 9. The owner of a building being rented by another company is called the lessor.

T F 10. A capital lease is a temporary rental agreement that usually requires the renter to return the leased property to the owner at the end of the lease or negotiate a new rental agreement.

Name_____   **Section**_____

MATCHING

In the spaces provided, write the letter of the definition for each of the following terms:

     a. Original cost minus accumulated depreciation.
     b. The purchase of two or more assets at a single price.
     c. The excess amount paid for a business over the fair market values of the individual assets and liabilities purchased.
     d. Increasing the cost of an asset for an expenditure that benefits more than one period.
     e. Allocating the cost of an intangible asset over its useful life.
     f. Proceeds minus book value.
     g. A name for the decrease in the value of long-term operating assets.
     h. A franchise is an example of this type of asset.
     i. Allocating the original cost of plant and equipment over the useful life.
     j. Another name for salvage value.

1. _____   Book value

2. _____   Gain or loss

3. _____   Amortization

4. _____   Impairment

5. _____   Depreciation

6. _____   Basket purchase

7. _____   Intangible asset

8. _____   Residual value

9. _____   Capitalization

10. _____   Goodwill

Name_____   Section_____

MULTIPLE CHOICE

1. On January 1, 2005, Gecho purchased computer equipment for $23,000 with an estimated useful life of four years and a salvage value of $400. If the double-declining-balance method of depreciation is used and the equipment is sold on December 31, 2006, for $250, Gecho will have a
   a. $250 gain
   b. $3,124 gain
   c. $3,600 loss
   d. $5,500 loss

2. A machine is purchased on January 1, 2006, for $36,000 cash. The machine has an estimated useful life of four years and a salvage value of $8,600. If the double-declining-balance method of depreciation is used, what will be the machine's book value as of December 31, 2007?
   a. $8,600
   b. $9,000
   c. $9,400
   d. $15,450

3. Trans-State Movers purchased a truck on January 1, 2004, for $51,375. At the time of purchase, the truck was estimated to have a useful life of six years and a residual value of $3,375. In 2006, Trans-State determined that the truck had a total useful life of 10 years and the residual value is unchanged. If Trans-State uses straight-line depreciation, the 2006 depreciation expense for the truck will be
   a. $4,000
   b. $4,732
   c. $6,625
   d. $8,000

4. On January 1, 2005, Meri-Ann Corporation purchased computer equipment for $23,000. The equipment had an estimated useful life of four years and a salvage value of $400. Meri-Ann uses the sum-of-the-years'-digits method of depreciation. The accumulated depreciation at December 31, 2006, would be
   a. $9,040
   b. $9,200
   c. $15,820
   d. $16,100

5. Bridges Construction Company purchased for $205,500 a machine on January 1, 2005, which has an estimated useful life of eight years and a salvage value of $13,500. In 2007, the machine is determined to have a total useful life of five years and the salvage value will be $7,500. If Bridges uses straight-line depreciation, what will be the balance of the accumulated depreciation account on December 31, 2007?
   a. $50,000
   b. $72,000
   c. $122,000
   d. $98,000

Quiz Solutions

Quiz A		Quiz B		Quiz C	
1.	T	1.	a	1.	d
2.	F	2.	f	2.	b
3.	T	3.	e	3.	a
4.	T	4.	g	4.	c
5.	F	5.	i	5.	d
6.	T	6.	b		
7.	F	7.	h		
8.	T	8.	j		
9.	T	9.	d		
10.	F	10.	c		

MULTIPLE CHOICE

Measuring Long-Term Liabilities

1. The two major categories of liabilities on a typical balance sheet are
   a. Current Liabilities and Long-Term Liabilities
   b. Wages Payable and Long-Term Liabilities
   c. Accounts Payable and Notes Payable
   d. Current Liabilities and Bonds Payable

   ANS: A

2. Which of the following is LEAST likely to be classified as a long-term liability?
   a. Interest Payable
   b. Pension Liability
   c. Lease Liability
   d. Mortgage Payable

   ANS: A

3. Which of the following statements is false?
   a. A liability is an item that involves a future transfer of resources.
   b. A liability is an item that is measurable in monetary terms.
   c. A liability is an item that represents an obligation of an enterprise.
   d. A liability is an item that must be paid in cash.

   ANS: D

4. Which of the following is LEAST likely to be classified as a long-term liability?
   a. Salaries Payable
   b. Mortgage Payable
   c. Lease Obligations
   d. Deferred Income Taxes Payable

   ANS: A

5. Assuming an annual interest rate of 10 percent, what factor from the tables would be used to calculate the present value of a specified payment to be received nine years from today?
   a. 0.4241
   b. 0.4224
   c. 2.3579
   d. 2.3674

   ANS: A

6. Assuming an annual interest rate of 8 percent, what factor from the tables would be used to calculate the amount that should be deposited in a bank today to grow to a specified amount nine years from today?
   a. 0.5002
   b. 0.5019
   c. 1.9926
   d. 1.9990

   ANS: A

7. You are purchasing a home. You know the monthly mortgage payment amount that you can afford, and you want to calculate the corresponding mortgage total amount. The technique you will use is the
   a. Future amount of $1
   b. Present value of $1
   c. Future amount of an annuity of $1
   d. Present value of an annuity of $1

   ANS: D

8. An investor wants to withdraw $8,000 (including principal) from an investment fund at the end of each year for 10 years. How should the investor compute the required initial investment at the beginning of the first year if the fund earns 10 percent compounded annually?
   a. $8,000 times the amount of an annuity of $1 at 10 percent at the end of each year for 10 years
   b. $8,000 divided by the amount of an annuity of $1 at 10 percent at the end of each year for 10 years
   c. $8,000 times the present value of an annuity of $1 at 10 percent at the end of each year for 10 years
   d. $8,000 divided by the present value of an annuity of $1 at 10 percent at the end of each year for 10 years

   ANS: C

9. Measuring and recording liabilities created in noncash transactions is based on the
   a. Cost principle
   b. Time value of money
   c. Matching principle
   d. Future value of money

   ANS: B

10. For a 10-year bond paying semiannual interest, how many compounding periods are there over the life of the bond?
    a. 5
    b. 10
    c. 15
    d. 20

    ANS: D

11. You have just purchased an automobile for $30,000 and will be financing it at 12 percent interest compounded monthly for five years. Your monthly payment will be
    a. $1,376.00
    b. $367.33
    c. $511.41
    d. $667.33

    ANS: D

12. If Cheng Corporation can invest $10,000 at 10 percent interest compounded annually, approximately how many years will it take for the $10,000 to grow to $20,000?
    a. Slightly more than 5 years
    b. Slightly more than 7 years
    c. Slightly more than 10 years
    d. Slightly more than 25 years

    ANS: B

13. If Kitna Company can invest $10,000 at 8 percent interest compounded annually, approximately how many years will it take for the $10,000 to grow to $20,000?
    a. 7 years
    b. 8 years
    c. 9 years
    d. 10 years

    ANS: C

14. The present value of $1 discounted for 10 years at 8 percent compounded annually is 0.4632. The present value of an annuity of $1 discounted for 10 years at 8 percent compounded annually is 6.7101. Given this information, how much would you receive for a 10-year, $1,000, 10 percent bond if interest is paid annually and the market rate of interest is 8 percent?
    a. $671.01
    b. $1,134.21
    c. $463.20
    d. $1,108.07

    ANS: B

15. Which of the following has the smallest present value?
    a. $2,000 discounted for 4 years at 8 percent compounded annually
    b. $2,000 discounted for 4 years at 8 percent compounded semiannually
    c. $3,000 discounted for 4 years at 8 percent compounded annually
    d. $3,000 discounted for 4 years at 8 percent compounded semiannually

    ANS: B

16. The present value of a $500 annuity for 10 years at 10 percent interest compounded annually is
    a. Less than $5,000
    b. Greater than $5,000
    c. Exactly $5,000
    d. Not determinable from the above data

    ANS: A

17. What is the approximate present value of $100 to be received in one year if interest is 12 percent compounded annually?
    a. $80
    b. $84
    c. $87
    d. $89

    ANS: D

18. The present value of $1,000 to be received in three years when interest is 12 percent compounded quarterly is computed by discounting at
    a. 3 percent for 12 periods
    b. 12 percent for 3 periods
    c. 4 percent for 9 periods
    d. 6 percent for 6 periods

    ANS: A

19. A one-year, $18,000, 8 percent note is signed on April 1. If the note is prematurely repaid on November 1 of the same year (without penalty), how much interest expense is incurred?
    a. $700
    b. $840
    c. $980
    d. $1,440

    ANS: B

20. What is the approximate present value of $100 to be received in two years if interest is 10 percent compounded annually?
    a. $83
    b. $90
    c. $110
    d. $121

    ANS: A

21. The present value of $1 discounted for 10 years at 8 percent compounded annually is 0.4632. The present value of an annuity of $1 discounted for 10 years at 8 percent compounded annually is 6.7101. Given this information, the present value of $80 to be received in 10 years at 8 percent compounded annually is
    a. $11.92
    b. $37.06
    c. $172.71
    d. $536.81

    ANS: B

22. The present value of $1 discounted for eight years at 10 percent compounded annually is 0.4665. The present value of an annuity of $1 discounted for eight years at 10 percent compounded annually is 5.3349. Given this information, how much must be invested today so that $100 can be received each year for eight years if money is worth 10 percent compounded annually?
    a. $46.65
    b. $214.36
    c. $187.44
    d. $533.49

    ANS: D

23. The present value of $1 discounted for eight years at 10 percent compounded annually is 0.4665. The present value of an annuity of $1 discounted for eight years at 10 percent compounded annually is 5.3349. Given this information and assuming a market interest rate of 10 percent, if equipment is purchased by issuing an eight-year, noninterest-bearing note for $300,000, the equipment would be entered in the accounting records at
    a. $56,233
    b. $112,466
    c. $139,950
    d. $300,000

    ANS: C

24. The present value of $1 discounted for 10 years at 8 percent compounded annually is 0.4632. The present value of an annuity of $1 discounted for 10 years at 8 percent compounded annually is 6.7101. Given this information and assuming a market interest rate of 8 percent, if equipment is purchased by issuing a 10-year, $200,000 interest-bearing note at a stated rate of 8 percent (payable annually), the equipment would be entered in the accounting records at
    a. $29,806
    b. $92,640
    c. $185,280
    d. $200,000

    ANS: D

25. The present value of $2,500 to be received in four years when interest is 12 percent compounded quarterly is computed by discounting at
    a. 12 percent for 4 periods
    b. 6 percent for 8 periods
    c. 4 percent for 12 periods
    d. 3 percent for 16 periods

    ANS: D

26. Which of the following has the smallest present value?
    a. $3,500 discounted for 6 years at 8 percent compounded annually
    b. $3,500 discounted for 6 years at 8 percent compounded semiannually
    c. $3,500 discounted for 6 years at 8 percent compounded quarterly
    d. $4,000 discounted for 6 years at 8 percent compounded annually

    ANS: C

27. Arsenio plans to invest $10,000 at the end of each of the next 10 years. Assume that Arsenio will earn interest at an annual rate of 6 percent compounded annually. The investment at the end of 10 years would be (rounded)
    a. $137,390
    b. $131,808
    c. $106,000
    d. $100,000

    ANS: B

28. Assuming an interest rate of 10 percent, an ordinary annuity of six annual $40,000 payments will grow to
    a. $169,220
    b. $308,624
    c. $748,160
    d. $806,590

    ANS: B

29. Assume you are going to purchase a house. You have $20,000 to use as a down payment and can afford a payment of $8,000 per year for 30 years. If interest is 8 percent per year, what is the largest purchase price of the house that you can buy?
    a. $20,795
    b. $225,156
    c. $260,000
    d. $110,062

    ANS: D

30. Suppose you want to determine the payments you will have to make on a loan for a house. The house will cost $100,000, and your bank requires a 20 percent down payment. The remainder will be financed at 12 percent compounded annually for 25 years. What will be the annual payment?
    a. $750
    b. $4,704
    c. $5,882
    d. $10,200

    ANS: D

Accounting for Long-Term Liabilities

31. Which of the following is LEAST likely to be classified as a current liability?
    a. Wages Payable
    b. Income Taxes Payable
    c. Unemployment Taxes Payable
    d. Bonds Payable

    ANS: D

32. The entry to record the annual lease payment on a capitalized lease includes a
    a. Credit to Lease Obligation
    b. Debit to Cash
    c. Credit to Depreciation Expense
    d. Debit to Interest Expense

    ANS: D

33. A long-term, noncancelable lease for a period that is equal to the life of the leased asset is accounted for as a(n)
    a. Operating lease
    b. Rental agreement
    c. Capital lease
    d. None of the above

    ANS: C

34. Generally accepted accounting principles specify that a long-term noncancelable lease for a period equal to the life of the equipment is
    a. An operating lease
    b. Essentially equivalent to a purchase
    c. Not mentioned in the financial statements unless payment is reasonably possible
    d. Expensed in the year signed

    ANS: B

35. Which of the following is NOT true?
    a. Bonds allow a company to borrow a lot of money from a lot of different people.
    b. Notes involve borrowing a lot of money from one lender.
    c. Mortgages typically have a lower interest rate because of collateral on the loan.
    d. Leases typically require a lower down payment as there are no risks associated with product obsolescence.

    ANS: A

36. If no interest payments are made on a note, then the difference between the present value of the cash flows associated with the note and the face value of the note represents
    a. Principal
    b. Amortization
    c. Interest
    d. Principal reduction

    ANS: C

37. Which of the following is prepared to identify how much of each mortgage payment is interest and how much is principal reduction?
    a. Mortgage depreciation schedule
    b. Mortgage amortization schedule
    c. Mortgage depletion schedule
    d. Mortgage reduction schedule

    ANS: B

38. At the end of each year, a mortgage is reported under how many sections of the balance sheet?
    a. 1
    b. 2
    c. 3
    d. 4

    ANS: B

39. Which of the following is an example of off-balance-sheet financing?
    a. Mortgages
    b. Bonds
    c. Operating leases
    d. Notes payable

    ANS: C

40. The amount of a company's future operating lease payments must be disclosed in the
    a. Current liabilities section of the balance sheet
    b. Long-term liabilities section of the balance sheet
    c. Notes to the financial statements
    d. Operating expenses section of the income statement

    ANS: C

41. A four-month, $6,500 note payable at 9 percent incurs interest (rounded to the nearest whole dollar) of
    a. $195
    b. $146
    c. $292
    d. $585

    ANS: A

42. The following entry is made to record the second monthly payment on a $60,000, 9 percent mortgage:

Account A	450	
Account B	32	
Account C		482

    Given this entry, the amount of interest included with this payment is
    a. $450
    b. $32
    c. $482
    d. Not determinable, without more information

    ANS: A

43. On January 1, Wadsworth Corp. leased a mainframe computer from IMB for $20,000 per year (payable on each December 31) for 10 years. The lease is a capital lease, and the current market rate of interest is 12 percent. The market value of the computer is $113,000, which is equal to its discounted present value at 12 percent. Given these data, interest expense on the lease for the first year is
    a. $20,000
    b. $13,560
    c. $12,000
    d. $6,440

    ANS: B

44. On January 1, Wadsworth Corp. leased a mainframe computer from IMB for $20,000 per year (payable on each December 31) for 10 years. The lease is a capital lease, and the current market rate of interest is 12 percent. The market value of the computer is $113,000, which is equal to its discounted present value at 12 percent. Given these data, the amount of the lease obligation at the end of the first year is
    a. $113,000
    b. $200,000
    c. $99,440
    d. $106,560

    ANS: D

45. A one-year, $15,000, 12 percent note is signed on April 1. If the note is prematurely repaid on September 1 of the same year, how much interest expense is incurred?
    a. $1,800
    b. $900
    c. $750
    d. $600

    ANS: C

46. Interest expense on a three-month, 14 percent, $1,500 note payable would be approximately
    a. $210
    b. $140
    c. $70
    d. $52.50

    ANS: D

47. An $18,000, 8 percent, one-year note is accepted by the bank on April 1. If the note is prematurely repaid on November 1 of the same year (without penalty), how much interest is paid?
    a. $700
    b. $840
    c. $980
    d. $1,440

    ANS: B

48. The present value of $2,000 received each year for six years and discounted at 9 percent is approximately
    a. $8,972
    b. $1,193
    c. $3,543
    d. $15,047

    ANS: A

49. If interest is 8 percent, $100 received one year from now is approximately equivalent to
    a. $80 today
    b. $93 today
    c. $108 today
    d. $120 today

    ANS: B

50. A 10-year lease requiring payments of $25,000 per year is signed. The entry to record the first payment would probably include a debit to Lease Obligation that is of a
    a. Larger amount than the debit to Interest Expense
    b. Smaller amount than the debit to Interest Expense
    c. Smaller amount than the debit to Cash
    d. Larger amount than the credit to Cash

    ANS: B

51. Which of the following notes would have the largest present value?
    a. A 10-year, $10,000, 6 percent note
    b. A 10-year, $10,000, 4 percent note
    c. A 10-year, $10,000, 12 percent note
    d. A 10-year, $10,000, 8 percent note

    ANS: C
    Example—N = 10, I = any rate, PMT = a – 600, b – 400, c – 1200, d – 800, FV = 10,000
    Using 10%, a = 7542, b = 6313, c = 11228, d = 8771

52. Which of the following notes would have the smallest present value?
    a. A 10-year, $10,000, 6 percent note
    b. A 10-year, $10,000, 4 percent note
    c. A 10-year, $10,000, 12 percent note
    d. A 10-year, $10,000, 8 percent note

    ANS: B
    Example—N = 10, I = any rate, PMT = a – 600, b – 400, c – 1200, d – 800, FV = 10,000
    Using 10%, a = 7542, b = 6313, c = 11228, d = 8771

The Nature of Bonds

53. Which of the following is one of the ways bonds can be categorized?
    a. The extent to which bondholders are protected
    b. How the bond interest is paid
    c. How the bonds mature
    d. All of the above

    ANS: D

54. Bonds that have a pledge of company assets are called
    a. Secured bonds
    b. Debenture bonds
    c. Registered bonds
    d. Convertible bonds

    ANS: A

55. When a company issues bonds that promise only to pay the face amount at the maturity date, the bonds issued are called
    a. Junk bonds
    b. Debenture bonds
    c. Term bonds
    d. Zero-coupon bonds

    ANS: D

56. High-risk bonds issued by companies in weak financial condition are called
    a. Zero-coupon bonds
    b. Junk bonds
    c. Debenture bonds
    d. Coupon bonds

    ANS: B

57. Which of the following is NOT a synonymous term to the others?
    a. Principal
    b. Face value
    c. Maturity value
    d. Present value

    ANS: D

58. Which of the following is an advantage of debt financing?
    a. Borrowed money must be repaid.
    b. Interest must usually be paid on borrowed money.
    c. Interest payments are tax deductible.
    d. Debt holders rank ahead of equity holders in cases of liquidation.

    ANS: C

59. Debentures are
    a. Unsecured bonds
    b. Secured bonds
    c. Ordinary bonds
    d. Serial bonds

    ANS: A

60. Callable bonds
    a. Can be redeemed by the issuer at some time at a pre-specified price
    b. Can be converted to stock
    c. Mature in a series of payments
    d. None of the above

    ANS: A

61. The issuance price of a bond does NOT depend on the
    a. Face value of the bond
    b. Riskiness of the bond
    c. Method used to amortize the bond discount or premium
    d. Effective interest rate

    ANS: C

62. The effective interest rate on bonds is higher than the stated rate when bonds sell
    a. At face value
    b. Above face value
    c. Below face value
    d. At maturity value

    ANS: C

Determining a Bond's Issuance Price

63. If the effective interest rate equals the stated interest rate, a bond will sell at
    a. A premium
    b. A discount
    c. Face value
    d. Unable to determine from the data given

    ANS: C

64. Bonds usually sell at a discount when
    a. Investors are willing to invest in the bonds at the stated interest rate
    b. Investors are willing to invest in the bonds at rates that are lower than the stated interest rate
    c. Investors are willing to invest in the bonds only at rates that are higher than the stated interest rate
    d. A capital gain is expected

    ANS: C

65. When do bonds usually sell at a premium?
    a. When the market rate of interest is greater than the stated rate of interest on the bonds
    b. When the stated rate of interest on the bonds is greater than the market rate of interest
    c. When the price of the bonds is greater than their maturity value
    d. None of the above

    ANS: B

66. The effective interest rate on bonds is lower than the stated rate when bonds sell
    a. At maturity value
    b. Above face value
    c. Below face value
    d. At face value

    ANS: B

67. The effective interest rate on bonds is higher than the stated rate when bonds sell
    a. At maturity value
    b. Above face value
    c. Below face value
    d. At face value

    ANS: C

68. Bonds usually sell at a premium when
    a. Investors are willing to invest in the bonds at the stated interest rate
    b. Investors are willing to invest in the bonds at rates that are lower than the stated interest rate
    c. Investors are willing to invest in the bonds only at rates that are higher than the stated interest rate
    d. The bond issuer expects a capital gain

    ANS: B

69. The method of bond amortization that results in a varying amount of amortization each period is
    a. Straight-line amortization
    b. Effective-interest amortization
    c. Accelerated amortization
    d. None of the above

    ANS: B

70. To compute the price to pay for a bond, you use
    a. Only the present value of $1 concept
    b. Only the present value of an annuity of $1 concept
    c. Both a and b
    d. Neither a nor b

    ANS: C

71. If the market rate of interest is 12 percent and a company is issuing long-term bonds paying 10 percent, at what percent would those liabilities have to be discounted, assuming semiannual compounding?
    a. 5 percent
    b. 6 percent
    c. 10 percent
    d. 12 percent

    ANS: B

72. Flute Corporation issued $200,000, 10-year, 9 percent bonds at a time when the market rate of interest was 12 percent. These bonds will be issued for
    a. $200,000
    b. More than $200,000
    c. Less than $200,000
    d. An unknown price; more information is needed

    ANS: C

73. Flute Corporation issued $200,000, 10-year, 9 percent bonds at a time when the market rate of interest was 7 percent. These bonds will be issued for
    a. $200,000
    b. More than $200,000
    c. Less than $200,000
    d. An unknown price; more information is needed

    ANS: B

74. Flute Corporation issued $200,000, 10-year, 9 percent bonds at a time when the market rate of interest was 9 percent. These bonds will be issued for
    a. $200,000
    b. More than $200,000
    c. Less than $200,000
    d. An unknown price; more information is needed

    ANS: A

75. LaFluer Corporation issued $300,000 of 15-year bonds on January 1. The bonds pay interest on January 1 and July 1 with a stated rate of 8 percent. If the market rate of interest at the time the bonds are sold is 6 percent, what will be the issuance price (approximate) of the bonds?
    a. $358,805
    b. $299,994
    c. $300,004
    d. $476,404

    ANS: A
    Note: If you use textbook tables, A is correct at $358,805. If you use a calculator, A should be $358,801.

76. LaFluer Corporation issued $300,000 of 15-year bonds on January 1. The bonds pay interest on January 1 and July 1 with a stated rate of 8 percent. If the market rate of interest at the time the bonds are sold is 10 percent, what will be the issuance price (approximate) of the bonds?
    a. $278,345
    b. $277,248
    c. $254,366
    d. $253,890

    ANS: D
    Note: If you use textbook tables, D is correct at $253,890. If you use a calculator, D should be $253,883.

Accounting for Bonds Payable Issued at Face Value

77. When bonds are first issued, the liability is entered in the bonds payable account at the bond's
    a. Face value
    b. Face value plus any discount
    c. Issuance price when that amount is greater or less than face value
    d. Face value plus accrued interest

    ANS: A

78. The entry to record a bond retirement at maturity usually involves
    a. No gain or loss
    b. A credit to Gain on Retirement
    c. A debit to Loss on Retirement
    d. A credit to Bonds Payable

    ANS: A

79. Just before bonds are retired, the balance in the bonds payable account is equal to the bond's
    a. Face value
    b. Face value plus any discount or premium amortized
    c. Issuance price
    d. Face value plus interest to be paid

    ANS: A

80. A bond retired before maturity usually involves a
    a. Debit to Gain on Retirement of Bond
    b. Credit to Bond Interest Expense
    c. Debit to Cash
    d. Debit to Bonds Payable

    ANS: D

81. If a gain occurs on the early retirement of bonds, it is
    a. Not reported in the financial statements
    b. Reported under the "Other revenues and gains" section of the income statement
    c. Only reported in the notes to the financial statements
    d. Reported as an extraordinary gain in the income statement

    ANS: B

EXPANDED MATERIAL

Bonds Issued at a Discount or at a Premium

82. The effective interest rate on bonds is also called
     a. The stated rate
     b. The yield rate
     c. The nominal rate
     d. None of the above

     ANS: B

83. Which of the following is true of a premium on bonds payable?
     a. It is a contra-stockholders' equity account.
     b. It is an account that appears only on the books of the investor.
     c. It increases when amortization entries are made until it reaches its maturity value.
     d. It decreases when amortization entries are made until its balance reaches zero at the
         maturity date.

     ANS: D

84. A bond discount is reported on the financial statements in the
     a. Liabilities section of the balance sheet
     b. Expenses section of the income statement
     c. Assets section of the balance sheet
     d. Revenues section of the income statement

     ANS: A

85. The net amount of a bond liability that appears on the balance sheet is the
     a. Call price of the bond plus bond discount or minus bond premium
     b. Face value of the bond plus related premium or minus related discount
     c. Face value of the bond plus related discount or minus related premium
     d. Maturity value of the bond plus related discount or minus related premium

     ANS: B

86. When a company issues bonds, how are unamortized bond discounts and premiums classified on
     the balance sheet?
     a. Bond discounts are classified as assets, and bond premiums are classified as contra-asset
         accounts.
     b. Bond discounts are classified as expenses, and bond premiums are classified as revenues.
     c. Bond premiums are classified as additions to, and bond discounts are classified as
         deductions from, the face value of bonds.
     d. None of the above

     ANS: C

87. When interest expense is calculated using the effective-interest amortization method, interest expense (assuming that interest is paid annually) always equals the
    a. Actual amount of interest paid
    b. Bond carrying value multiplied by the stated interest rate
    c. Bond carrying value multiplied by the effective-interest rate
    d. Maturity value of the bonds multiplied by the effective-interest rate

    ANS: C

88. The effective-interest method of amortizing bond premiums
    a. Is too complicated for practical use
    b. Recognizes the time value of money
    c. Is another name for the straight-line method
    d. Is needed to determine the amount of cash to be paid to bondholders at each interest date

    ANS: B

89. The net amount required to retire a bond before maturity (assuming no call premium and constant interest rates) is the
    a. Issuance price of the bond plus any unamortized discount or minus any unamortized premium
    b. Face value of the bond plus any unamortized premium or minus any unamortized discount
    c. Face value of the bond plus any unamortized discount or minus any unamortized premium
    d. Maturity value of the bond plus any unamortized discount or minus any unamortized premium

    ANS: B

90. On January 1, 2006, $50,000 of 20-year, 6 percent debentures were issued for $56,275.20. Interest payment dates on the bonds are January 1 and July 1. When using the straight-line method, the amount of premium to be amortized on July 1, 2006, is
    a. $313.76
    b. $156.88
    c. $776.50
    d. $93.11

    ANS: B

91. The total interest expense on a $200,000, 10 percent, 10-year bond issued at 105 would be
    a. $190,000
    b. $195,000
    c. $200,000
    d. $210,000

    ANS: A

92. The effective interest rate of a 10-year, 8 percent, $1,000 bond issued at 103 would be approximately
    a. 7.6 percent
    b. 7.8 percent
    c. 8.0 percent
    d. 8.2 percent

    ANS: A

93. On January 1, 2006, Cabuki Corporation issued $500,000 of 10 percent, 10-year bonds at 88.5. Interest is payable on December 31. If the market rate of interest was 12 percent at the time the bonds were issued, how much cash was paid for interest in 2006?
    a. $44,250
    b. $50,000
    c. $53,100
    d. $60,000

    ANS: B

94. On January 1, 2006, Cabuki Corporation issued $500,000 of 10 percent, 10-year bonds at 88.5. Interest is payable on December 31. If the market rate of interest was 12 percent at the time the bonds were issued, how much was interest expense in 2006?
    a. $44,250
    b. $50,000
    c. $53,100
    d. $60,000

    ANS: C

95. Kwancom Corporation, a calendar-year firm, is authorized to issue $200,000 of 10 percent, 20-year bonds dated January 1, 2006, with interest payable on January 1 and July 1 of each year. The entry to account for the discount amortization and accrual of interest on December 31, 2006, would include a
    a. Debit to Discount on Bonds Payable
    b. Credit to Cash
    c. Credit to Interest Payable
    d. Debit to Bonds Payable

    ANS: C

96. Assuming the straight-line method of amortization is used, the average yearly interest expense on a $250,000, 11 percent, 20-year bond issued at 106 would be
    a. $26,750
    b. $27,500
    c. $28,250
    d. $29,500

    ANS: A

97. On January 1, 2006, Santos Hospital issued a $250,000, 10 percent, five-year bond for $231,601. Interest is payable on June 30 and December 31. Santos uses the effective-interest method to amortize all premiums and discounts. Assuming an effective interest rate of 12 percent, how much interest expense should be recorded on June 30, 2006?
    a. $11,935.14
    b. $12,500.00
    c. $13,896.06
    d. $14,729.82

    ANS: C

98. On January 1, 2006, Santos Hospital issued a $250,000, 10 percent, five-year bond for $231,601. Interest is payable on June 30 and December 31. Santos uses the effective-interest method to amortize all premiums and discounts. Assuming an effective interest rate of 12 percent, approximately how much discount will be amortized on December 31, 2006?
    a. $2,230
    b. $1,480
    c. $1,396
    d. $987

    ANS: B

99. A $50,000 bond with a carrying value of $52,000 was called at 103 and retired. In recording the retirement, the issuing company should record
    a. No gain or loss
    b. A $1,500 loss
    c. A $2,000 gain
    d. A $500 gain

    ANS: D

100. A $50,000 bond with a carrying value of $52,000 was called at 107 and retired. In recording the retirement, the issuing company should record
    a. No gain or loss
    b. A $1,500 loss
    c. A $2,000 gain
    d. A $500 gain

    ANS: B

101. Riverview County issued a $500,000, 10 percent, 10-year bond on January 1, 2006, for 113.6 when the effective interest rate was 8 percent. Interest is payable on June 30 and December 31. Riverview uses the effective-interest method to amortize all premiums and discounts. How much premium or discount should be amortized on June 30, 2006?
    a. $2,790
    b. $2,280
    c. $2,000
    d. $1,970

    ANS: B

102. Riverview County issued a $500,000, 10 percent, 10-year bond on January 1, 2006, for 113.6 when the effective interest rate was 8 percent. Interest is payable on June 30 and December 31. Riverview uses the effective-interest method to amortize all premiums and discounts. How much interest expense should Riverview record on December 31, 2006?
    a. $25,000.00
    b. $23,810.15
    c. $22,628.80
    d. $19,920.10

    ANS: C

103. Smith Corporation issued a $100,000, 10-year, 10 percent bond on January 1, 2004, for $112,000. Smith uses the straight-line method of amortization. On April 1, 2007, Smith reacquired the bonds for retirement when they were selling at 102 on the open market. How much gain or loss should Smith recognize on the retirement of the bonds?
    a. $2,000 loss
    b. $3,900 gain
    c. $6,100 gain
    d. $8,200 loss

    ANS: C

Using Debt-Related Financial Ratios

104. Which of the following ratios is used to evaluate a company's ability to meet its periodic interest payments?
    a. Times interest paid ratio
    b. Times interest earned ratio
    c. Times interest recorded ratio
    d. Times interest expensed ratio

    ANS: B

105. Which of the following is NOT used to evaluate a company's financial leverage?
    a. Debt ratio
    b. Times interest earned ratio
    c. Debt-to-equity ratio
    d. None of the above

    ANS: B

106. Hakeem, Inc. reported the following data in its 2005 financial statements: total liabilities, 24,000; total stockholders' equity, $12,000; net income, $2,700; income tax expense, $1,800; and interest expense, $1,500. The debt-to-equity ratio is
    a. 0.50
    b. 0.67
    c. 3.00
    d. 2.00

    ANS: D

107. Hakeem, Inc. reported the following data in its 2005 financial statements: total liabilities, $24,000; total stockholders' equity, $12,000; net income, $2,700; income tax expense, $1,800; and interest expense, $1,500. The debt ratio is
    a. 50 percent
    b. 67 percent
    c. 300 percent
    d. 200 percent

    ANS: B

108.   Hakeem, Inc. reported the following data in its 2005 financial statements: total liabilities, $24,000; total stockholders' equity, $12,000; net income, $2,700; income tax expense, $1,800; and interest expense, $1,500. The times interest earned ratio is
a.   4.0 times
b.   1.8 times
c.   2.8 times
d.   3.0 times

ANS: A

PROBLEMS

1.   On January 1, 2005, Watters Corporation leased a truck. The lease agreement specified payments of $15,000 per year (payable each year on January 2, starting in 2006) for six years. The market rate of interest for lease transactions of this type is 12 percent compounded annually.

1.   What is the present value of the lease? (Round to the nearest whole dollar.)
2.   Prepare journal entries for the initiation of the lease on January 1, 2005, and for the required entries on December 31, 2005, and January 2, 2006. (Round to the nearest whole dollar.)

ANS:

1. $61,671   [$15,000 × 4.1114 (Table II, 6 periods at 12%)] or N = 6, I/Yr = 12, PMT = 15,000

2.   01/01/05   Leased Truck   61,671
                       Lease Obligation............................   61,671

      12/31/05   Interest Expense...............................   7,401
                       Lease Interest Payable   7,401

      01/02/06   Lease Interest Payable   7,401
                       Lease Obligation..............................   7,599
                           Cash   15,000

2.   On June 1, 2006, Bellamy Corporation borrowed $400,000 on a 15-year mortgage to purchase land and a building. The land and building are pledged as collateral on the mortgage, which has an interest rate of 12 percent compounded monthly. The payments of $4,800 are made at the end of each month, beginning on June 30, 2006. (Round amounts to the nearest whole dollar.)

1.   Prepare the journal entry for the purchase of the land and building, assuming that $100,000 is assignable to the land.
2.   Prepare journal entries for the monthly payments on June 30, July 31, and August 31. (Round amounts to the nearest whole dollar.)
3.   Calculate the balance in the mortgage liability account after the August 31 payment.

ANS:

1. 06/01/06   Land   100,000
                  Building..   300,000
                       Mortgage Payable   400,000

2. 06/30/06   Mortgage Payable   800
                  Interest Expense   4,000
                       Cash   4,800

    07/31/06   Mortgage Payable   808
                  Interest Expense   3,992
                       Cash..   4,800

    08/31/06   Mortgage Payable   816
                  Interest Expense   3,984
                       Cash..   4,800

3. ($400,000 – $800 – $808 – $816) = $397,576

3. On January 1, 2005, Xero Corporation borrowed $40,000 on a two-year interest-bearing note
    from Regional Bank at an annual interest rate of 10 percent (Note A). Also on January 1, 2005,
    Xero borrowed $25,000 from United Bank, signing a three-year interest-bearing note at an annual
    interest rate of 12 percent (Note B). For both notes, interest is payable yearly on January 1.
    Prepare the following journal entries. (Round all amounts to the nearest whole dollar.)

    1. January 1, 2005 borrowings on:
        a. Note A
        b. Note B
    2. Recognition of interest on December 31, 2005. (Interest on both notes can be in one
        entry.)
    3. Interest payment on January 1, 2006. (Interest on both notes can be in one entry.)
    4. Repayment of Note B on January 1, 2008.

ANS:

1. 01/01/05   Cash   40,000
                       Notes Payable (Note A)   40,000

    01/01/05   Cash   25,000
                       Notes Payable (Note B)   25,000

2. 12/31/05   Interest Expense............................   7,000
                       Interest Payable........................   7,000
                       ($40,000 × 0.10) + ($25,000 × 0.12)

3. 01/01/06   Interest Payable............................   7,000
                          Cash   7,000

4. 01/01/08   Notes Payable (Note B)   25,000
                          Interest Payable............................   3,000
                          Cash   28,000
                          ($25,000 × 0.12) Interest expense
                          would have been recognized on 12/31/2007.

4. On March 1, 2006, Lloyd Corporation sold $400,000 of 12 percent, five-year bonds at a yield of 10 percent compounded semiannually. Interest is payable on March 1 and September 1 of each year. The corporation is a calendar-year corporation. Bond premiums and discounts are amortized on interest-paying dates and at year-end. (Round amounts to the nearest whole dollar.)

Prepare the journal entries that are appropriate to account for these bonds on the following dates: March 1, 2006; September 1, 2006; and December 31, 2006. Use the effective-interest method of amortization.

ANS:

03/01/06   Cash...   430,881*
                  Bond Payable   400,000
                  Bond Premium   30,881

09/01/06   Bond Interest Expense   21,544
                  Bond Premium   2,456
                      Cash   24,000

12/31/06   Bond Interest Expense.............................   14,281
                  Bond Premium   1,719
                      Bond Interest Payable.....................   16,000

* Using a calculator results in $430,887.

5. Meecham Corporation reported the following data in its financial statements for 2005:

Current liabilities	$36,000		Interest expense	$6,000
Long-term liabilities	60,000		Income tax expense	2,400
Stockholders' equity	50,000		Net income	5,600

Compute the following:
1. Debt-to-equity ratio
2. Debt ratio
3. Times interest earned ratio

ANS:

1. Debt-to-equity ratio   = Total liabilities ÷ Total stockholders' equity
    = ($36,000 + $60,000) ÷ $50,000
    = <u>1.92</u>

2. Debt ratio   = Total liabilities ÷ Total assets
    = ($36,000 + $60,000) ÷ ($36,000 + $60,000 + $50,000)
    = <u>65.75%</u>

3. Times interest earned ratio   = Income before interest and taxes ÷ Interest expense
    = ($5,600 + $2,400 + $6,000) ÷ $6,000
    = <u>2.33 times</u>

Name_____   Section_____

TRUE/FALSE

Circle T or F to indicate whether each of the following statements is true or false.

T   F   1.   The more frequent the compounding period, the larger the present value of the future sum.

T   F   2.   An annuity is a series of equally spaced payments of unequal amounts.

T   F   3.   The leased asset and the lease liability accounts for a capital lease will usually have different balances each period throughout the life of a lease.

T   F   4.   A lease in which ownership is transferred to the lessee at the end of the lease term must usually be capitalized.

T   F   5.   The retirement of bonds at maturity is recorded by debiting Bonds Payable and crediting Cash.

T   F   6.   The face value of a bond will equal its present value if the effective and stated interest rates are different.

T   F   7.   Issuing bonds is considered to be a form of equity financing.

T   F   8.   Bonds that are secured with the issuer's assets are often referred to as "debentures."

T   F   9.   The market price of bonds is influenced by the general economic conditions and the financial status of the company selling the bonds.

T   F   10.   The present value of the principal and interest on a bond may be lower than the maturity value of the bond.

Name_____   Section_____

MATCHING

In the spaces provided, write the letter of the definition for each of the following terms:

    a. The actual interest rate earned on a bond investment.

    b. A person or an organization leasing property and agreeing to pay periodic rental payments throughout the lease term.

    c. The present value today of $1 to be received at the end of each of a certain number of periods at a specified interest rate.

    d. Series of equally spaced payments.

    e. Money borrowed to purchase a specific asset, usually real estate; usually requires monthly payments.

    f. Bonds for which no collateral has been pledged.

    g. Another name for the face value of bonds.

    h. The rate of interest printed on the bond.

    i. When bonds initially sell at amounts above face value.

    j. When bonds initially sell at amounts below face value.

1. _____ Lessee

2. _____ Present value of an annuity

3. _____ Annuity

4. _____ Mortgage payable

5. _____ Discount

6. _____ Premium

7. _____ Principal

8. _____ Stated interest rate

9. _____ Effective interest rate

10. _____ Debentures

Quiz Solutions

Quiz A

1. F
2. F
3. T
4. T
5. T
6. F
7. F
8. F
9. T
10. T

Quiz B

1. B
2. C
3. D
4. E
5. J
6. I
7. G
8. H
9. A
10. F

MULTIPLE CHOICE

Raising Equity Financing

1. Which form of financing allows the source of the funds to share in the wealth if the company that received the financing does well?
   a. A loan
   b. An investment
   c. Both a and b
   d. Neither a nor b

   ANS: B

2. Which form of financing requires repayment, regardless of whether the company receiving the funds does well?
   a. A loan
   b. An investment
   c. Both a and b
   d. Neither a nor b

   ANS: A

3. Which type of business organization is characterized by unlimited liability and limited life?
   a. Proprietorship
   b. Partnership
   c. Corporation
   d. All of the above
   e. Only a and b

   ANS: E

4. Which of the following types of business organization is owned by one person?
   a. Corporation
   b. Partnership
   c. Proprietorship
   d. All of the above

   ANS: C

5. Which of the following types of business organization is NOT a separate legal entity from its owner or owners?
   a. Proprietorship
   b. Partnership
   c. Corporation
   d. Both a and b

   ANS: D

6. Which of the following events would NOT dissolve a partnership?
    a. The retirement of a partner
    b. The earning of a partnership loss
    c. The admission of a new partner
    d. The bankruptcy of a partner

    ANS: B

Corporations and Corporate Stock

7. Which type of business organization allows the business to be a separate, distinct entity from the owners?
    a. Proprietorship
    b. Partnership
    c. Corporation
    d. All of the above

    ANS: C

8. Which of the following is a characteristic of corporations?
    a. They pay taxes on their profits.
    b. They provide their investors with no liability.
    c. A change in ownership usually affects the corporation's legal and economic status.
    d. In case of bankruptcy, stockholders receive corporate assets before the claims of debtholders are satisfied.

    ANS: A

9. The right of current stockholders to purchase additional shares in order to maintain the same percentage ownership of new shares is called
    a. Liquidation
    b. The voting rights privilege
    c. Preemptive right
    d. The cumulative preference

    ANS: C

10. Which of the following organizations has a retained earnings account?
    a. Partnership
    b. Proprietorship
    c. Corporation
    d. All of the above

    ANS: C

11. Which of the following is NOT true of a corporation?
    a. A corporation has easy transferability of ownership.
    b. A corporation is taxed separately from its owners.
    c. A corporation has the ability to raise large amounts of capital.
    d. The owners of a corporation have unlimited liability.

    ANS: D

12. Which of the following statements is true of a corporation?
    a. Ownership rights can be transferred only after lengthy legal proceedings.
    b. In the case of bankruptcy, owners are not personally liable to debtholders.
    c. By law, the income of both the corporation and the owners is always taxed together.
    d. Incorporation allows a company to enjoy increased freedom from government regulations.

    ANS: B

13. Which type of business organization is characterized by limited liability?
    a. Corporation
    b. Proprietorship
    c. Partnership
    d. All of the above

    ANS: A

14. Which of the following is a characteristic of the corporate form of business organization?
    a. Unlimited liability
    b. Limited life
    c. Ease of formation
    d. Double taxation

    ANS: D

15. Which of the following is NOT a basic right of a common stockholder?
    a. The right to vote for the board of directors
    b. The preemptive right
    c. The right to receive a dividend
    d. The right to receive all excess assets once the obligations to others have been satisfied

    ANS: C

16. Which of the basic stockholder rights do preferred stockholders normally give up?
    a. The right to vote
    b. The preemptive right
    c. The right to receive dividends when they are declared
    d. The right to excess assets after creditor claims are satisfied

    ANS: A

Accounting for Stock

17. Which of the following is NOT true regarding "legal capital"?
    a. It is intended as a means to protect a company's creditors.
    b. It represents an amount that cannot be returned to the owners so long as the corporation exists.
    c. The dollar amount of legal capital is established by federal statutes.
    d. It is intended to prevent corporations from paying excessive dividends.

    ANS: C

18. When common stock is issued in exchange for a noncash asset, the acquired asset should usually be recorded at an amount equal to
    a. The book value of the noncash asset
    b. The par value of the stock
    c. The market value of the stock
    d. None of the above

    ANS: C

19. A paid-in capital account can be credited with all of the following transactions, EXCEPT
    a. A stock dividend
    b. The issuance of no-par stock with a stated value
    c. The reissuance of treasury stock
    d. The purchase of treasury stock

    ANS: D

20. Treasury stock is stock that is
    a. Authorized but not issued
    b. Issued and outstanding
    c. Issued but not outstanding
    d. Authorized and outstanding

    ANS: C

21. A loss on the sale of treasury stock is recognized when treasury stock is sold at
    a. A higher price than the stock's market value
    b. A higher price than the stock's cost
    c. A higher price than the stock's par or stated value
    d. None of the above

    ANS: D

22. Treasury stock is classified on the balance sheet as
    a. A current asset
    b. A long-term investment
    c. Contributed capital
    d. Contra-stockholders' equity

    ANS: D

23. If treasury stock is sold for less than its cost, and there were no previous treasury stock sales, the difference between the sales price and the cost is debited to
    a. Paid-In Capital, Treasury Stock
    b. Common Stock
    c. Retained Earnings
    d. Paid-In Capital in Excess of Par

    ANS: C

24. Compared with preferred stock, common stock usually has a favorable preference in terms of
    a. Dividends
    b. Voting rights
    c. Liquidated assets
    d. Resale value

    ANS: B

25. When common stock is issued in exchange for a noncash asset, the acquired asset should usually be recorded at an amount equal to the
    a. Book value of the stock
    b. Book value of the noncash asset
    c. Market value of the noncash asset
    d. Undepreciated cost of the noncash asset

    ANS: C

26. Which of the following statements is true of treasury stock?
    a. It is classified as an asset on the balance sheet.
    b. It allows management to vote for members of the board of directors.
    c. It is considered outstanding stock.
    d. It usually has a debit balance.

    ANS: D

27. When 10,000 shares of $10 par-value common stock are issued at $15 per share, Paid-In Capital in Excess of Par, Common Stock is credited for
    a. $150,000
    b. $100,000
    c. $50,000
    d. None of the above

    ANS: C

28. On January 1, 2006, Georgi Company was authorized to issue 10,000 shares of $2 par common stock and 5,000 shares of $5 preferred stock. Given this information, if Georgi Company issued 2,000 shares of common stock for land with a book value of $15,000 (market value, $10,000), the entry to record the transaction would include a
    a. Debit to Land of $10,000
    b. Credit to Common Stock of $15,000
    c. Credit to Paid-In Capital in Excess of Par, Common Stock of $11,000
    d. Debit to Land of $15,000

    ANS: A

29. On January 1, 2006, Georgi Company was authorized to issue 10,000 shares of $2 par common stock and 5,000 shares of $5 preferred stock. Given this information, if Georgi Company issued 3,000 shares of common stock for $7 per share on January 10, 2006, the entry to record the issuance of the stock would include a
    a. Debit to Cash of $6,000
    b. Credit to Paid-In Capital in Excess of Par, Common Stock of $6,000
    c. Credit to Common Stock of $6,000
    d. Debit to Cash of $15,000

    ANS: C

30. Moony Corporation had 20,000 shares of $4 par-value common stock outstanding on January 1, 2006. On January 10, 2006, the firm purchased 2,000 of its outstanding shares for $18 per share. On July 22, 2006, it reissued 1,000 shares at $22 per share. Given this information, the entry to record the purchase of this stock on January 10 would include a debit to
    a. Treasury Stock of $36,000
    b. Common Stock of $36,000
    c. Treasury Stock of $8,000
    d. Common Stock of $8,000

    ANS: A

31. Moony Corporation had 20,000 shares of $4 par-value common stock outstanding on January 1, 2006. On January 10, 2006, the firm purchased 2,000 of its outstanding shares for $18 per share. On July 22, 2006, it reissued 1,000 shares at $22 per share. Given this information, the entry to record the reissuance of the stock on July 22 would include a credit to
    a. Treasury Stock of $4,000
    b. Common Stock of $4,000
    c. Paid-In Capital of $18,000
    d. Paid-In Capital, Treasury Stock of $4,000

    ANS: D

32. Moony Corporation had 20,000 shares of $4 par-value common stock outstanding on January 1, 2006. On January 10, 2006, the firm purchased 2,000 of its outstanding shares for $18 per share. On July 22, 2006, it reissued 1,000 shares at $22 per share. Given this information, the entry to record the reissuing of the remaining 1,000 shares on August 17, 2006, at $12 per share would probably include a
    a. Credit to Treasury Stock of $4,000
    b. Debit to Retained Earnings of $2,000
    c. Debit to Paid-In Capital, Treasury Stock of $6,000
    d. Debit to Loss on Sale of Stock of $6,000

    ANS: B

33. During the year, Little Company purchased 5,000 shares of its $3 par common stock at $20 per share and later sold it for $18 per share. How much did total stockholders' equity change because of these treasury stock transactions?
    a. $100,000
    b. $90,000
    c. $10,000
    d. $15,000

    ANS: C

Retained Earnings

34. Which of the following is NOT an important date associated with dividends?
    a. Dividend payment date
    b. Date of information
    c. Date of record
    d. Declaration date

    ANS: B

35. Which of the following statements about retained earnings is true?
    a. It is the amount of cash that has been retained from a company's earnings.
    b. It is the amount of creditors' claims on assets.
    c. It is never increased when treasury stock is bought or sold.
    d. None of the above is true.

    ANS: C

36. When do dividends become liabilities?
    a. On the date of record
    b. On the declaration date
    c. On the payment date
    d. Dividends are never liabilities because a company is not legally required to pay dividends

    ANS: B

37. The declaration of a common stock dividend decreases
    a. A company's retained earnings balance
    b. The par value of outstanding stock
    c. The number of shares of outstanding stock
    d. The amount of cash

    ANS: A

38. The declaration and payment of cash dividends
    a. Reduce the amount of resources a company has to invest in productive assets
    b. Sometimes do not reduce a company's retained earnings balance
    c. Reduce a company's net income
    d. Sometimes do not reduce a company's cash balance

    ANS: A

39. The declaration and distribution of stock dividends
    a. Reduce the amount of resources a company has to invest in productive assets
    b. Sometimes do not reduce a company's retained earnings balance
    c. Reduce a company's net income
    d. Do not reduce a company's cash balance

    ANS: D

40. Which of the following dividend preferences is associated with common stock?
    a. Cumulative-dividend preference
    b. Current-dividend preference
    c. Both a and b
    d. Neither a nor b

    ANS: D

41. Dividends in arrears on preferred stock are classified as
    a. A current liability account
    b. A stockholder's equity account
    c. A long-term liability account
    d. None of the above

    ANS: D

42. Dividends in arrears on preferred stock are
    a. A current liability account
    b. A stockholder's equity account
    c. A long-term liability account
    d. Disclosed in the notes to the financial statements

    ANS: D

43. As compared with preferred stock, common stock usually has favorable preferences in terms of
    a. Liquidated assets
    b. Dividends
    c. Voting rights
    d. Both a and c

    ANS: C

44. The declaration of dividends by a company always
    a. Decreases the balance in Retained Earnings
    b. Reduces the Cash balance
    c. Increases the balance in Retained Earnings
    d. Increases the balance in Common Stock

    ANS: A

45. Dividends in arrears are associated with the
    a. Current-dividend preference
    b. Cumulative-dividend preference
    c. Noncumulative-dividend preference
    d. None of the above

    ANS: B

46. Dividends declared are reported on the
    a. Income statement as an expense
    b. Balance sheet as a liability
    c. Statement of retained earnings
    d. Income statement as a revenue

    ANS: C

47. The dividend payout ratio is a measure of
    a. Percentage of net income paid in dividends
    b. Capital structure
    c. Common stock outstanding
    d. Efficiency

    ANS: A

48. Reiser Co. has 8,000 shares of no-par common stock with a $50 stated value and 3,000 shares of $40 par, 5 percent noncumulative preferred stock outstanding. If the company declares cash dividends of $22,000, the total amount of the dividend paid to preferred stockholders is
    a. $5,000
    b. $11,000
    c. $6,000
    d. $5,500

    ANS: C

49. The Retained Earnings balance of Goa Company was $23,400 on January 1, 2006. Net income for 2006 was $13,240. If Retained Earnings had a credit balance of $10,500 after closing entries were posted on December 31, 2006, and if additional stock of $6,500 was issued during the year, dividends declared during 2006 were
    a. $19,400
    b. $26,140
    c. $32,640
    d. None of the above

    ANS: B

50. Pelletier Corporation has the following stock outstanding:

Preferred stock (6 percent, $10 par, 45,000 shares authorized,10,000 shares issued and outstanding)	$100,000
Common stock ($7 par, 250,000 shares authorized, 120,000 shares issued and outstanding)	840,000

Given this information, if Pelletier pays a $9,000 cash dividend, and if the preferred stock is noncumulative, common stockholders will receive
a. $3,000
b. $9,000
c. $6,000
d. $4,500

ANS: A

51. Pelletier Corporation has the following stock outstanding:

Preferred stock (6 percent, $10 par, 45,000 shares authorized,10,000 shares issued and outstanding)	$100,000
Common stock ($7 par, 250,000 shares authorized, 120,000 shares issued and outstanding)	840,000

Given this information, if Pelletier pays a $64,000 dividend, and if the preferred stock is cumulative and two years' dividends are in arrears, common stockholders will receive
a. $32,000
b. $52,000
c. $58,000
d. $46,000

ANS: D

52. Pelletier Corporation has the following stock outstanding:

Preferred stock (6 percent, $10 par, 45,000 shares authorized,10,000 shares issued and outstanding)	$100,000
Common stock ($7 par, 250,000 shares authorized, 120,000 shares issued and outstanding)	840,000

Given this information, if Pelletier pays a $64,000 dividend, and if the preferred stock is noncumulative and the two previous years' dividends have not been paid, common stockholders will receive
a. $32,000
b. $52,000
c. $58,000
d. $46,000

ANS: C

53. Pelletier Corporation has the following stock outstanding:

Preferred stock (6 percent, $10 par, 45,000 shares authorized, 10,000 shares
  issued and outstanding) $100,000
Common stock ($7 par, 250,000 shares authorized, 120,000 shares issued and
  outstanding) 840,000

Given this information, if Pelletier pays a $108,000 dividend, and if the preferred stock is
cumulative and three years' dividends are in arrears, preferred stock will receive
a. $18,000
b. $24,000
c. $90,000
d. $84,000

ANS: B

54. The following information is available for Snipes Company:

	2006	2005
Current assets	$12,000	$11,800
Current liabilities	4,200	3,700
Long-term assets	9,200	7,500
Long-term liabilities	6,000	5,600
Stockholders' equity	11,000	10,000
Net sales	44,000	38,000
Net income	1,600	1,400
Dividends paid	900	800

The dividend payout ratio for 2006 is
a. 17.77 percent
b. 88.89 percent
c. 57.14 percent
d. 56.25 percent

ANS: D

Other Equity Items

55. The term used to describe the equity section of the balance sheet that reports the effect on equity
that results from market-related gains and losses that are NOT included in the computation of net
income is
a. Equity income
b. Market income
c. Accumulated other comprehensive income
d. Valuation income

ANS: C

56. The purpose of a statement of stockholders' equity is to
    a. Report the balances in the stockholders' equity accounts as of a particular date
    b. Reconcile beginning and ending balances of all stockholders' equity accounts reported on the balance sheet
    c. Report changes in all stockholders' equity accounts except Retained Earnings
    d. Summarize treasury stock transactions for a period of time

    ANS: B

57. The foreign currency translation adjustment is reported in the
    a. Gains and losses section of the income statement
    b. Equity section of the balance sheet
    c. Extraordinary items section of the income statement
    d. Investments section of the balance sheet

    ANS: B

58. Unrealized gains and losses on available-for-sale securities are reported in the
    a. Gains and losses section of the income statement
    b. Equity section of the balance sheet
    c. Extraordinary items section of the income statement
    d. Investments section of the balance sheet

    ANS: B

59. Which of the following is NOT a component of comprehensive income?
    a. Net income
    b. Foreign currency translation adjustment
    c. Unrealized gains and losses on available-for-sale securities
    d. Treasury stock

    ANS: D

60. Which of the following would NOT appear on a statement of stockholders' equity?
    a. Unrealized gains and losses on trading securities
    b. Accumulated other comprehensive income
    c. Treasury stock
    d. Additional paid-in capital

    ANS: A

EXPANDED MATERIAL

Accounting for Stock Dividends

61. A small stock dividend is one that is less than
    a. 10 percent
    b. 15 percent
    c. 20 percent
    d. 25 percent

    ANS: D

62. In a large stock dividend, the amount transferred out of retained earnings is equal to
    a. The market value of the newly issued shares
    b. The par value of the newly issued shares
    c. The realized value of the newly issued shares
    d. None of the above

    ANS: B

63. In a small stock dividend, the amount transferred out of retained earnings is equal to
    a. The market value of the newly issued shares
    b. The par value of the newly issued shares
    c. The realized value of the newly issued shares
    d. None of the above

    ANS: A

64. A 2-for-1 stock split
    a. Reduces the par value of all authorized stock by one-half
    b. Increases both retained earnings and the number of shares of stock outstanding
    c. Decreases the amount of retained earnings
    d. Changes the total amount of stockholders' equity

    ANS: A

65. A 2-for-1 stock split
    a. Increases retained earnings by 50 percent
    b. Increases the par value of all authorized stock by one-half
    c. Doubles the number of shares of stock outstanding
    d. Requires a transfer of retained earnings to contributed capital

    ANS: C

66. Which of the following transactions would NOT ultimately affect the total amount of owners' equity?
    a. The declaration of cash dividends
    b. The payment of property dividends
    c. The distribution of stock dividends
    d. A prior-period adjustment

    ANS: C

67. Which of the following transactions CANNOT change the total amount of stockholders' equity?
    a. Reissuance of treasury stock
    b. Purchase of treasury stock
    c. Declaration of a stock dividend
    d. Any of the above transactions can change total stockholders' equity

    ANS: C

68. Archer Corporation has 2,000,000 authorized shares of $9 par-value common stock, with 300,000 shares issued and outstanding. After a 3-for-1 stock split, Archer Corporation would have
    a. 900,000 shares of common stock issued and outstanding at $3 par
    b. 100,000 shares of common stock issued and outstanding at $27 par
    c. 6,000,000 shares of common stock outstanding at $3 par
    d. 666,667 shares of stock outstanding at $27 per share

    ANS: A

69. Cedar Corporation has 200,000 shares of $15 par common stock outstanding. If the corporation declares a 27,000 share stock dividend when the market value of the stock is $24 per share, what amount should be debited to Retained Earnings?
    a. $648,000
    b. $243,000
    c. $405,000
    d. None of the above

    ANS: A

70. Sequoia Corporation has 40,000 shares of $14 par-value common stock outstanding. If the corporation declares a 15 percent stock dividend and the market value of the stock on the date of declaration is $22 per share, what amount should be credited to Paid-In Capital?
    a. $132,000
    b. $48,000
    c. $0
    d. $84,000

    ANS: B

71. Bud Company has 14,000 shares of common stock authorized, of which 10,000 shares have been issued and 9,000 are currently outstanding. If the company declares a 10 percent stock dividend, how many shares of stock will it issue?
    a. 900
    b. 1,000
    c. 1,400
    d. None of the above

    ANS: A

Prior-Period Adjustments

72. Prior-period adjustments are reported on the
    a. Income statement
    b. Balance sheet
    c. Statement of changes in financial position
    d. Statement of retained earnings

    ANS: D

PROBLEMS

1. The stockholders' equity section of the balance sheet for Juarez Corporation as of December 31, 2006, is as follows:

Stockholders' Equity

Preferred stock (6 percent, $12 par, cumulative, 100,000 shares authorized)		$ 600,000
Common stock (no par, $5 stated value, 100,000 shares authorized)		800,000
Paid-in capital in excess of stated value, common stock ..		450,000
Total contributed capital		$1,850,000
Retained earnings:		
Retained earnings, unrestricted	$600,000	
Retained earnings, restricted	200,000	800,000
Total contributed capital and retained earnings		$2,650,000
Less: Treasury stock, common (5,000 shares at $15 per share)		(75,000)
Total stockholders' equity		$2,575,000

1. How many shares of preferred stock have been issued?
2. How many shares of common stock have been issued?
3. How many shares of preferred stock are outstanding?
4. How many shares of common stock are outstanding?

ANS:

1. $600,000 ÷ $12 par = 50,000 shares
2. $800,000 ÷ $5 stated value = 160,000 shares
3. $600,000 ÷ $12 par = 50,000 shares (no preferred treasury stock)
4. 160,000 shares issued – 5,000 treasury shares = 155,000 shares

2. On January 1, 2006, Dkembe Corporation was authorized to issue 100,000 shares of common
    stock, par value $5 per share, and 20,000 shares of 5 percent cumulative preferred stock, par
    value $40 per share.

    Prepare journal entries to record the following 2006 transactions:

    1. Issued 60,000 shares of common stock at $12 per share.
    2. Issued 12,000 shares of preferred stock at $56 per share.
    3. Reacquired 1,000 shares of common stock at $12 per share.
    4. Reissued 200 of the treasury shares for $2,600.
    5. Declared a cash dividend sufficient to meet the current-dividend preference on
        preferred stock and pay common stockholders $1 per share.

    ANS:

    1. Cash...   720,000
            Common Stock   300,000
            Paid-In Capital in Excess of Par Value,
                Common Stock   420,000
                Issued 60,000 shares of common stock at $12 per
                share.

    2. Cash   672,000
            Preferred Stock   480,000
            Paid-In Capital in Excess of Par, Preferred
                Stock   192,000
                Issued 12,000 shares of preferred stock at $56 per
                share.

    3. Treasury Stock...   12,000
            Cash   12,000
                Reacquired 1,000 shares of common stock at $12
                per share.

    4. Cash...   2,600
            Paid-In Capital, Treasury Stock..........................   200
            Treasury Stock..   2,400
                Reissued 200 shares of treasury stock at $13 per
                share; cost of shares reissued, $12 per share.

    5. Dividends, Common...   59,200
        Dividends, Preferred...   24,000
            Dividends Payable, Preferred Stock   24,000
            Dividends Payable, Common Stock   59,200
                Declared current-year dividend on preferred stock
                ($480,000 × 0.05 = $24,000) and a $1 per share
                dividend on common stock (60,000 common shares
                issued – 1,000 treasury shares purchased + 200
                treasury shares reissued = 59,200 shares of
                common outstanding).

3. Assume that 2,000 shares of common stock with a par value of $12 and a market price of $16 per share are issued in exchange for land with a fair market value of $32,000.

1. Prepare the journal entry to record the transaction.
2. If the land's appraised fair market value were $33,000, what would be the correct entry to record the transaction?
3. Prepare the necessary journal entry, assuming the same facts as in (2), except that the stock is not actively traded and therefore its market price is unknown.
4. Prepare the necessary journal entry, assuming the stock has a par value of $10 and a market price of $15 per share.

ANS:

1. Land.. 32,000
      Common Stock... 24,000
      Paid-In Capital in Excess of Par Value,
         Common Stock 8,000
         Issued 2,000 shares of $12 par common stock,
         market price $16 per share, in exchange for land.

2. Same entry as in (1); the land would be valued at the fair market value of the stock given up, which is $32,000.

3. Land.. 33,000
      Common Stock... 24,000
      Paid-In Capital in Excess of Par, Common Stock 9,000
         Issued 2,000 shares of $12 par common stock in
         exchange for land with an appraised fair market
         value of $33,000.

4. Land.. 30,000
      Common Stock... 20,000
      Paid-In Capital in Excess of Par, Common Stock 10,000
         Issued 2,000 shares of $10 par common stock,
         market price $15 per share, in exchange for land.

4. Provide the necessary journal entries to record the following:

   1. Oscar Corporation was granted a charter authorizing the issuance of 300,000 shares of $1 par-value common stock.
   2. The company issued 150,000 shares of common stock at a price of $6 per share.
   3. The company reacquired 4,000 shares of its own stock at $7 per share, to be held in treasury.
   4. Another 4,000 shares were reacquired at $8 per share.
   5. Of the shares reacquired in (3), 1,500 were reissued for $9 per share.
   6. Of the shares reacquired in (4), 1,000 were reissued at $6.40 per share.
   7. Given the preceding transactions, what is the balance in the treasury stock account?

   ANS:

   1. No entry required.

   2. Cash 900,000
         Common Stock   150,000
         Paid-In Capital in Excess of Par, Common Stock   750,000
            Issued 150,000 shares of $1 par common stock,
            market price $6 per share.

   3. Treasury Stock 28,000
         Cash   28,000
            Reacquired 4,000 shares at $7 per share.

   4. Treasury Stock 32,000
         Cash   32,000
            Reacquired 4,000 shares at $8 per share.

   5. Cash 13,500
         Treasury Stock   10,500
         Paid-In Capital, Treasury Stock   3,000
            Reissued 1,500 shares of treasury stock,
            cost of $7, market price of $9.

   6. Cash 6,400
      Paid-In Capital, Treasury Stock 1,600
         Treasury Stock   8,000
            Reissued 1,000 shares of treasury stock, cost
            of $8, market price of $6.40.

   7. Balance in treasury stock is $28,000 + $32,000 − $10,500 − $8,000 = $41,500
      or (2,500 × $7) + (3,000 × $8) = $41,500.

5. The accounting records of Janeway Corporation reveal the following data:

December 31, 2004 balances		2005 transactions	
Common stock	$ 80,000	Net income	$25,000
Additional paid-in capital	120,000	Translation adjustment	2,500
Retained earnings	60,000	Unrealized loss on available-	
Accumulated other		for-sale securities	(1,200)
comprehensive income	5,000	Dividends paid	12,000

1. Compute the comprehensive income for 2005.
2. Prepare the statement of stockholders' equity for 2005.

ANS:

1. Comprehensive income = $25,000 + $2,500 – $1,200 = $26,300

2.

Janeway Corporation
Statement of Stockholders' Equity
For the Year Ended December 31, 2005

	Common Stock	Additional Paid-In Capital	Retained Earnings	Accumulated Other Comprehensive Income	Total
Balance, January 1, 2005	$80,000	$120,000	$60,000	$5,000	$265,000
Net income—2005			25,000		$ 25,000
Translation adjustment				2,500	2,500
Unrealized loss on AFSS				(1,200)	(1,200)
Comprehensive income					$ 26,300
Dividends			(12,000)		$ (12,000)
Balance, December 31, 2005	$80,000	$120,000	$73,000	$6,300	$279,300

Chapter 12—Equity Financing—Quiz A

Name_____   Section_____

TRUE/FALSE

Circle T or F to indicate whether each of the following statements is true or false.

T F   1.   The retained earnings account is always reduced when a stock dividend is declared.

T F   2.   When treasury stock is reissued at a price that exceeds its cost, the excess is credited to an equity account.

T F   3.   Management may sometimes buy back its own stock so that the stock can be reissued to employees.

T F   4.   The market value of a stock, rather than its par value, is used when a company exchanges stock for capital assets.

T F   5.   The total number of shares of issued stock is always the same as the total number of shares of authorized stock.

T F   6.   Corporations are legally obligated to pay preferred stock dividends.

T F   7.   Cash dividends are not paid on treasury stock.

T F   8.   When preferred stock is cumulative, dividends in arrears is not a current liability.

T F   9.   Total stockholders' equity is affected by the payment of cash dividends, but is not reduced by the declaration of cash dividends.

T F 10.   When total liabilities exceed total assets, stockholders' equity must have a deficit balance.

Name_____   Section_____

MATCHING

In the spaces provided, write the letter of the definition for each of the following terms:

a. A class of stock that usually conveys voting rights to its holders.
b. The right of preferred stockholders to receive dividends for the current period before any dividends can be paid to common stockholders.
c. The amounts and types of stock that can be issued by a corporation.
d. An amount equal to the par value of stock times the number of shares issued.
e. This right is not granted to holders of noncumulative preferred stock.
f. The amount of dividends on cumulative preferred stock that were not declared in prior periods.
g. A class of stock that usually conveys dividend and liquidation preferences to its holders.
h. Shares of stock that have been issued but are not currently outstanding.
i. The total amount invested in a corporation by its owners in exchange for shares of stock.
j. The time when those who will receive a dividend are identified.

1. _____ Dividends in arrears

2. _____ Legal capital

3. _____ Cumulative-dividend preference

4. _____ Treasury stock

5. _____ Common stock

6. _____ Preferred stock

7. _____ Current-dividend preference

8. _____ Contributed capital

9. _____ Authorized stock

10. _____ Date of record

Quiz Solutions

Quiz A

1. T
2. T
3. T
4. T
5. F
6. F
7. T
8. T
9. F
10. T

Quiz B

1. f
2. d
3. e
4. h
5. a
6. g
7. b
8. i
9. c
10. j

MULTIPLE CHOICE

Why Companies Invest in Other Companies

1. Which of the following is NOT typically a reason why one company would invest in another company?
    a. To diversify product offerings
    b. To ensure a supply of raw materials
    c. To recruit key personnel
    d. To acquire a new product

    ANS: C

2. Which of the following is NOT typically a reason why one company would invest in another company?
    a. To earn higher returns than those offered by banks
    b. To make a safer investment than those offered by banks
    c. To influence the board of directors
    d. To make use of seasonal increases in cash flows

    ANS: B

Classifying a Security

3. Which type of securities is purchased with the intent of selling them in the near future?
    a. Marketable equity securities
    b. Available-for-sale securities
    c. Trading securities
    d. Held-to-maturity securities

    ANS: C

4. Unless there is compelling evidence to the contrary, significant influence is presumed when a company owns
    a. 20 to 50 percent of the outstanding voting stock of another company
    b. 50 percent or more of the outstanding voting stock of another company
    c. 0 to 20 percent of the outstanding voting stock of another company
    d. 10 to 40 percent of the outstanding voting stock of another company

    ANS: A

5. Harvey Corporation purchased 1,200 of the 3,000 outstanding shares of Michael Company common stock for $50 per share. Given this information, Harvey Corporation should account for the investment in Michael Company stock using the
    a. Cost method
    b. Equity method
    c. Effective-amortization method
    d. Straight-line amortization method

    ANS: B

6. Which category includes only debt securities?
    a. Marketable equity securities
    b. Available-for-sale securities
    c. Trading securities
    d. Held-to-maturity securities

    ANS: D

7. Accounting for investments under the equity method generally applies when the level of ownership in another company is at what percentage?
    a. Less than 20 percent
    b. 20 percent to 30 percent
    c. 20 percent to 50 percent
    d. More than 50 percent

    ANS: C

8. The equity method of accounting for an investment in the common stock of another company should be used when the investment
    a. Is composed of common stock and it is the investor's intent to vote the common stock
    b. Ensures a source of supply such as raw materials
    c. Enables the investor to exercise significant influence over the investee
    d. Gives the investor voting control over the investee

    ANS: C

9. Consolidated financial statements are typically prepared when one company has
    a. Accounted for its investment in another company by the equity method
    b. Significant influence over the operating and financial policies of another company
    c. The controlling financial interest in another company
    d. A substantial equity interest in the net assets of another company

    ANS: C

10. What are the two general types of securities purchased by companies?
    a. Debt and bonds
    b. Debt and equity
    c. Stock and equity
    d. Common and preferred

    ANS: B

11. Which category of security does NOT include equity securities?
    a. Available-for-sale
    b. Trading
    c. Equity method
    d. Held-to-maturity

    ANS: D

12. The equity method is used to account for an investment of more than 20 percent of another company's
    a. Bonds
    b. Preferred stock
    c. Common stock
    d. Convertible bonds

    ANS: C

13. Which of the following is NOT one of the acceptable classifications for investments?
    a. Trading securities
    b. Available-for-sale securities
    c. Equity method securities
    d. Control securities

    ANS: D

Accounting for Trading and Available-for-Sale Securities

14. If a trading security is sold, the investment account is
    a. Debited for the market value of the security
    b. Credited for the cost of the security
    c. Credited for the market value of the security
    d. Debited for the cost of the security

    ANS: B

15. Unrealized holding gains or losses which are recognized in income are from securities classified as
    a. Trading
    b. Available-for-sale
    c. Held-to-maturity
    d. Income producing

    ANS: A

16. On January 1, 2005, Mellie Company purchased a $10,000, 10 percent bond, at face value. Interest is paid annually each January 1. The entry related to this investment on December 31, 2005, would include a
    a. Debit to Interest Receivable for $1,000
    b. Credit to Interest Expense for $1,000
    c. Debit to Interest Revenue for $1,000
    d. Credit to Cash for $1,000

    ANS: A

17. Augsburg Corporation recorded the following transactions for its long-term investments during 2006:

> May 22   Purchased 1,000 shares of Miller Corporation stock at $55 per share plus brokerage fees of $1,000 and classified the shares as trading securities. Miller Corporation has 30,000 shares outstanding.
>
> June 30   Received a cash dividend of $0.80 per share on Miller Corporation stock.
>
> Aug. 26   Sold 400 shares of Miller Corporation stock for $60 per share.
>
> Dec. 31   Miller common stock had a closing market price of $50 per share. The decline is considered to be temporary.

Given this information, on August 26, Augsburg should
 a. Credit Investment in Trading Securities for $22,000
 b. Credit Realized Gain on Sale of Securities for $1,600
 c. Credit Realized Gain on Sale of Securities for $1,200
 d. Debit Dividend Revenue for $23,600

ANS: B

18. On January 5, 2006, Gannon Corporation purchased 100 shares of Hedney Company stock at $12 per share and paid a $50 brokerage commission. Gannon classified the shares as available-for-sale securities. On May 31, 2006, the entry to record the receipt of the 60-cent-per-share dividend would include a credit to
 a. Dividend Revenue for $100
 b. Long-Term Investments for $60
 c. Dividend Revenue for $60
 d. Long-Term Investments for $100

ANS: C

19. If 300 shares of stock are purchased for $38 per share and are sold one year later for $41 per share, what is the net gain or loss on the sale? (Assume that there are no transaction costs.)
 a. $900 gain
 b. $900 loss
 c. $300 gain
 d. $300 loss

ANS: A

20. In July 2005, Leaf Company acquired 5,000 shares of the common stock of Ryan Corporation and classified the shares as trading securities. The following January, Ryan announced a $100,000 net income for 2005 and declared a cash dividend of $0.50 per share on its 100,000 shares of outstanding common stock. The Leaf Company dividend revenue from Ryan Corporation in January 2006 would be
 a. $0
 b. $2,500
 c. $5,000
 d. $10,000

ANS: B

Accounting for Changes in Value of Securities

21. Changes in fair value of securities are reported in the income statement for which type of securities?
    a. Marketable equity securities
    b. Available-for-sale securities
    c. Trading securities
    d. Held-to-maturity securities

    ANS: C

22. Changes in fair value of securities are reported in the stockholders' equity section of the balance sheet for which type of securities?
    a. Marketable equity securities
    b. Available-for-sale securities
    c. Trading securities
    d. Held-to-maturity securities

    ANS: B

23. Unrealized losses on trading securities are
    a. Classified as contra-owners' equity accounts
    b. Recorded only when the stock is sold
    c. Classified as a contra-investment asset account
    d. Included in a section on the income statement

    ANS: D

24. A net unrealized increase in the value of available-for-sale securities (considered as a whole) should be reflected in the current financial statements as
    a. An extraordinary item on the income statement which increases retained earnings
    b. A current revenue resulting from holding securities
    c. Only a disclosure in the notes to the financial statements
    d. A valuation allowance which is included in the equity section of the balance sheet

    ANS: D

25. A net unrealized decrease in the value of available-for-sale securities (considered as a whole) should be reflected in the current financial statements as
    a. An extraordinary item on the income statement which reduces retained earnings
    b. A current liability resulting from holding securities
    c. Only a disclosure in the notes to the financial statements
    d. A valuation allowance which is included in the equity section of the balance sheet

    ANS: D

26. Augsburg Corporation recorded the following transactions for its short-term investments during 2006:

May 22   Purchased 1,000 shares of Miller Corporation stock at $55 per share plus brokerage fees of $1,000 and classified the shares as trading securities. Miller Corporation has 30,000 shares outstanding.
June 30   Received a cash dividend of $0.80 per share on Miller Corporation stock.
Aug. 26   Sold 400 shares of Miller Corporation stock for $60 per share.
Dec. 31   Miller common stock had a closing market price of $53 per share. The decline is considered to be temporary.

Given this information, the adjusting entry that Augsburg needs to make on December 31 is
a. Market Adjustment—Trading Securities 1,800
        Unrealized Loss on Trading Securities—Income 1,800
b. Unrealized Loss on Trading Securities—Income 1,800
        Market Adjustment—Trading Securities 1,800
c. Market Adjustment—Trading Securities 3,000
        Unrealized Loss on Trading Securities—Income 3,000
d. Unrealized Loss on Trading Securities—Income 3,000
        Market Adjustment—Trading Securities 3,000

ANS: B

27. During 2006, Fisher Corp. acquired 200 shares of Wychek stock at $20 per share. Fisher accounted for the stock as trading securities. The market price per share of Wychek's stock as of December 31, 2006 and 2007, is $15 and $25, respectively. How much unrealized gain or loss on long-term investments should Fisher report on its December 31, 2006 income statement?
a. $1,000 unrealized loss
b. $3,000 unrealized loss
c. $500 unrealized gain
d. No unrealized gain or loss

ANS: D

28. During 2006, Fisher Corporation acquired 200 shares of Wychek stock at $20 per share. Fisher Corporation accounted for the stock as available-for-sale securities. All declines in market value are considered to be temporary. The market price per share of Wychek's stock as of December 31, 2006 and 2007, is $15 and $25, respectively. Given this information, the correct adjusting entry by Fisher at December 31, 2007, would include a credit to
a. Market Adjustment—Available-for-Sale Securities of $1,000
b. Unrealized Increase in Value of Available-for-Sale Securities—Equity of $2,000
c. Market Adjustment—Available-for-Sale Securities of $2,000
d. Unrealized Increase in Value of Available-for-Sale Securities—Equity of $1,000

ANS: B

29. On March 1, one hundred shares of stock were originally purchased for $62 per share and are being held as trading securities. The price decreased to $58 per share on July 1 and then increased to $66 on December 31. At what amount should the investment be valued in the December 31 balance sheet?
    a. $5,800
    b. $6,200
    c. $6,600
    d. Some other amount

    ANS: C

30. On January 2, 2006, Murray Corporation bought 15 percent of Castro Corporation's capital stock for $60,000 and classified it as available-for-sale securities. Castro's net income for the year ended December 31, 2006, was $100,000. During 2006, Castro declared a dividend of $140,000. On December 31, 2006, the fair value of the Castro stock owned by Murray had increased to $90,000. How much should Murray show on its 2006 income statement as income from this investment?
    a. $3,150
    b. $15,000
    c. $21,000
    d. $51,000

    ANS: C

31. On January 2, 2006, Rockne Co. acquired 2,000 shares of Rice Company common stock for $8,000 and classified these shares as available-for-sale securities. During 2006, Rockne received $6,000 of cash dividends. The fair value of Rice's stock on December 31, 2006, was $7 per share. What amount should Rockne report in 2006 related to Rice Company?
    a. Revenue of $6,000
    b. Revenue of $12,000
    c. A $14,000 decrease in the investment account
    d. A $14,000 increase in the investment account

    ANS: A

32. On January 1, 2006, Ya-Ling Co. paid $500,000 for 20,000 shares of Chen Co.'s common stock and classified these shares as trading securities. The fair value of Chen Co.'s stock at December 31, 2006, is $27 per share. What is the net asset amount (which includes both investments and any related market adjustments) attributable to the investment in Chen that will be included on Ya-Ling's balance sheet at December 31, 2006?
    a. $0
    b. $40,000
    c. $500,000
    d. $540,000

    ANS: D

33. Nguyen Inc. began business on January 1, 2006, and at December 31, 2006, Nguyen had the following investment portfolios of equity securities:

	Trading	Available-for-Sale
Total cost	$150,000	$225,000
Total market value	110,000	195,000

Unrealized losses at December 31, 2006, should be recorded with corresponding charges against Income and Stockholders' Equity of
a. $70,000 and $0, respectively
b. $40,000 and $30,000, respectively
c. $30,000 and 40,000, respectively
d. $0 and $70,000, respectively

ANS: B

EXPANDED MATERIAL

Accounting for Held-to-Maturity Securities

34. When investors purchase bonds between interest dates, they
a. Earn "extra" interest
b. Do not earn any interest until after the first interest date has passed
c. Must purchase the accrued interest from the seller
d. Receive interest based on the market price at the beginning of the period

ANS: C

35. The total amount of interest earned when bonds are purchased at a premium is the amount of the cash interest payments
a. Plus the discount
b. Minus the discount
c. Plus the premium
d. Minus the premium

ANS: D

36. When bonds that are held as a long-term investment are sold before their maturity dates, the difference between the sales price and the balance in the investment account is
a. Debited or credited to Capital Stock
b. Recorded as a gain or loss on the sale
c. Recorded directly to Retained Earnings
d. Recorded as interest revenue or expense

ANS: B

37. The amortization of a bond discount
    a. Increases the amount of interest revenue earned on an investment in bonds
    b. Decreases the amount of interest revenue earned on an investment in bonds
    c. Decreases the balance of the investment account
    d. Does not affect the balance in the investment account

    ANS: A

38. The journal entry to record the amortization of a premium resulting from an investment in bonds would cause
    a. An increase in Investment in Bonds
    b. An increase in Bond Interest Revenue
    c. A decrease in Bond Interest Revenue
    d. No change in Investment in Bonds

    ANS: C

39. The entry to amortize an investment in bonds purchased at a discount includes a debit to
    a. Investment in Bonds
    b. Interest Expense
    c. Cash
    d. Bond Discount

    ANS: A

40. If a 10 percent, $8,000 face value bond sells for $7,000, the effective interest rate will be
    a. Less than 10 percent
    b. Greater than 10 percent
    c. Equal to 10 percent
    d. Unknown; more information is needed

    ANS: B

41. On April 1, 2006, Fiedler purchased $10,000 of Hun Corporation Bonds at 96 plus accrued interest. The bonds pay interest of 10 percent semiannually on March 1 and September 1. To record this acquisition, Fiedler should debit Investments in Held-to-Maturity Securities—Hun Bonds for
    a. $9,600
    b. $9,700
    c. $10,000
    d. $10,100

    ANS: A

42. On April 1, 2006, Bering Inc. purchased $20,000 of Warner Corporation's 10-year, 8 percent bonds at par plus accrued interest. Interest is payable on June 30 and December 31. How much interest revenue should Bering report on its December 31, 2006 income statement as a result of this investment?
    a. $1,248
    b. $1,200
    c. $824
    d. $800

    ANS: B

43. Farve purchased ten $1,000, 10 percent bonds issued by Marino Corporation for 104 on July 1, 2006. The bonds will mature on July 1, 2016, and pay interest on June 30 and December 31. Farve uses the straight-line method to amortize premiums and discounts. How much interest revenue should Farve recognize from its investment for the year ending December 31, 2006?
    a. $480
    b. $485
    c. $500
    d. $520

    ANS: A

44. Simpson Corporation purchased $20,000 of Tekservice Corporation's 12 percent bonds for $18,230 plus accrued interest on March 1, 2006. The bonds mature on January 1, 2016, and interest is payable on June 30 and December 31. How much discount or premium should be amortized on June 30, 2006, under the straight-line method?
    a. $90.00
    b. $88.50
    c. $60.00
    d. $59.00

    ANS: C

45. Simpson Corporation purchased $20,000 of Tekservice Corporation's 12 percent bonds at 92 plus accrued interest on March 1, 2006. The bonds mature on January 1, 2016, and interest is payable on June 30 and December 31. How much did Simpson pay in total on March 1, 2006?
    a. $20,000
    b. $18,800
    c. $18,400
    d. $18,000

    ANS: B

46. On January 1, 2006, Young Inc. purchased $50,000 of Montana Corporation 14 percent bonds for $53,000. Interest is payable semiannually. If Young desires a 12 percent rate of return, how much premium should be amortized on June 30, 2006, using the effective-interest method?
    a. $3,180
    b. $1,855
    c. $320
    d. $210

    ANS: C

Investments in Debt and Equity Securities   **339**

47. Cleveland purchased $100,000 of Rob Company's 10-year, 9 percent bonds for $83,050 on July 1, 2006. Cleveland purchased the bonds to yield 12 percent interest. If Cleveland uses the effective-interest method to amortize discounts, how much interest revenue should Cleveland recognize for 2006 as a result of the investment?
    a. $7,474
    b. $6,000
    c. $5,767
    d. $4,983

    ANS: D

48. On January 1, 2006, Roswell purchased ten $1,000, 12 percent, 10-year bonds issued by E. T. Corporation at 101. The bonds pay interest on June 30 and December 31. When the bonds showed an unamortized balance of $10,070, Roswell sold them for $10,050. How much gain or loss should Roswell record on the sale?
    a. $100 gain
    b. $50 gain
    c. $30 loss
    d. $20 loss

    ANS: D

49. Poway Inc. purchased $20,000 of SD Corporation's 12 percent, 10-year bonds on January 1, 2005, for $21,200 plus accrued interest. Interest on the bonds is payable on April 1 and October 1. On January 1, 2006, Poway sold the bonds for 102 plus accrued interest. As a result of the sale, Poway should debit Cash for
    a. $21,036
    b. $21,624
    c. $21,000
    d. $21,200

    ANS: C

50. Mel Company purchased $60,000 of Gibson Company's 20-year, 8 percent bonds at 98 on July 1, 2006. The bonds pay interest each January 1 and July 1, and they mature on July 1, 2023. Given this information, the entry to record the purchase of Gibson Company bonds would include a
    a. Debit to Held-to-Maturity Securities of $58,800
    b. Debit to Held-to-Maturity Securities of $60,000
    c. Credit to Cash of $60,000
    d. Credit to Interest Revenue of $5,000

    ANS: A

51. Mel Company purchased $60,000 of Gibson Company's 20-year, 8 percent bonds at 98 on November 1, 2006. The bonds pay interest each January 1 and July 1, and they mature on July 1, 2023. Given this information, the entry to record the purchase of Gibson Company bonds would include a
    a. Debit to Interest Receivable of $800
    b. Debit to Held-to-Maturity Securities of $60,000
    c. Credit to Cash of $60,400
    d. Credit to Interest Revenue of $1,600

    ANS: C

52. Mel Company purchased $60,000 of Gibson Company's 20-year, 8 percent bonds at 98 on July 1, 2006. The bonds pay interest each January 1 and July 1, and they mature on July 1, 2023. Given this information, the entry needed on December 31, 2006 (year-end), to account for the interest on Gibson Company's bonds would include a debit to
   a. Cash of $4,800
   b. Cash of $2,400
   c. Interest Receivable of $4,800
   d. Interest Receivable of $2,400

   ANS: D

Accounting for Equity Investments Using the Equity Method

53. When the equity method is used to account for long-term investments in stock, the receipt of dividends is recorded as a credit to
   a. The investment account
   b. Dividend Revenue
   c. Cash
   d. Interest Revenue

   ANS: A

54. When an investor uses the equity method to account for investments in common stock, the investment account will be increased when the investor recognizes
   a. A proportionate share of the net income of the investee
   b. A cash dividend received from the investee
   c. Periodic amortization of the goodwill related to the purchase
   d. Depreciation related to the excess of market value over book value of the investee's depreciable assets at the date of purchase by the investor

   ANS: A

55. When an investor uses the equity method to account for investments in common stock, cash dividends received by the investor from the investee should be recorded as
   a. An increase in the investment account
   b. A deduction from the investment account
   c. Dividend revenue
   d. A deduction from the investor's share of the investee's profits

   ANS: B

56. Bart Corporation purchased 1,200 of the 3,000 outstanding shares of Starr Company common stock for $50 per share. Given this information, when Bart Corporation receives a cash dividend from Starr Company, which of the following accounts should be credited?
   a. Revenue from Investments
   b. Dividend Revenue
   c. Investment in Equity Method Securities
   d. None of the above

   ANS: C

57. On March 17, 2006, Jose Inc. acquired 17,000 shares of Luis Corporation stock at $39 per share. Jose has 50,000 shares outstanding. On December 31, 2006, Luis common stock had a closing market price of $24 per share. Assuming that the decline in market price is considered to be temporary, at December 31, Luis would
    a. Make an adjusting entry, including a debit to Unrealized Loss on Equity Method Securities of $255,000
    b. Make an adjusting entry, including a credit to Market Adjustment on Equity Method Securities of $408,000
    c. Make an adjusting entry, including a credit to Investment in Luis Stock of $255,000
    d. Do nothing; an adjusting entry is not required

    ANS: D

58. Sharpe Inc. had the following activities related to long-term investments during 2006:

July 6	Purchased 12,000 shares of Berlin Tours for $15 per share.
Aug. 16	Received a $1.20-per-share cash dividend from Berlin Tours.
Dec. 31	Berlin announced earnings for the year of $166,800. Berlin has 36,000 shares of stock outstanding.

    Given this information, how much revenue should Sharpe report in 2006 for its investment in Berlin stock?
    a. $14,400
    b. $55,600
    c. $70,000
    d. $84,400

    ANS: B

59. In 2006, Rune had the following activities in long-term investments:

April 6	Purchased 2,000 shares of Arledge stock for $3.25 per share plus brokerage fees of $500.
July 7	Received a cash dividend of $0.70 per share on Arledge stock.
Dec. 31	Arledge reported net income of $50,000. Arledge has 8,000 shares of common stock outstanding.

    What should be the balance in the investment in equity method securities—Arledge stock account as of December 31, 2006?
    a. $17,600
    b. $18,100
    c. $19,500
    d. $20,900

    ANS: B

60. On January 2, 2005, U.S. Buyers, Inc. purchased 5,000 shares of the 20,000 shares outstanding of Latino Corporation stock for $15,000. The following information was reported by Latino during 2005:

Net income..	$45,000
Dividends..	$1.75 per share
Market price, 12/31/05...	$2.50 per share

U.S. Buyers, Inc. sold all of its Latino Corporation stock on March 1, 2006, for $3.10 per share. The total amount U.S. Buyers, Inc. should report on the sale is
   a. $3,500 gain
   b. $3,000 loss
   c. $2,000 loss
   d. $1,950 loss

ANS: C

Basics of Consolidated Financial Statements

61. Financial statements in which financial data for two or more companies are combined as a single entity are called
   a. Conventional statements
   b. Consolidated statements
   c. Audited statements
   d. Constitutional statements

ANS: B

62. Johnson Company owns 90 percent of the outstanding stock of Smith Company. The equity of the remaining 10 percent of Smith Company stock is called the
   a. Parent
   b. Minority interest
   c. Majority interest
   d. Subsidiary

ANS: B

63. In general, consolidated financial statements should be prepared
   a. When a corporation owns more than 20 percent of the common stock of another company
   b. When a corporation owns more than 50 percent of the common stock of another company
   c. Only when a corporation owns 100 percent of the common stock of another company
   d. Whenever the market value of the stock investment is significantly lower than its cost

ANS: B

PROBLEMS

1. On February 1, 2005, Pike Company purchased the following trading securities:

Security	Cost
1	$ 9,000
2	12,000
3	26,000

On August 15, 2005, Pike Company sold Security 2 for $10,000.

On December 31, 2005, market prices were as follows: Security 1, $8,500 and Security 2, $27,500.

1. Prepare journal entries to record the events of 2005.
2. Illustrate how the investment related accounts would be reported on the balance sheet and income statement for 2005.

ANS:

1.

Feb.	1	Investment in Trading Securities..........	47,000	
		Cash...		47,000
Aug.	15	Cash	10,000	
		Realized Loss on Sale of Trading Securities...	2,000	
		Investment in Trading Securities......		12,000
Dec.	31	Market Adjustment—Trading Securities	1,000	
		Unrealized Gain on Trading.............. Securities—Income..........................		1,000

2.

Pike Company
Partial Balance Sheet
December 31, 2005

Current assets:		
Trading securities..	$35,000	
Plus: Market adjustment—trading securities................	1,000	$36,000

Pike Company
Partial Income Statement
For the Year Ended December 31, 2005

Other revenue:	
Unrealized gain on trading securities—income............	$ 1,000
Other expenses:	
Realized loss on sale of trading securities	(2,000)

2. In June 2006, Wade Company had excess cash that would not be needed until March 1, 2007. Management decided to invest the money in a short-term investment in trading securities. Wade owned no investment securities before June 2006. The following transactions relate to these investments:

June 20   Purchased 5,000 shares of Delano Corporation stock. The price paid (including brokerage fees) was $52,250.
Sept. 2   Received a cash dividend of $0.60 per share on Delano stock.
Oct. 5   Sold 2,000 shares of Delano stock at $10.50 per share. Paid a selling commission of $200.
Dec. 31   The market price of Delano stock was $11.00.

Give the journal entries necessary to account for the investment in Delano Corporation during 2006.

ANS:

| June 20 | Investment in Trading Securities, Delano Corporation | 52,250 | |
| | Cash | | 52,250 |

Sept. 28	Cash	3,000	
	Dividend Revenue		3,000
	($0.60 × 5,000 shares = $3,000)		

Oct. 5	Cash	20,800	
	Realized Loss on Sale of Trading Securities	100	
	Investment in Trading Securities, Delano Corporation		20,900
	(Cash = $10.50 × 2,000 shares − $200 commission = $20,800; short-term investment = $52,250 × 2/5; loss = $20,800 − $20,900)		

Dec. 31	Market Adjustment—Trading Securities	1,650	
	Unrealized Gain on Trading Securities— Income		1,650
	[$11.00 × 3,000 shares − ($52,250 − $20,900) = $1,650]		

3. Barry Inc. carries the following marketable equity securities on its books at December 31, 2005 and 2006. All securities were purchased during 2005, and there were no beginning balances in any market adjustment accounts.

Trading securities:

	Cost	Market December 31, 2005	Market December 31, 2006
D Company.........	$ 50,000	$ 26,000	$ 40,000
E Company	26,000	40,000	40,000
F Company..........	70,000	60,000	50,000
Total	$146,000	$126,000	$130,000

Available-for-sale securities:

	Cost	Market December 31, 2005	Market December 31, 2006
G Company.........	$420,000	$360,000	$300,000
H Company.........	100,000	120,000	140,000
Total	$520,000	$480,000	$440,000

1. Give the journal entries necessary to record the valuations for both trading and available-for-sale securities at December 31, 2005 and 2006.
2. What net effect would these valuations have on 2005 and 2006 income?

ANS:

1. 2005
   Dec. 31   Unrealized Loss on Trading Securities—
   Income 20,000
       Market Adjustment—Trading Securities.....   20,000

   31   Unrealized Decrease in Value of Available-for-
   Sale Securities—Equity 40,000
       Market Adjustment—Available-for-Sale
       Securities..   40,000

   2006
   Dec. 31   Market Adjustment—Trading Securities.......... 4,000
       Unrealized Gain on Trading Securities—
       Income   4,000

   31   Unrealized Decrease in Value of Available-
   for-Sale Securities—Equity 40,000
       Market Adjustment—Available-for-Sale
       Securities..   40,000

2. Effect of valuation entries on 2005 net income:
   Recognized decline in value of trading securities .... $(20,000)

   Effect of valuation entries on 2006 net income:
   Recognized increase in value of trading securities........... $ 4,000

4. Don Ono purchased Yoko bonds with a face value of $30,000 in the secondary market on March 1, 2006, at a price of $28,340 plus a brokerage fee of $280 and accrued interest. Interest at 10 percent is payable on January 1 and July 1 each year. The bonds were originally issued on January 1, 2005, and mature on January 1, 2008. Don plans to amortize the discount once a year at December 31 on a straight-line basis.

    1. Prepare the journal entries to record the investment in the bonds on March 1, 2006, and the receipt of the first interest payment on July 1, 2006.
    2. Prepare the journal entry necessary on December 31, 2006, to properly report Don's income for 2006.
    3. Compute the amount of interest revenue that Don earned on these bonds in 2006.

ANS:

1. 2006

Mar. 1	Investment in Held-to-Maturity Securities	28,620	
	Bond Interest Receivable	500	
	Cash		29,120
July 1	Cash	1,500	
	Bond Interest Receivable		500
	Interest Revenue		1,000

2. 2006

Dec. 31	Bond Interest Receivable	1,500	
	Investment in Held-to-Maturity Securities	627	
	Interest Revenue		2,127
	[($30,000 − $28,620)/22 months =		
	$62.73; $62.73 × 10 months = $627]		

3. $1,000 + $2,127 = $3,127

5. Andy Company held a bond investment with a face value of $72,000. The company decided to sell the bonds on April 15, 2006, at a quoted price of 103.5. On that date, the carrying value of the bonds was $72,350. The sale is subject to a brokerage commission of $360.

Prepare the journal entry on April 15, 2006, for the sale of the bond investment. (Ignore accrued interest.)

ANS:

Cash	74,160	
Investment in Held-to-Maturity Securities		72,350
Gain on Sale of Bonds		1,810
[($72,000 × 1.035) − $360 = $74,160;		
$74,160 − $72,350 = $1,810]		

6. On January 1, 2006, Shane Corporation acquired 30 percent (13,000 shares) of Matthews Services Inc. common stock for $1,300,000 as a long-term investment. Data from Matthews' 2006 financial statements include the following:

Net income...	$330,000
Less cash dividends paid...	160,000
Increase in retained earnings..	$170,000

The market value of Matthews Services Inc. common stock on December 31, 2006, was $98 per share. Shane does not have any other investments in securities.

Prepare the necessary journal entries for Shane's investment in Matthews Services Inc. common stock assuming Shane uses the following methods to account for its investment in Matthews Services:

1. Classified as available-for-sale securities.
2. The equity method.

ANS:

1. | | | |
    |---|---|---|
    | Investment in Available-for-Sale Securities—
    Matthews Services Inc. Stock.............................. | 1,300,000 | |
    | Cash .... | | 1,300,000 |
    | | | |
    | Cash ($160,000 × 30%) .... | 48,000 | |
    | Dividend Revenue.. | | 48,000 |
    | | | |
    | Unrealized Increase/Decrease in Value of Available-
    for-Sale Securities—Equity (13,000 shares × $2) | 26,000 | |
    | Market Adjustment—Available-for-Sale Securities | | 26,000 |

2. | | | |
    |---|---|---|
    | Investment in Equity Method Securities................. | 1,300,000 | |
    | Cash .... | | 1,300,000 |
    | | | |
    | Cash .... | 48,000 | |
    | Investment in Equity Method Securities............. | | 48,000 |
    | | | |
    | Investment in Equity Method Securities
    ($330,000 × 30%)... | 99,000 | |
    | Revenue from Investment in Equity Method
        Securities... | | 99,000 |

Name_____   Section_____

TRUE/FALSE

Circle T or F to indicate whether each of the following statements is true or false.

T F 1. The equity method is usually used to account for investments in stock when more than 20 percent of the outstanding voting stock of another company is owned.

T F 2. The equity method records changes in the value of the investment as the net assets of the investee change.

T F 3. From 10 to 20 percent ownership of the outstanding voting stock of another company is not classified as "significant influence."

T F 4. When an investor purchases a stock or a bond of an issuing corporation, the commission and broker's fee are included in the cost of the asset.

T F 5. Trading securities, available-for-sale securities, and held-to-maturity securities are all shown on the balance sheet at current market value.

T F 6. Trading securities are held with the intent of selling the securities should the need for cash arise or to realize gains arising from short-term changes in price.

T F 7. Dividends received on stock classified as available-for-sale securities are shown as dividend revenue on the income statement.

T F 8. Changes in value of bond investments classified as held-to-maturity securities are shown as an adjustment to owners' equity.

T F 9. Dividends received on stock classified as trading securities are shown as dividend revenue on the income statement.

T F 10. The market adjustment account for trading securities will have a credit balance when the current market value exceeds cost for the portfolio of trading securities (considered as a whole).

Name_____   Section_____

TRUE/FALSE

Circle T or F to indicate whether each of the following statements is true or false.

T   F   1.   When bonds are purchased between interest dates, accrued interest from the last interest payment date to the date of purchase is not paid to the former bondholder.

T   F   2.   An investor in corporate bonds usually records the bond premium or bond discount in the same account as the principal amount of bonds purchased.

T   F   3.   It is relatively rare for bonds to be sold between interest dates because of the complications of accounting for accrued interest.

T   F   4.   A New York Bond Exchange quotation of a particular corporation's bonds indicates only the stated rate and not the effective (yield) rate of interest on the bonds.

T   F   5.   The method of recording interest on a bond investment purchased between interest dates is to credit Bond Interest Receivable.

T   F   6.   When bonds are purchased between interest dates, the investing company must amortize any premium or discount over the period the bonds are held as an investment.

T   F   7.   When bonds are purchased at a premium, the amount of amortization decreases each successive period when using the effective-interest method of amortization.

T   F   8.   The straight-line method of amortizing a premium or discount on a bond investment results in an amount of revenue earned that always meets generally accepted accounting standards.

T   F   9.   When long-term investments in bonds and stocks are written down to market value at the end of the year, the amount of the write-down in each case is reported as an unrealized loss in the stockholders' equity section of the balance sheet.

T   F   10.   When bonds are purchased at a premium and amortized under the effective-interest method, the amount of interest earned would decline each successive period.

Name_____   Section_____

MATCHING

In the spaces provided, write the letter of the term for each of the following definitions:

    a. Trading securities
    b. Realized gains and losses
    c. Equity securities
    d. Market Adjustment—Trading Securities
    e. Available-for-sale securities
    f. Held-to-maturity securities
    g. Consolidated financial statements
    h. Unrealized Increase/Decrease in Value of Available-for Sale Securities—Equity
    i. Unrealized gains and losses
    j. Equity method

1. _____ Gains and losses resulting from the sale of securities in an arm's-length transaction.

2. _____ A method of accounting for equity securities when the amount of stock purchased is between 20 and 50 percent of the total stock outstanding of the investee.

3. _____ An account used to track the difference between the historical cost and the market value of a company's portfolio of trading securities.

4. _____ Debt and equity securities purchased with the intent of selling them should the need for cash arise or to realize short-term gains.

5. _____ Debt securities purchased by an investor with the intent of holding the securities until they mature.

6. _____ Shares of ownership in a corporation that can change significantly in value and that provide for a return to investors in the form of dividends.

7. _____ Gains and losses resulting from changes in the value of securities that are still being held.

8. _____ Financial statements that represent the combined financial results of two or more companies.

9. _____ Debt and equity securities not classified as trading, held-to-maturity, or equity method securities.

10. _____ This account is disclosed in the stockholders' equity section of the balance sheet, and its balance is carried from year to year.

Name_____   Section_____

MULTIPLE CHOICE

1. On January 1, 2006, Tomas Corporation purchased $100,000 of 10-year, 10 percent bonds for $113,592 to yield 8 percent annually. The bonds pay interest on January 1 and July 1 of each year. If Tomas uses the effective-interest method of amortization, how much interest revenue will the company record for the first six months? (rounded)
   a. $5,456
   b. $5,000
   c. $4,544
   d. $4,456

2. On January 2, 2005, Manudo, Inc., purchased $400,000 of 10 percent, 10-year bonds for $436,000. The bonds pay interest on January 1 and July 1 of each year. Manudo uses straight-line amortization for all premiums or discounts. On July 1, 2008, Manudo sold the bonds for $416,000. How much gain or loss should Manudo record on the sale?
   a. $3,400 gain
   b. $3,400 loss
   c. $7,400 gain
   d. $7,400 loss

3. On January 1, 2005, the Nevada Company purchased $800,000 of Utah Company's 10 percent, 20-year bonds at 104 and classified the investment as held-to-maturity securities. The bonds pay interest on January 1 and July 1 of each year. Nevada uses straight-line amortization for all premiums and discounts. The entry for the receipt of the semiannual interest on July 1, 2005, is
   a. Cash.. 40,000
         Investment in Held to Maturity Securities ...   800
            Bond Interest Revenue   40,800
   b. Cash.. 40,000
         Investment in Held-to Maturity Securities   800
            Bond Interest Revenue   39,200
   c. Cash.. 40,000
            Bond Interest Revenue   40,000
   d. Cash.. 40,800
            Bond Interest Revenue   40,800

4. Cleveland purchased $200,000 of Clair Company's 10-year, 9 percent bonds for $166,100 on July 1, 2006. Cleveland purchased the bonds to yield 12 percent interest. If Cleveland uses the effective-interest method to amortize discounts, how much interest revenue should Cleveland recognize for 2006 as a result of the investment?
   a. $14,948
   b. $12,000
   c. $11,534
   d. $9,966

5. Rouen Corporation recorded the following transactions for its short-term investments during 2006:

April 22   Purchased 1,000 shares of Miller Corporation stock at $110 per share plus brokerage fees of $2,000 and classified the shares as trading securities. Miller Corporation has 30,000 shares outstanding.
June 30   Received a cash dividend of $0.80 per share on Miller Corporation stock.
Sept. 26   Sold 400 shares of Miller Corporation stock for $120 per share.
Dec. 31   Miller common stock had a closing market price of $106 per share. The decline is considered to be temporary.

Given this information, the adjusting entry that Rouen needs to make on December 31 is
a. Market Adjustment—Trading Securities 3,600
       Unrealized Loss on Trading Securities—Income ...   3,600
b. Unrealized Loss on Trading Securities—Income   3,600
       Market Adjustment—Trading Securities   3,600
c. Market Adjustment—Trading Securities 6,000
       Unrealized Loss on Trading Securities—Income ...   6,000
d. Unrealized Loss on Trading Securities—Income   6,000
       Market Adjustment—Trading Securities   6,000

Quiz Solutions

Quiz A	Quiz B	Quiz C	Quiz D
1. T	1. F	1. b	1. c
2. T	2. T	2. j	2. d
3. T	3. F	3. d	3. b
4. T	4. F	4. a	4. d
5. F	5. F	5. f	5. b
6. T	6. T	6. c	
7. T	7. F	7. i	
8. F	8. F	8. g	
9. T	9. T	9. e	
10. F	10. T	10. h	

MULTIPLE CHOICE

The Purpose of a Statement of Cash Flows

1. The statement of cash flows replaces the
   a. Balance sheet
   b. Statement of financial position
   c. Income statement
   d. Statement of changes in financial position

   ANS: D

2. The statement of cash flows
   a. Is a required statement only for those companies using cash-basis accounting
   b. Provides a connecting link between two consecutive income statements
   c. Is intended primarily to provide necessary information for assessing the profitability of an entity
   d. Summarizes all cash inflows and outflows of an entity for a given period of time

   ANS: D

3. Which of the following is NOT a purpose of the statement of cash flows?
   a. It provides information about an entity's cash receipts and payments over a period of time.
   b. It provides investors with information about the investing and financing activities of an entity.
   c. It highlights changes in managerial strategy regarding investments and finances.
   d. It measures the profitability of an entity.

   ANS: D

4. Which of the following statements is NOT true?
   a. The statement of cash flows provides details as to how the cash account changed during a period.
   b. The statement of cash flows does not replace the income statement.
   c. The statement of cash flows includes transactions that are not already reflected in the balance sheet and income statement.
   d. The statement of cash flows sheds some light on a company's ability to generate income in the future.

   ANS: C

5. In addition to the three primary financial statements, which of the following is also required under GAAP?
   a. Statement of financial position
   b. Statement of cash flows
   c. Statement of changes in working capital
   d. Statement of cash equivalents

   ANS: B

Information Reported in the Statement of Cash Flows

6. Those transactions and events that enter into the determination of net income are reported under which section of the statement of cash flows?
    a. Significant noncash investing and financial activities
    b. Financial activities
    c. Investing activities
    d. Operating activities

    ANS: D

7. Which of the following is the proper sequencing of activities on the statement of cash flows?
    a. Operating, investing, and financing
    b. Operating, financing, and investing
    c. Investing, operating, and financing
    d. Investing, financing, and operating

    ANS: A

8. Which of the following would NOT be included in the operating activities section of the statement of cash flows?
    a. Interest received
    b. Interest paid
    c. Dividends received
    d. Dividends paid

    ANS: D

9. Significant noncash financing and investing transactions are
    a. Listed in the body of a statement of cash flows
    b. Reported in a narrative or in a separate schedule
    c. Reported under the financing and investing activities sections
    d. Converted to cash equivalents

    ANS: B

10. Which of the following would NOT be considered cash or cash equivalents for purposes of preparing a statement of cash flows?
    a. Money market funds
    b. Checking accounts
    c. Treasury bills
    d. Notes receivable

    ANS: D

11. Which of the following would be reported as a cash flow from financing activities?
    a. Cash receipts from the sale of equipment
    b. Cash receipts from interest on notes receivable
    c. Cash receipts from dividends on long-term investments
    d. Cash receipts from the issuance of long-term debt

    ANS: D

12. The exchange of debt for equipment would be shown
    a. On a statement of cash flows as an operating activity
    b. On a statement of cash flows as an investing activity
    c. On a statement of cash flows as a financing activity
    d. As a supplementary disclosure

    ANS: D

13. Which of the following would be classified as an investing activity on a statement of cash flows?
    a. Cash received from dividends
    b. Cash paid for interest
    c. Cash received from the sale of land
    d. Cash used to repay principal amounts borrowed

    ANS: C

14. Which of the following would be classified as an operating activity on a statement of cash flows?
    a. Cash received from selling equity securities
    b. Cash received as dividends on investments
    c. Cash dividends paid to stockholders
    d. Cash paid to purchase treasury stock

    ANS: B

15. A statement of cash flows will help investors understand all the following, EXCEPT
    a. How a new building was financed
    b. Why inventory increased
    c. How much long-term debt was retired
    d. Whether or not a company paid dividends

    ANS: B

16. Which of the following would NOT be reported as an investing activity on a statement of cash flows?
    a. Collection of a long-term note receivable
    b. Amounts borrowed
    c. Extending loans to other entities
    d. Sale of a building

    ANS: B

17. Which of the following would be reported as a financing activity on a statement of cash flows?
    a. Receipt of a dividend
    b. Purchase of treasury stock
    c. Proceeds from the sale of land
    d. Payment of interest

    ANS: B

18. Which of the following would be reported as an operating activity on a statement of cash flows?
    a. Payment of taxes
    b. Payment of dividends
    c. Repayment of a loan
    d. Purchase of a building

    ANS: A

19. The repayment of the principal on a loan used to finance the purchase of equipment should be classified as a(n)
    a. Operating activity
    b. Investing activity
    c. Financing activity
    d. Noncash transaction

    ANS: C

20. Significant noncash financing transactions
    a. Are included parenthetically on a statement of cash flows
    b. Should not be disclosed at all since they are irrelevant to actual performance
    c. Should not be disclosed on a statement of cash flows but should appear elsewhere
    d. Are deducted from net income to determine cash provided by operating activities on a statement of cash flows

    ANS: C

21. Simpson purchased money market funds with cash during the current year. This transaction will result in a decrease in cash from
    a. Operating activities
    b. Financing activities
    c. Investing activities
    d. None of the above

    ANS: D

22. Durning Company loaned $1,000,000 at 8 percent interest to Silva Company. The interest revenue would be classified as a(n)
    a. Operating activity
    b. Investing activity
    c. Financing activity
    d. Noncash transaction

    ANS: A

23. Durning Company loaned $1,000,000 at 8 percent interest to Silva Company. The loan would be classified as a(n)
    a. Operating activity
    b. Investing activity
    c. Financing activity
    d. Noncash transaction

    ANS: B

Preparing a Statement of Cash Flows

24. Which of the following transactions is LEAST likely to be a separate item on a statement of cash flows prepared using the indirect method?
    a. The collection of accounts receivable
    b. The sale of equipment
    c. The issuance of stock
    d. The payment of dividends

    ANS: A

25. If depreciation expense is $20,000 and the beginning and ending Accumulated Depreciation balances are $100,000 and $110,000, respectively, cash paid for depreciation is
    a. $0
    b. $10,000
    c. $20,000
    d. $100,000

    ANS: A

26. If sales revenue for the period is $200,000 and the beginning and ending Accounts Receivable balances are $20,000 and $15,000, respectively, cash collected from customers is
    a. $200,000
    b. $205,000
    c. $195,000
    d. $235,000

    ANS: B

27. If interest revenue for the period is $4,000 and the beginning and ending Interest Receivable balances are $500 and $2,000, respectively, cash received from interest is
    a. $6,000
    b. $6,500
    c. $5,500
    d. $2,500

    ANS: D

28. If cost of goods sold is $100,000 and the beginning and ending Inventory balances are $20,000 and $16,000, respectively, net purchases are
    a. $96,000
    b. $100,000
    c. $104,000
    d. $136,000

    ANS: A

29. If cost of goods sold is $80,000 and the beginning and ending Accounts Payable balances are $10,000 and $15,000, respectively, cash paid to suppliers is
    a. $75,000
    b. $80,000
    c. $85,000
    d. Not determinable from the information given

    ANS: D

30. If net purchases are $126,000 and the beginning and ending Accounts Payable balances are $16,000 and $6,000, respectively, cash paid to suppliers is
    a. $136,000
    b. $116,000
    c. $126,000
    d. Not determinable from the information given

    ANS: A

31. If wages expense is $40,000 and the beginning and ending Wages Payable balances are $4,000 and $8,000, respectively, cash paid to employees is
    a. $36,000
    b. $40,000
    c. $44,000
    d. Not determinable from the information given

    ANS: A

32. If insurance expense is $5,000 and the beginning and ending Prepaid Insurance balances are $1,000 and $1,500, respectively, cash paid for insurance is
    a. $4,500
    b. $5,000
    c. $5,500
    d. Not determinable from the information given

    ANS: C

Analyzing Financial Statement to Prepare Statement of Cash Flows

33. The method that begins with net income or net loss and adjusts that number for items that did not affect cash is called the
    a. Direct method
    b. Operating method
    c. Indirect method
    d. Cash-equivalent method

    ANS: C

34. Which of the following would be deducted from net income on a statement of cash flows prepared using the indirect method?
    a. A gain from the sale of equipment
    b. A decrease in accounts receivable
    c. An increase in accounts payable
    d. Dividends paid

    ANS: A

35. Which of the following would be added to net income on a statement of cash flows prepared using the indirect method?
    a. A gain from the sale of equipment
    b. A decrease in accounts receivable
    c. A decrease in accounts payable
    d. Dividends received

    ANS: B

36. The purchase of inventory on account would increase
    a. Cash from operating activities
    b. Cash from financing activities
    c. Working capital
    d. None of the above

    ANS: D

37. The direct and indirect methods will usually show different amounts of cash flows from
    a. Operating activities
    b. Financing activities
    c. Investing activities
    d. None of the above

    ANS: D

38. Which of the following would NOT be added to net income on a statement of cash flows prepared by the indirect method?
    a. An increase in accounts payable
    b. A decrease in accounts receivable
    c. A gain from the sale of equipment
    d. Depreciation expense

    ANS: C

39. Which of the following would NOT be added to net income on a statement of cash flows prepared by the indirect method?
    a. An increase in accounts payable
    b. An increase in dividends payable
    c. Depreciation expense
    d. All of the above would be added

    ANS: B

40. Which of the following items would be reported on a statement of cash flows prepared by the indirect method but not by the direct method?
    a. Depreciation expense
    b. Cash received from the sale of a building
    c. Cash received from issuance of stock
    d. Cash paid for dividends

    ANS: A

41. A loss from the sale of a building would be reported on an indirect method statement of cash flows as a(n)
    a. Addition to net income
    b. Deduction from net income
    c. Cash inflow from financing activities
    d. Cash outflow from investing activities

    ANS: A

42. The indirect method of preparing a statement of cash flows
    a. Results in the same net cash flow from operating activities as the direct method
    b. Is the method most often used in practice
    c. Involves adjusting the net income figure for any noncash expenses
    d. All of the above

    ANS: D

43. The approach to preparing a statement of cash flows that adjusts net income to cash flows from operations is the
    a. All financial resources method
    b. Direct method
    c. Indirect method
    d. Worksheet method

    ANS: C

44. The method by which cash flows are presented on a statement of cash flows as operating cash receipts and payments is the
    a. All financial resources method
    b. Direct method
    c. Indirect method
    d. Working capital method

    ANS: B

45. The direct method of presenting a statement of cash flows
    a. Classifies activities differently from the indirect method
    b. Involves reconciling accrual net income to net cash flows from operating activities
    c. Shows the major classes of operating cash receipts and payments
    d. Includes noncash financing transactions

    ANS: C

46. Chen Company's financial statements show a net income of $184,000. The following items also appear on Chen's balance sheet:

Depreciation expense	$40,000
Accounts receivable decrease	12,000
Inventory increase	28,000
Accounts payable increase	8,000

What is Chen's net cash flow from operating activities?
a. $216,000
b. $136,000
c. $232,000
d. $272,000

ANS: A

47. Garcia Company's financial statements show a net loss of $90,000. The following items also appear on Garcia's balance sheet:

Depreciation expense	$42,000
Accounts receivable increase	72,000
Inventory decrease	24,000
Accounts payable decrease	12,000
Accrued liabilities increase	18,000

What is Garcia's net cash flow from operating activities?
a. $42,000
b. $78,000
c. $174,000
d. ($90,000)

ANS: D

48. Worthy Company's financial statements show a net income of $180,000. The following items also appear on Worthy's balance sheet:

Amortization expense	$48,000
Accounts receivable decrease	45,000
Inventory decrease	21,000
Interest payable increase	30,000

What is Worthy's net cash flow from operating activities?
a. $138,000
b. $222,000
c. $282,000
d. $324,000

ANS: D

49. Booth Company's financial statements show a net income of $143,000. The following items also appear on Booth's balance sheet:

Depreciation expense	$32,000
Accounts receivable decrease	36,000
Prepaid rent increase	22,000
Accounts payable decrease	26,000

What is Booth's net cash flow from operating activities?
a. $121,000
b. $163,000
c. $177,000
d. $157,000

ANS: B

50. The following information relates to Equipment and related accounts of El Sheikh Corporation:

Equipment, beginning balance	$130,000
Equipment, ending balance	150,000
Equipment sold during the year: Cost	10,000
Book value	2,000
Fully depreciated equipment written off during the year	5,000
Accumulated Depreciation, beginning balance	90,000
Accumulated Depreciation, ending balance	84,500

Assuming that all equipment purchases are for cash, how much cash was used to purchase equipment during the year?
a. $21,000
b. $25,000
c. $35,000
d. $39,000

ANS: C

51. The following information relates to Equipment and related accounts of El Sheikh Corporation:

Equipment, beginning balance	$130,000
Equipment, ending balance	150,000
Equipment sold during the year: Cost	10,000
Book value	2,000
Fully depreciated equipment written off during the year	5,000
Accumulated Depreciation, beginning balance	90,000
Accumulated Depreciation, ending balance	84,500

Assuming that the indirect method is used, the depreciation expense that would be added to net income in computing cash flows from operations would be
a. $4,500
b. $7,500
c. $10,500
d. $11,500

ANS: B

52. The following financial information is available for Ligutti Company:

	2006	2005
Cash and cash equivalents	$ 12,000	$15,000
Accounts receivable	25,000	22,000
Buildings	108,000	45,000
Accumulated depreciation	(20,000)	(16,000)
Land	30,000	20,000
	$155,000	$86,000
Accounts payable	$ 26,000	$22,000
Long-term notes payable	50,000	20,000
Common stock	50,000	30,000
Retained earnings	29,000	14,000
	$155,000	$86,000

Additional information:
- Dividends paid totaled $10,000.
- Net income was $30,000.
- No buildings were sold during the year.

What was the net cash provided by (used in) operating activities?
a. $33,000
b. $30,000
c. $26,000
d. $35,000

ANS: D

53. The following financial information is available for Ligutti Company:

	2006	2005
Cash and cash equivalents	$ 12,000	$15,000
Accounts receivable	25,000	22,000
Buildings	108,000	45,000
Accumulated depreciation	(20,000)	(16,000)
Land	30,000	20,000
	$155,000	$86,000
Accounts payable	$ 26,000	$22,000
Long-term notes payable	50,000	20,000
Common stock	50,000	30,000
Retained earnings	29,000	14,000
	$155,000	$86,000

Additional information:
- Dividends paid totaled $15,000.
- Net income was $30,000.
- No buildings were sold during the year.

What was the net cash provided by (used in) financing activities?
a. $25,000
b. $35,000
c. $10,000
d. $45,000

ANS: B

54. The following financial information is available for Ligutti Company:

	2006	2005
Cash and cash equivalents	$ 12,000	$15,000
Accounts receivable..	25,000	22,000
Buildings...	108,000	45,000
Accumulated depreciation	(20,000)	(16,000)
Land	30,000	20,000
	$155,000	$86,000
Accounts payable..	$ 26,000	$22,000
Long-term notes payable	50,000	20,000
Common stock...	50,000	30,000
Retained earnings...	29,000	14,000
	$155,000	$86,000

Additional information:
• Dividends paid totaled $10,000.
• Net income was $30,000.
• No buildings were sold during the year.

What was the net cash provided by (used in) investing activities?
a. ($63,000)
b. ($73,000)
c. $63,000
d. $73,000

ANS: B

55. Ojeda Corporation had the following cash flows during 2006. The company uses the direct method of preparing a statement of cash flows.

Cash receipt from the issuance of stock	$20,000
Cash received from customers	9,000
Dividends received on long-term investments	4,000
Cash paid for wages	7,000
Cash paid for insurance	500
Cash paid for dividends	3,000
Cash paid to purchase building	30,000
Loan made to another company	10,000

Given this information, net cash inflow (outflow) from operating activities is
a. $8,500
b. $5,500
c. $3,500
d. $15,000

ANS: B

56. Selected balance sheet and income statement data for Fowler Inc. are presented below. The company uses the direct method in preparing its statement of cash flows.

Partial Balance Sheet

	Beginning of Year	End of Year
Accounts Receivable	$10,000	$ 12,000
Inventories	20,000	24,000
Prepaid Insurance	1,500	2,000
Prepaid Rent	1,500	1,000
Accounts Payable	12,000	14,000
Wages Payable	13,000	15,000
Unearned Rent	10,000	6,000

Partial Income Statement

Rent Revenue	$ 20,000
Sales Revenue	100,000
Cost of Goods Sold	60,000
Insurance Expense	10,000
Rent Expense	6,000
Wages Expense	30,000

Given this information, cash collected from customers is
a. $98,000
b. $100,000
c. $102,000
d. $122,000

ANS: A

57. Selected balance sheet and income statement data for Fowler Inc. are presented below. The company uses the direct method in preparing its statement of cash flows.

Partial Balance Sheet

	Beginning of Year	End of Year
Accounts Receivable	$10,000	$ 12,000
Inventories	20,000	24,000
Prepaid Insurance	1,500	2,000
Prepaid Rent	1,500	1,000
Accounts Payable	12,000	14,000
Wages Payable	13,000	15,000
Unearned Rent	10,000	6,000

Partial Income Statement

Rent Revenue	$ 20,000
Sales Revenue	100,000
Cost of Goods Sold	60,000
Insurance Expense	10,000
Rent Expense	6,000
Wages Expense	30,000

Given this information, cash collected for rent is
a. $16,000
b. $20,000
c. $24,000
d. $24,500

ANS: A

58. Selected balance sheet and income statement data for Fowler Inc. are presented below. The company uses the direct method in preparing its statement of cash flows.

Partial Balance Sheet

	Beginning of Year	End of Year
Accounts Receivable	$10,000	$ 12,000
Inventories	20,000	24,000
Prepaid Insurance	1,500	2,000
Prepaid Rent	1,500	1,000
Accounts Payable	12,000	14,000
Wages Payable	13,000	15,000
Unearned Rent	10,000	6,000

Partial Income Statement

Rent Revenue	$ 20,000
Sales Revenue	100,000
Cost of Goods Sold	60,000
Insurance Expense	10,000
Rent Expense	6,000
Wages Expense	30,000

Given this information, cash paid for insurance is
a. $9,500
b. $10,000
c. $10,500
d. Not determinable from the information given

ANS: C

59. Selected balance sheet and income statement data for Fowler Inc. are presented below. The company uses the direct method in preparing its statement of cash flows.

Partial Balance Sheet

	Beginning of Year	End of Year
Accounts Receivable..	$10,000	$ 12,000
Inventories	20,000	24,000
Prepaid Insurance...	1,500	2,000
Prepaid Rent..	1,500	1,000
Accounts Payable..	12,000	14,000
Wages Payable...	13,000	15,000
Unearned Rent	10,000	6,000

Partial Income Statement

Rent Revenue..	$ 20,000
Sales Revenue..	100,000
Cost of Goods Sold..	60,000
Insurance Expense	10,000
Rent Expense	6,000
Wages Expense...	30,000

Given this information, cash paid for inventory is
a. $58,000
b. $60,000
c. $62,000
d. $64,000

ANS: C

60. Selected balance sheet and income statement data for Fowler Inc. are presented below. The company uses the direct method in preparing its statement of cash flows.

Partial Balance Sheet

	Beginning of Year	End of Year
Accounts Receivable	$10,000	$ 12,000
Inventories	20,000	24,000
Prepaid Insurance	1,500	2,000
Prepaid Rent	1,500	1,000
Accounts Payable	12,000	14,000
Wages Payable	13,000	15,000
Unearned Rent	10,000	6,000

Partial Income Statement

Rent Revenue	$ 20,000
Sales Revenue	100,000
Cost of Goods Sold	60,000
Insurance Expense	10,000
Rent Expense	6,000
Wages Expense	30,000

Given this information, cash paid for wages is
a. $28,000
b. $30,000
c. $32,000
d. Not determinable from the information given

ANS: A

61. Selected balance sheet and income statement data for Fowler Inc. are presented below. The company uses the direct method in preparing its statement of cash flows.

Partial Balance Sheet

	Beginning of Year	End of Year
Accounts Receivable...	$10,000	$ 12,000
Inventories	20,000	24,000
Prepaid Insurance..	1,500	2,000
Prepaid Rent..	1,500	1,000
Accounts Payable...	12,000	14,000
Wages Payable...	13,000	15,000
Unearned Rent	10,000	6,000

Partial Income Statement

Rent Revenue...	$ 20,000
Sales Revenue..	100,000
Cost of Goods Sold..	60,000
Insurance Expense	10,000
Rent Expense	6,000
Wages Expense...	30,000

Given this information, cash paid for rent is
a. $5,500
b. $6,000
c. $6,500
d. Not determinable from the information given

ANS: A

62. In 2006, Riner Company paid $5,000 to satisfy its 2005 tax liability, $32,000 for its 2003 tax liability, and still owed taxes payable of $8,000 at year-end. How much should Riner report as a cash outflow for tax payments on the 2006 statement of cash flows?
a. $37,000
b. $27,000
c. $40,000
d. $45,000

ANS: A

63. The following data were taken from the 2005 financial statements of Melfi Corporation:

Cost of Goods Sold	$350,000
Beginning Inventory	40,000
Ending Inventory	60,000
Beginning Accounts Payable	25,000
Ending Accounts Payable	20,000

How much cash did Melfi pay for inventory in 2005?
a. $335,000
b. $325,000
c. $375,000
d. $365,000

ANS: C

64. The following information appeared on the 2006 income statement of Kane Company:

Depreciation expense	$ 25,000
Patent amortization expense	10,000
Loss on sale of machinery	6,000
Gain on sale of securities	3,000
Net income	120,000

Based on this information, what is Kane's net cash provided by operations?
a. $164,000
b. $158,000
c. $120,000
d. $82,000

ANS: B

65. In 2005, Franco Manufacturing had sales of $750,000, beginning Accounts Receivable of $65,000, and ending Accounts Receivable of $85,000. Cash collected from customers for the year totaled
a. $750,000
b. $770,000
c. $815,000
d. $730,000

ANS: D

66. Chen Corporation had the following cash flows during 2006. The company uses the direct method of preparing a statement of cash flows.

Cash receipt from the issuance of stock	$20,000
Cash received from customers	10,000
Dividends received on long-term investments	5,000
Cash paid for wages	6,000
Cash paid for insurance	500
Cash paid for dividends	3,000
Cash paid to purchase building	30,000
Loan made to another company	10,000

Given this information, net cash inflow (outflow) from investing activities is
a. ($10,000)
b. ($30,000)
c. ($40,000)
d. ($43,000)

ANS: C

67. Chen Corporation had the following cash flows during 2006. The company uses the direct method of preparing a statement of cash flows.

Cash receipt from the issuance of stock	$20,000
Cash received from customers	10,000
Dividends received on long-term investments	5,000
Cash paid for wages	6,000
Cash paid for insurance	500
Cash paid for dividends	3,000
Cash paid to purchase building	30,000
Loan made to another company	10,000

Given this information, net cash inflow (outflow) from financing activities is
a. $20,000
b. $17,000
c. ($3,000)
d. ($13,000)

ANS: B

68. Chen Corporation had the following cash flows during 2006. The company uses the direct method of preparing a statement of cash flows.

Cash receipt from the issuance of stock....................................	$20,000
Cash received from customers..	10,000
Dividends received on long-term investments............................	5,000
Cash paid for wages...	6,000
Cash paid for insurance	500
Cash paid for dividends	3,000
Cash paid to purchase building.......................................	30,000
Loan made to another company.......................................	10,000

Given this information, net cash inflow (outflow) from ALL activities is
a. $5,500
b. $10,000
c. ($14,500)
d. ($24,500)

ANS: C

69. Zhong Corporation's Retained Earnings balance increased by $50,000 during the year. Zhong also paid $15,000 in cash dividends that had been declared last year and declared dividends of $20,000 for the current year (but has not paid them at year-end). Zhong's net income for the current year must be
a. $30,000
b. $70,000
c. $65,000
d. $50,000

ANS: B

70. Compton Inc. had the following cash transactions during 2005:

Sales receipts	$1,000,000
Inventory payments	750,000
Interest payments...	10,000
Wage payments...	60,000
Dividend receipts...	5,000
Interest receipts..	3,000
Equipment purchased..	75,000
Stock of Rojas Company purchased	25,000
Stock issued	150,000
Repaid a note (nonoperating)..	50,000

What was Compton's net cash provided by (used in) operating activities?
a. $1,008,000
b. $180,000
c. $258,000
d. $188,000

ANS: D

71. Compton Inc. had the following cash transactions during 2005:

Sales receipts	$1,000,000
Inventory payments	750,000
Interest payments	10,000
Wage payments	60,000
Dividend receipts	5,000
Interest receipts	3,000
Equipment purchased	75,000
Stock of Rojas Company purchased	25,000
Stock issued	150,000
Repaid a note (nonoperating)	50,000

What was Compton's net cash provided by (used in) financing activities?
a. $100,000
b. $150,000
c. $50,000
d. $75,000

ANS: A

72. Compton Inc. had the following cash transactions during 2005:

Sales receipts	$1,000,000
Inventory payments	750,000
Interest payments	10,000
Wage payments	60,000
Dividend receipts	5,000
Interest receipts	3,000
Equipment purchased	75,000
Stock of Rojas Company purchased	25,000
Stock issued	150,000
Repaid a note (nonoperating)	50,000

What was Compton's net increase in cash for the year?
a. $153,000
b. $133,000
c. $188,000
d. $288,000

ANS: C

73. Analysis using cash flow information is restricted to
a. Vertical analysis
b. Horizontal analysis
c. Relationships among the categories in the statement of cash flows
d. All of the above

ANS: C

74. Which of the following cash flow patterns do growing companies follow?
    a. Cash reserves are being used to finance operating shortfalls and pay long-term creditors and investors.
    b. Cash is being borrowed to cover cash shortages from operations and to purchase fixed assets.
    c. Cash generated by operations is used to buy fixed assets and pay down debt.
    d. Operating cash flow shortages are covered from the sale of fixed assets, borrowing, or stockholder contributions.

    ANS: B

75. If a company is to succeed over the long-term, positive cash flows are necessary from
    a. Operating activities
    b. Investing activities
    c. Financing activities
    d. Both investing and financing activities

    ANS: A

PROBLEMS

1. Santini Company had the following selected transactions during the past year:

   a. Sold (issued) 5,000 shares of common stock, $1 par, for $10 per share.
   b. Sold equipment for $5,000. The original cost was $20,000; the book value was $5,500.
   c. Paid $30,000 of its accounts payable.
   d. Borrowed $60,000 from First National Bank and signed a note to repay in six months, with 12 percent interest.
   e. Purchased equipment costing $80,000 by paying cash of $20,000 and signing a 12 percent note for the remainder.
   f. Purchased treasury stock for $20,000.
   g. Recorded depreciation expense of $8,000.

   1. Prepare journal entries for each of the transactions above.
   2. For each transaction, indicate the amount of cash inflow or cash outflow and how each of these cash flows would be classified on a statement of cash flows.

ANS:

1.

a.	Cash	50,000	
	Common Stock		5,000
	Paid-In Capital in Excess of Par		45,000

b.	Cash	5,000	
	Accumulated Depreciation	14,500	
	Loss on Sale of Equipment	500	
	Equipment		20,000

c.	Accounts Payable	30,000	
	Cash		30,000

d.	Cash	60,000	
	Notes Payable		60,000

e.	Equipment	80,000	
	Cash		20,000
	Notes Payable		60,000

f.	Treasury Stock	20,000	
	Cash		20,000

g.	Depreciation Expense	8,000	
	Accumulated Depreciation		8,000

2.
a. The $50,000 cash inflow would be classified as a financing activity.
b. The $5,000 cash inflow is reported as an investing activity. Under the indirect method, the $500 loss would be added to net income.
c. The $30,000 cash outflow would be classified as an operating activity.
d. The $60,000 cash inflow would be classified as a financing activity.
e. The $20,000 cash outflow would be reported as an investing activity. $60,000 of the transaction is reported in a note or separate schedule as a significant noncash transaction.
f. The $20,000 cash outflow is reported as a financing activity.
g. There is no cash flow from this transaction. Under the indirect method, the $8,000 would be added to net income.

2. From the following data for Vargas Company, determine the net cash flow provided (used) by operating activities.

Net income	$50,000
Depreciation for the year	35,000
Dividends declared during the year	30,000

	Beginning of Year	End of Year
Cash and cash equivalents	$35,000	$42,000
Accounts receivable	25,000	27,000
Inventory	83,000	80,000
Prepaid expenses	7,000	8,000
Accounts payable	28,000	22,000
Accrued liabilities	2,000	7,000
Dividends payable	23,000	25,000

ANS:

Net income	$50,000
Add (deduct) adjustments to cash basis:	
Depreciation	35,000
Increase in accounts receivable	(2,000)
Decrease in inventory	3,000
Increase in prepaid expenses	(1,000)
Decrease in accounts payable	(6,000)
Increase in accrued liabilities	5,000
Net cash flow provided by operating activities	$84,000

Note: The amount of cash paid for dividends was $28,000 ($30,000 declared plus $23,000 payable at beginning of year less $25,000 payable at year-end). However, dividend payments are classified as a financing activity, not as an operating activity.

3. Goodson Company reports the following selected information at year-end:

Sales revenue	$750,000
Interest revenue	6,000
Cost of goods sold	360,000
Wages expense	280,000
Depreciation expense	43,000
Other (cash) operating expenses	95,000
Proceeds from sale of equipment	37,000

	Beginning of Year	End of Year
Accounts receivable	$ 55,000	$ 49,000
Interest receivable	4,200	3,400
Inventory	221,000	225,000
Accounts payable	33,000	38,000
Wages payable	26,000	18,000

Using the direct method, compute the amount of net cash flow provided (used) by operating activities for Goodson Company.

ANS:

Cash receipts from:
Sales revenue	$750,000	
+ Beginning accounts receivable	55,000	
− Ending accounts receivable	(49,000)	
Cash collected from customers		$ 756,000

Interest revenue	$ 6,000	
+ Beginning interest receivable	4,200	
− Ending interest receivable	(3,400)	
Cash collected from interest		6,800
Total cash receipts from operations		$ 762,800

Cash payments to:
Cost of goods sold	$360,000	
− Beginning inventory	(221,000)	
+ Ending inventory	225,000	

Purchases	$364,000	
+ Beginning accounts payable	33,000	
− Ending accounts payable	(38,000)	
Cash paid for inventory		$(359,000)

Wages expense	$280,000	
+ Beginning wages payable	26,000	
− Ending wages payable	(18,000)	
Cash paid for wages		(288,000)

Cash paid for other operating expenses		(95,000)

Total cash payments for operations		$(742,000)

Net cash flow provided from operating activities		$ 20,800

Note: The proceeds from sale of equipment is an investing activity. Depreciation is a noncash item and can be ignored when using the direct method.

4. From the following information for Epperson Company, prepare a statement of cash flows for the year ended December 31, 2006, using the indirect method.

Amortization of patent	$ 8,000
Depreciation expense	14,000
Net income	50,000
Payment of dividends	58,000
Purchase of equipment	33,500
Retirement of long-term debt	20,000
Issuance of common stock	30,000
Cash received in the sale of land (includes $5,000 gain)	42,000
Decrease in accounts receivable	2,500
Increase in inventory	1,500
Increase in accounts payable	1,200
Cash balance, January 1, 2006	34,800
Cash balance, December 31, 2006	?

ANS:

Epperson Company
Statement of Cash Flows
For the Year Ended December 31, 2006

Cash Flows from Operating Activities:		
Net income	$50,000	
Add (deduct) adjustments to cash basis:		
Amortization of patent	8,000	
Depreciation	14,000	
Gain on sale of land	(5,000)	
Decrease in accounts receivable	2,500	
Increase in inventory	(1,500)	
Increase in accounts payable	1,200	
Net cash flows provided by operating activities		$69,200
Cash Flows from Investing Activities:		
Cash receipts from sale of land	$42,000	
Cash payments for purchase of equipment	(33,500)	
Net cash flows provided by investing activities		8,500
Cash Flows from Financing Activities:		
Cash receipts from issuance of common stock	$30,000	
Cash payments for dividends	(58,000)	
Cash payments to retire long-term debt	(20,000)	
Net cash flows used in financing activities		(48,000)
Net increase in cash		$29,700
Beginning cash balance		34,800
Ending cash balance		$64,500

5.

Ciomara Corporation
Balance Sheet
December 31, 2005

Assets	2005	2004
Cash	$ 11,000	$ 46,500
Accounts receivable..	120,000	115,500
Land...	75,000	60,000
Equipment..	70,000	90,000
Accumulated depreciation	(13,500)	(19,500)
Total assets..	$262,500	$292,500
Liabilities and Stockholders' Equity		
Accounts payable..	$ 6,000	$ 9,000
Long-term debt	20,000	28,500
Common stock..	190,000	172,500
Retained earnings...	46,500	82,500
Total liabilities & stockholders' equity............................	$262,500	$292,500

Other data:
1. Net loss for 2005 is $30,000.
2. Equipment with a cost of $20,000 and accumulated depreciation of $15,000 was sold for $8,000.
3. Dividends of $6,000 were paid.

Prepare a statement of cash flows for the year ended December 31, 2005, using the indirect method.

ANS:

Ciomara Corporation
Statement of Cash Flows
For the Year Ended December 31, 2005

Cash Flows from Operating Activities:

Net loss		$(30,000)
Add (deduct) adjustments to cash basis:		
Depreciation..	$ 9,000 *	
Gain on sale of equipment	(3,000)**	
Increase in accounts receivable...................................	(4,500)	
Decrease in accounts payable	(3,000)	(1,500)
Net cash flows used by operating activities.................		$(31,500)
Cash Flows from Investing Activities:		
Cash receipt from sale of equipment	$ 8,000	
Cash payment for purchase of land..............................	(15,000)	
Net cash flows used by investing activities		(7,000)
Cash Flows from Financing Activities:		
Cash receipts from sale of common stock	$ 17,500	
Cash payment to retire long-term debt	(8,500)	
Cash payment for dividends	(6,000)	
Net cash flows provided by financing activities...........		3,000
Net decrease in cash..		$(35,500)
Beginning cash balance		46,500
Ending cash balance		$ 11,000

*	Beginning accumulated depreciation....	$19,500
	Accumulated depreciation on sale	−15,000
		$ 4,500
	Ending accumulated depreciation.........	13,500
	Depreciation expense............................	$ 9,000
**	Cost of equipment................................	$20,000
	Accumulated depreciation	−15,000
	Book value...	$ 5,000
	Proceeds from sale of equipment..........	8,000
	Gain on sale of equipment....................	$ 3,000

Name_____   Section_____

TRUE/FALSE

Circle T or F to indicate whether each of the following statements is true or false.

T F   1.   Cash received from selling securities of other entities is classified as an investing activity on a statement of cash flows.

T F   2.   When the indirect method is used to prepare a statement of cash flows, a decrease in prepaid insurance is added to net income.

T F   3.   Noncash transactions such as refinancing long-term debt with stock are reported directly on a statement of cash flows.

T F   4.   Accountants (preparers) generally favor the direct method of preparing a statement of cash flows over the indirect method.

T F   5.   The payment of cash dividends is classified as a financing activity.

T F   6.   Interest paid on long-term debt is classified as an operating activity.

T F   7.   Dividends received on long-term investments are classified as an operating activity.

T F   8.   With the indirect method of preparing a statement of cash flows, a decrease in accounts receivable would be added to net income.

T F   9.   The statement of cash flows generally explains changes in the cash and cash equivalents balances of two successive balance sheets.

T F   10. The financing and investing activity sections of a statement of cash flows differ between the direct and the indirect methods.

Name_____   Section_____

MATCHING

In the spaces provided, write the letter of the term for each of the following definitions:

    a.   Obtaining resources from and repaying resources to owners and creditors.
    b.   Short-term, highly liquid investments.
    c.   One of three primary financial statements.
    d.   Financial resources flowing into and out of an entity.
    e.   Shows the main classes of cash receipts and payments for operations.
    f.   Transactions involving the purchase or sale of assets generally classified as noncurrent.
    g.   Depreciation expense.
    h.   Transactions that enter into the determination of net income.
    i.   Details the adjustments to net income to compute net cash flow from operations.
    j.   Authoritative guidance for preparing a statement of cash flows.

1. _____   Cash equivalents

2. _____   Cash flows

3. _____   Investing activities

4. _____   Financing activities

5. _____   Operating activities

6. _____   Noncash item

7. _____   Direct method

8. _____   Indirect method

9. _____   Statement of cash flows

10. _____   FASB Statement No. 95

Name_____   Section_____

MULTIPLE CHOICE

1. Noncash investing and financing activities, if material, are
    a. Reported in the statement of cash flows as the "all financial resources concept"
    b. Reported in the statement of cash flows only if the indirect method is used
    c. Disclosed in a note or separate schedule accompanying the statement of cash flows
    d. Not reported or disclosed because they have no impact on cash

2. A gain on the sale of machinery in the ordinary course of business should be presented in a statement of cash flows (indirect method) as a(n)
    a. Deduction from net income
    b. Addition to net income
    c. Inflow and outflow of cash
    d. Outflow of cash

3. In its accrual-basis income statement for the year ended December 31, 2006, Nelson Company reported revenue of $3,500,000. Additional information is as follows:

Accounts receivable—December 31, 2005	$1,010,000
Net income for 2006	140,000
Accounts receivable—December 31, 2006	750,000

    Nelson should report cash collected from customers in its 2006 statement of cash flows (direct method) in the amount of
    a. $3,240,000
    b. $3,100,000
    c. $3,380,000
    d. $3,760,000

4. Didericksen Company's income statement for the year ended December 31, 2006, reported net income of $360,000. The financial statements also disclosed the following information:

Amortization	$20,000	Increase in salaries payable	$ 28,000
Depreciation	60,000	Dividends paid	120,000
Increase in accounts receivable	20,000	Purchase of equipment	150,000
Increase in inventory	48,000	Increase in long-term note	
Decrease in accounts payable	76,000	payable	300,000

    Net cash provided by operating activities for 2006 should be reported as
    a. $84,000
    b. $204,000
    c. $234,000
    d. $324,000

5. The following information is available from the financial statements of Worthington Corporation for the year ended December 31, 2006.

Net income............................	$396,000	Increase in accounts payable.....	$24,000
Depreciation expense.............	102,000	Payment of dividends................	54,000
Decrease in accounts receivable	104,000	Purchase of available-for-	
Increase in inventories............	90,000	sale securities......................	22,000
		Decrease in income taxes	
		payable...............................	16,000

What is Worthington Corporation's net cash flows from operating activities?
a. $440,000
b. $466,000
c. $520,000
d. $542,000

Quiz Solutions

Quiz A	Quiz B	Quiz C
1. T	1. b	1. c
2. T	2. d	2. a
3. F	3. f	3. d
4. F	4. a	4. d
5. T	5. h	5. c
6. T	6. g	
7. T	7. e	
8. T	8. i	
9. T	9. c	
10. F	10. j